WORKING FOR A
JAPANESE COMPANY

WORKING
FOR A
JAPANESE
COMPANY

Insights into the Multicultural Workplace

Robert M. March

KODANSHA INTERNATIONAL
Tokyo • New York • London

Distributed in the United States by Kodansha America, Inc., 575
Lexington Avenue, New York, New York 10022, and in the United
Kingdom and continental Europe by Kodansha Europe, Ltd.,
95 Aldwych, London WC2B 4JF.
Published by Kodansha International, Ltd., 17-14 Otowa 1-chome,
Bunkyo-ku, Tokyo 112-8652, and Kodansha America, Inc.
Copyright © 1992 by Kodansha International, Ltd.
All right reserved. Printed in Japan.

First Edition 1992
First Paperback Edition 1996
00 01 02 03   6 5 4 3

LCC 92-10037
ISBN 4-7700-2085-6

ACKNOWLEDGMENTS

Many people in Japan, the USA, the United Kingdom, and Australia have assisted me generously.

My editor, Leslie M. Pockell at Kodansha International, Tokyo, supported the book enthusiastically from the start and helped me over the many rough spots, up to four rewrites in some places, until we were satisfied. Lucy Marshall of Japan Net Australia, Diane Sasaki of Culture Shock Inc., Tokyo, Judy Van Dyck of Oregon State University, and Jennifer Stanley of Stanley & Associates, London, were highly supportive, helping to arrange interviews and sometimes providing conceptual input as well. Lucy also attended some interviews which she kindly recorded and transcribed for me. I have had many valuable discussions during the course of this project with Professor Larry Rosenberg of the University of Maryland in Tokyo, while Professor Kichiro ["Kich"] Hayashi of Aoyama Gakuin University, Tokyo, was a stimulating interlocutor in the early stages of the project.

Many people permitted me to interview them, although some prefer not to be named, and I have referred to them by pseudonyms. However, I can publicly thank: Yuki Akimoto, Wal Anderson, Robin Fenstermaker, Peter Forrest, Robert Gavey, Jean

Goldsmith, Akira Kodama, Bruno Modica, Roger March, Arnie Papp, Carolyn Pearson, Margaret Price, Anthony Robinson, Susan Slater, Cliff Stratton, and Yukiko Tanabe.

I am very grateful to my wife, Anna, for her support throughout the project, and particulary for her help in typing the many "final" versions of the manuscript.

CONTENTS

INTRODUCTION

When the Japanese raided Pearl Harbor in 1941, the US government and its advisers were convinced that they had become engaged in war with the most alien enemy they had ever faced. As Ruth Benedict (1946) has written, Americans saw the Japanese as people of immense contradictions: polite but also arrogant, rigid but also adaptable, loyal but also treacherous, submissive but also not easily amenable to control. "In no other war," she reported, "had it been necessary to take into account such exceedingly different habits of acting and thinking" (*The Chrysanthemum and the Sword*, p. 5).

Fifty years later, some millions of Japanese and non-Japanese people are daily working and living together with one another in the Americas, Europe, Asia, Oceania as well as Japan—as bosses or workers, as friends or neighbors, as lovers or spouses, as clients or colleagues. How is that possible? Have the Japanese changed so much? There is no question that there have been changes in the Japanese personality in the last fifty years. The crude ultranationalism has gone. The education system of a great industrial power produces people of broader perspectives and greater urbanized sophistication than the predominantly agricultural society of prewar

Japan. But though they have changed somewhat in that half century, the Japanese still remain vastly different from most other societies in their psychology and social customs. The people who know this best and avoid making superficial judgments (good or otherwise) about them, are those who work or live with the Japanese on a day-to-day basis.

The Japanese have an expression, *"onaji kama no meshi o ku,"* which translates as "eating rice from the same pot." The expression dates from feudal times when apprentices or young men in training lived together in dormitories and ate rice together, taken from the one central rice pot. Even today, the saying has strong nuances of intimacy for the Japanese; it means to live together in a companionable way, to share the pleasantries of the same table with your peers. Japanese businessmen use this phrase often when they talk about others they are close to. In Japan, someone you have lived with and shared rice with is like family. Many Japanese businessmen began their working life by living with other single co-workers in a dormitory, and they share that "rice" bond with them and, vicariously, with those of their seniors or juniors who had also lodged in the same dormitory.

The closer we look at the family-like bonds between Japanese co-workers, the better the understanding we will achieve of the effectiveness of Japanese organizations. But creating family-type bonds with foreigners, or getting a sense of companionableness in daily life together, turns out to be a universal problem whenever Japanese and Westerners (in particular) work together. Whether they work together in a Japanese company in Japan or its subsidiary abroad, or in a foreign company in Japan or one abroad, everyday problems of misunderstanding, confusion, and miscommunication often become commonplace, occasionally reaching chronic and corrosive levels. Some of the problems are to be attributed to the special conditions of work and living to be found in all cross-cultural relationships and multicultural organizations; some are specifically due to the extreme gap in values, culture, and customs between Japan and the West; and others are due to the lack of know-how in managing crosscultural relationships or multicultural organizations.

I first became involved in these problems in 1979, when the English president of the Japanese subsidiary of a foreign multinational consumer goods maker spoke to me about the problems occurring on almost a daily basis between his Japanese and expatriate staff. At that time, the subsidiary had 18 expatriates assigned to it—a diverse array of specialists in marketing, production, finance, etc.—including Germans, Englishmen, Canadians, Australians, Belgians, and a Turk. By the time I had been consulted, the fundamental problems had become hopelessly confused with the negative feelings of the expatriates toward the Japanese managers and staff.

The president asked me what, if anything, could be done. Although it was a problem that foreign managers in Tokyo at that time knew about, when I asked colleagues for their suggestions about how to handle cross-cultural human relations problems, we found we were all in the dark. No one knew of any other work that had been done, save some sensitivity group training that had been attempted but given up when the Japanese refused to participate.

Eventually, I settled on what I hoped would be a simple, non-threatening design. We brought together, at one large conference table, 15 of the expatriates and an equal number of Japanese managers. Each member in turn was asked to relate an example of cross-cultural difficulty he had personally experienced or was familiar with. When he had finished, I then asked all the other members on the same side to say how they would have felt or behaved if it had happened to them. When that was done, I then invited all the members of the other side to say how they would have reacted (if it had happened to them), and how they interpreted the events of the case.

The day had many surprises in store for all of us. For one thing, we found that the interpretations of the cases, and the strength of identification with interpretations, were almost identical within each of the groups. That is, all the Japanese interpreted cases in the same way, as did the Westerners, in spite of the many different countries they came from. But the biggest shock was that almost invariably the Westerners' interpretation was the complete opposite of the Japanese!

In one, an expatriate production adviser, after discussion with his Japanese staff, came to the conclusion that a machine in the factory should be moved to improve production flow and accordingly ordered the change. On coming to the factory a day or two later, he was irritated to see that the machine was still in the same place. "Why hasn't it been moved?" he asked. "Ah," the foreman replied, "we haven't reached a consensus on that yet." That further irritated him. Surely it is a very simple matter to move a machine? "No," they said, "we must discuss it further." The next morning, the expatriate arrived early at the factory to find that the machine had been moved. The full story about the move, which he learned later, was this: One member of the work team, its youngest member, had been away visiting his sick mother when the move had first been requested, and no one, from the foreman down, was prepared to reach a decision until the young man returned. He had returned the previous night, been consulted, and the machine was immediately moved. Cases involving Japanese-style group consensus, when they lead to holdups in decision-making, are among the most difficult for Westerners to accept and generate a great deal of annoyance and incredulity, especially when, as does happen, the Westerners are left out of the decision-making group.

In another case, an expatriate who spoke no Japanese used an English-speaking man for liaison with the factory. Under extreme pressure to finish a certain project on time, the expatriate saw that his liaison man was doing a particular job in "completely the wrong way." He became quite annoyed with him and so implicitly belittled him. As a result, reported the expatriate, "I effectively lost him for three months." It was only when he took the liaison man out for a drink three months later and apologized for his behavior that relations improved, and he discovered that the solution the liaison man was going to propose would in fact have been quite a feasible one. The expatriate's mistake here, the Japanese managers pointed out, was not merely to have shown irritation and belittled the Japanese (for, they made clear, we are all human and imperfect), but to have let the situation go on for so long without repairing it. What Japanese conventions call for is that within two or three days the parties involved should go out for a drink and talk, in the course of which the offender (the expatriate in this case) should make clear that he knows he has made a mistake. This need not, in Japanese business culture, take the form of an explicit apology, and a mea culpa attitude of professed guilt is definitely not called for.

Again, a Western manager, to foster the international sophistication of his staff, arranged for six of his senior managers and their wives to attend a dinner party at his home. On the morning of the party date, the six men appeared sheepishly in his office and awkwardly told him that taking wives to a party was not a Japanese custom, and that they wanted to go without their wives. The expatriate was almost apoplectic. "That is the whole point!" he roared at them. "And why have you left it to the day of the dinner to tell me this?" "Ah," said the Japanese, "we know your wife is preparing all that food, so we have invited six junior men from our department to take the place of the wives." The party was cancelled. This case engendered a lot of emotional identification among the other expatriates—all of them expressing sympathetic annoyance. On the other hand, the Japanese all agreed that they would have gone along with the new arrangements, which, they were convinced, would have been extensively discussed beforehand by the Japanese staff.

This is just a small sampling of the cases reported that day. The themes that these cases of cross-cultural difference touch upon continue to be at least as prevalent as I found them in 1979, not surprising when we recognize the enormous increase since then in numbers of Japanese and non-Japanese working and living together. Some other themes of conflict that are commonplace today include: Western insistence upon specialist training for young staff versus Japanese insistence on broad, non-specialized training; serious conflicts in communications between bosses and subordinates—for example, Japanese subordinates failing to check their understanding of instructions from an American boss, or American subordinates asking "too many" questions of Japanese bosses; expatriate reluctance, in Japan or abroad, to become involved in social activity with local staff; differences in attitudes toward meetings, with Japanese demands for frequent lengthy meetings coming up against Western demands that they be kept few and short; differences in the status given to female employees; the disapproval in Japanese society of showing anger or hostility to others, versus the tendency among Westerners to at least tolerate and even admire men who are skillful at "putting others down" in a humorous or ironic way—not so in Japan, where they say, and believe, the proverb "*nama byoho wa ohkega no moto*": "crude tactics cause great injuries," and where they decry anger with "*tanki wa sonki*," or, "a short temper means a failed spirit."

While only a few published books and articles refer to the diversity of cross-cultural differences found when we analyze actual cases, media recognition has started to escalate. The December 3, 1990 issue of *Fortune*, for instance, ran a cover story entitled "Working for the Japanese." *Fortune* saw newsworthiness in the fact that more and more Americans (not to mention English, Australian, Chinese, etc. people) are now working for Japanese companies in their own countries, and experiencing both "fascination and frustration." The fascination is there for those who are able to use their specialist skills more effectively than in the past in American companies. However, *Fortune* adds, "though the Japanese are creating lots of jobs in the US, most of the best ones are still reserved for Japanese. Americans are often hired to fill a specific function, with little regard for long-term career development."

Two weeks later, *Business Week* ran a special report headed "Culture Shock at Home: Working For a Foreign Boss." Most of the story, however, was about Japanese companies, even though the Japanese employ considerably fewer Americans than do British, German, or Canadian companies. Where the *Fortune* article had been factual and evenhanded, *Business Week* led off with a story of discrimination suits pending against Fujitsu in California, which, they said, "were typical of the many filed in recent years by disgruntled former American executives of Japanese companies" (p. 80). Other complaints against the Japanese included: failure to give American middle managers decision-making power, lower compensation than in US companies, "management philosophies and methods that are alien to" Americans, and isolation from the "inner counsels" of decision making.

Another sign of the widening perception gaps and recognition of workplace difficulties between Japanese and Westerners was the 1987 US comedy movie *Gung Ho* (called *Working Class Man* in some countries). This amusingly portrayed relationships between Japanese managers and American workers in a Pennsylvania auto plant. As one Japanese reviewer shrewdly observed, no one had ever found anything amusing about British or Dutch investment in the USA. It took the great cultural gap between Japan and America to create a comedy. When the Japanese executives first arrive by plane in the plant town, the mayor and the townspeople roll out a red carpet for them at the airport. The Japanese take off their shoes before walking on the carpet. When the union representative is offered business cards by nine Japanese managers at the same time, he cannot figure out who is who, since all Japanese look alike to him, so he tears up the cards. After many misadventures and conflicts, the American workers and Japanese managers end up as one big happy family who have learned much from one another.

Workplace encounters between Japanese and non-Japanese do not only take place abroad. Since 1984, Japanese companies have been steadily increasing the numbers of foreigners they employ in Japan. Up to a quarter of a million foreigners, the majority blue-collar or semi-skilled, many of them illegal immigrants on tourist visas, are working in Japan in 1992, predominantly for small factories and businesses. Employers welcome them, since it has long been very difficult for small businesses to attract enough Japanese workers. The poorly educated, mostly Asian workers welcome the often dirty and difficult work, for they are paid wages undreamt of at home. In three to four years they may save enough to buy a house, and they are treated, by and large, satisfactorily. The Japanese media pay a lot of attention to the dilemma now facing Japan concerning these humble workers. Should they authorize the employment of semi-skilled foreigners in Japan in order to relieve the severe labor shortage? A further important advantage of this would be the diplomatic prestige Japan would acquire in both East and West Asia. On the other hand, the Japanese are loath to allow many foreigners into their country in the belief that it would lead to increases in crime and other social problems. While bureaucrats and politicians mull this problem over, Japanese small businesses are continuing to employ more illegal foreigners.

Not as much media attention in Japan is given to the less widespread but increasing employment of non-Japanese salaried and managerial workers, by the larger Japanese companies who are the subject of this book; there are no official figures, but the number in 1992 was probably around 12,000. With these small numbers, there is little interest among the Japanese in the topic, and most media reporting is in fact in the local English language media, with messages directed to non-Japanese readers in Japan. For instance, the *Japan Economic Journal* published a special issue on May 27, 1989, entitled "Japan's Foreign Workers." In this context, "foreign worker" meant salaried employee, usually white and college-educated, not Asian illegals (who did not get a mention). A survey of 2000 major Japanese companies listed on their stock exchange showed that one in every three is now hiring foreigners: as part of their "internationalization" drive or "to support their overseas operations," to "become familiar with other cultures" or to "broaden their horizons." What this means is that almost all of these foreigners are employed to facilitate the development of international knowledge and sensitivity.

Only a handful of Japanese companies are employing foreigners as regular (*sei shain*) employees. These include Sony, Toyota, Fujitsu, Bank of Tokyo, Kobe Steel, Seibu Department Store, C. Itoh, and a few other trading companies, securities houses, banks, construction companies, advertising agencies, and manufacturers. How successful this will be is hard to say right now. John Shook, the first foreigner ever to work for Toyota Motor Corporation in Japan, says "the whole company infrastructure is set up for the Japanese . . . we don't fit. If the company gets serious about hiring more foreigners, things will have to change." Another, who is the first foreigner to win promotion in a major company by regular examination (entirely in the Japanese language, exactly the same as for his Japanese colleagues), feels the same way.

"The only sure way for me to progress beyond *kacho* (section manager) is to settle permanently in Japan and take Japanese nationality, and that is out of the question," says Alfredo Villarante, a manager in a major computer company. Quality of life, and concern that their children's education and development would be unsatisfactory in Japan are big factors in these men's thinking about the future. Villarante, on long-term assignment from Japan to the US subsidiary, has already taken American nationality, an act that initially elicited some hostile reactions from the head office personnel department. John Shook of Toyota said in 1990 that he intended to leave Toyota and return "soon" to the US.

Expressed desires to become international, to employ more foreigners, to broaden their horizons, etc., are not just expressions of noble sentiments. Japanese multinationals face a severe shortage of managerial staff suitable for posting to their overseas subsidiaries. Many are now talking about the new policy of "localization" (which has various meanings including the promotion of local people to the most senior posts in overseas subsidiaries) as one that will be forced on them by the end of the decade. Japanese companies in many countries have given executive search firms open-ended commissions to find local high-quality managers who, with training, can become the local chief executive officer. The *Japan Economic Newspaper* has organized career forums for some years in the USA. These are job fairs where major Japanese companies look for bilingual American personnel. Unfortunately, there are many serious problems between local managers and expatriates, and local managers and head office managers, in the management of overseas subsidiaries. The *International Herald Tribune*, May 24, 1990, reported on what it described as segregationist policies in several Japanese corporations. These policies mean that Americans report only to other Americans, while Japanese report only to other Japanese officials. Some of the companies in fact claimed that their strategy from the beginning was that, in those areas having a direct relationship with Japan, communication would be handled by Japanese staff. Nissan America went further than this, according to the report. "The Japanese are there primarily to monitor the Americans' progress and to provide the sole link with Japan." The Japanese managers will, the memo says, "assist in the planning and checking of department activities, with the American staff carrying out and adjusting day-to-day operations."

Although US media reported this item in a way that was critical of the Japanese companies, it is hard for an outsider to comment without knowing all the facts. On the surface, such a policy or strategy seems to make very good sense. Telephone or fax communications between Americans in the US and Japanese in Tokyo usually become extended dialogue, in order for Tokyo, if it has final decision-making power or has to take any ultimate financial risk, to fully assess the issues. Very few non-Japanese have an understanding of, or even patience for, the kind of extended questioning that Japanese middle managers will engage in at any time. This is all supposing that there is no language problem—and it will be very rare for communication in this type of situation to be without its share of misunderstanding, mistakes, and bewildering confusion. In short, the Japanese companies reported on by the *Herald Tribune* were using policies that are very sensible in the short term. But in the long term, especially if one remembers the medium-term goal of "localization" that ought to be present for every Japanese multinational, it will only make sense if there is also ongoing training for both sides—Americans and Japanese— on how to communicate more effectively with each other on a day-to-day basis.

STRUCTURE OF THE BOOK

If this book were a novel, the main character would be the foreign white-collar/professional/managerial employee of the Japanese company, abroad or in Japan, and the supporting cast would include Japanese managers and staff, both in Japan and in other countries.

The main character comes to center stage only in Part 2 of the book. Part 1 serves as a prologue or statement of the context of the encounters that we deal with in Part 2. This statement of context helps to make more sense of Japanese behavior in the cross-cultural setting by recounting some of that nation's history of cross-cultural encounters, its people's unusual psychology of interpersonal relations, and the mutual perceptions and evaluations that are typical of modern-day encounters between Japanese and Americans (and other Westerners).

Part 2, based upon actual experiences of foreigners working for Japanese companies in the USA, UK, Australia, and Japan, answers a number of questions about their corporate life and experience: What cultural challenges and communication difficulties do foreign employees encounter in the different world of the Japanese corporation? What kinds of human relationships do they have with their Japanese colleagues and managers? Can they ever become true members of a Japanese corporation? How are they treated in the Japanese company? What are their conditions of work and employment? How involved and responsible do foreign employees become as managers and decision-makers in Japanese companies? This section reveals many constraints, barriers, and problems encountered by the foreign employee, the source of which seems largely to be Japanese management style and Japanese managers, especially abroad.

Chapter 10 provides a different perspective on the Japanese manager abroad by examining his problems from his point of view, and Chapter 11 offers an analysis and interpretation of all findings, which should provide a sounder basis for mutual understanding than presently exists. Finally, in a not-too-optimistic way, suggestions for the improvement of intercultural business relationships and Japanese corporate behavior abroad are presented, addressed both to the Japanese company and to present and potential foreign employees of these companies.

In puzzling out how to present the enormous amount of materials, especially in-depth interview data, I had collected during this project, I finally decided to minimize the number of direct quotations from a large number of people, for it made it difficult for readers of early drafts to keep the thread of connection and coherence across chapters. Although only a limited number of people then actually "speak" in the book, it has been my experience in the thirteen-plus years I have been studying this subject, that the human factors in the multicultural organization are extraordinarily similar from case to case, and that it is largely only details that differ.

PART
1

FIRST
ENCOUNTERS

CHAPTER
1
A BRIEF HISTORY

Living and working with foreigners can be quite unlike living and working with your own kind at home. Common sense may support that view, but why should it be so? The simplest answer is that our cultures differ in so many ways that we daily face surprises, shocks, and new learning experiences. We discover that the behavior, customs, ways of thinking, and habits that served us so well back home in ensuring a smooth and essentially harmonious daily life are not always helpful in adjusting to a new culture.

Interestingly enough, however, people differ widely in the ways they respond to living with foreigners. At its best, the cross-cultural experience can be (and this is often true of the Japanese-American encounter) like a marriage born out of romantic love. After a honeymoon period, life becomes a learning experience, as we discover that the "beloved" is both more and less than our romantic notions had led us to believe, and life may become a roller coaster of ups and downs until genuine mutual adjustment and perhaps lifelong friendship are achieved. At its worst, living in an alien environment can be like serving a prison term. You begin with minimal expectations, and whether the reality is better than the expectations or not, your main concern is to survive, serve out your time, and depart. A few people might be lucky enough to find that what promised to be a "prison" turned into a rewarding experience. And others, I have heard some say, have found that originally romantic "marriages" can turn into prisons.

Whichever it is, it is clear that there is no iron rule, no predictable outcome, for encounters and cohabitation between people as different from one another as Japanese and Westerners, or Japanese and most other Asians for that matter. Both sides find problems equally, find the other equally strange—and the historical epoch or era seems to make little difference. In the earliest modern Western encounters with Japan, in the sixteenth and seventeenth centuries, the Jesuit priests, who went to Japan to convert the heathen Japanese, found much to admire. The priest Organtino wrote frequently to colleagues in Europe, insisting that only the best missionaries be sent. "It must be understood," Organtino wrote in 1577, "that these people are in no sense barbarous. Excluding the advantage of religion, we ourselves in comparison with them are most barbarous. I learn something every day from the Japanese and I am sure that in the whole universe there is no people so well gifted by nature" (Sansom 1950, 174).

Francis Xavier, who spent the years 1549–51 trying to convert them to Christianity, was enthralled by the Japanese. "These," he said, "are the best people so far discovered, and it seems to me that among unbelievers no people can be found to excel them." But the good priest managed to alienate himself from many Japanese with his, to them, strange teachings. For instance, he became convinced that the Devil had founded all the Buddhist sects in Japan, and had this preached on the streets. Again, he preached that Japanese ancestor worship was wrong, and that all ancestors, not being saved, were condemned to hell. He called Buddhas "demons." Needless to say, Francis Xavier and his brother priests antagonized many Japanese, but still managed, over 35 years, to convert 150,000 or more.

In 1587, the unifying military leader Hideyoshi condemned the teachings of the missionaries and ordered them to leave Japan within 20 days. As Sansom puts it, Hideyoshi "well knew that the indigenous cult of Japan [Shinto] was the very foundation of the social order. It supported the whole pyramid of loyalties at whose summit he stood . . . he was undoubtedly right to regard Christian propaganda as subversive . . . the Jesuits were a challenge to the national tradition. . ." (p. 130). In spite of this edict, many missionaries continued, discreetly, to preach, but over the years Japanese Christians were increasingly persecuted, and churches and seminaries destroyed, culminating in the massacre of 37,000 Christian peasants in 1638. Perhaps a quarter of a million Japanese Christians were executed in all, until the country was finally closed off from foreign intercourse in 1641.

A better understanding of Japan's encounters with foreigners helps to illuminate the decision of the military government to close Japan to the world. It is true that the Japan of the time was self-contained and self-supporting, and therefore, as Sansom puts it, "there were no compelling reasons for cultural or commercial exchanges" (p. 178). Moreover, conservative sentiment against foreigners was as strong as in other countries. But, says Sansom, the closure of the country was motivated mostly by the real fear that outlying provinces (*han*) of Japan were conspiring with foreigners to gain firearms, artillery, and ships from them to seek the overthrow of the military government.

One of the most interesting historical figures in Japan's encounters with the West was the English sea pilot and shipwright William Adams. After his ship was disabled, he eventually reached Kyushu, the southernmost Japanese island, in the year 1600. A man of intelligence and wide competence, he was befriended by the shogun, Tokugawa Ieyasu. Adams, through Ieyasu's patronage and his own activities as a commercial agent and shipbuilder, became a man of wealth, influence, and renown in Japan. He married a Japanese and had two children, and took on a completely Japanese lifestyle. Though he acted often as an agent and interpreter for English and Dutch merchants, he was to remain, for the rest of his life, entirely Japanese in his dress and way of living. As a result, he was often regarded with suspicion by his fellow countrymen, who called him, unflatteringly, a "naturalized Japanner." James Clavell's novel *Shogun* is based upon the life of Adams.

Almost a century later, a German physician, Engelbert Kaempfer, spent three years at the Dutch trading post in Nagasaki. In spite of the fact that all Japanese dealing with the trading post were under oath to disclose nothing whatsoever about Japan to the foreigners—an obsession with secrecy that still persists in Japan today—Kaempfer was able to write an extraordinarily detailed and accurate account of Japan, in five volumes. Many Japanese were later to lament how well informed Europeans had become about Japan through his writings.

Apart from limited trading relations with the Dutch and Chinese and some isolated and unintentional visits by ship-wrecked foreign sailors, Japan closed its borders and all connections with foreign countries for over two centuries until the arrival, in the 1850s, of the American Commodore Perry, who was responsible for the successful negotiation of the reopening of Japanese ports to the West. Backing his demands unsubtly with a squadron of state-of-the-art warships, Perry was determined not to leave until the treaty was concluded, in spite of the delaying tactics used by the Japanese. For example, when Perry demanded that he meet with the highest-ranking local lord, the Japanese substituted an ordinary police officer, who pretended to be the lord. A major reason for doing this was that under the law of the day, only members of the samurai class were permitted to make direct requests to provincial lords. Nonsamurai who made direct appeals were subject, together with their family, to the death penalty. The Japanese wisely, with one eye on the massive cannonry in the harbor, did not tell Perry that he was violating the law of the land. Another factor in their delaying tactics was the long-standing Japanese doctrine of *joi-ron*, or policy of excluding foreigners; and they understandably wanted to avoid war with the United States.

Two years after agreement was reached with Perry, much to the consternation of the Japanese an American consul, Townsend Harris, arrived unexpectedly in Japan to negotiate a full commercial treaty. The Japanese authorities, who had barely gotten rid of Perry after agreeing to open up two minor and remote ports for provisioning and some trade, spent a year treating Harris to a series of delaying tactics, arguing interminably over points of detail. Sansom tells us that "the officials whom Harris encountered on his arrival at Shimoda in 1856 had been given orders to prevent any intimacy between Japanese and foreigners . . . he met with nothing but obstruction . . . and was surrounded by spies who tried to trap him into indiscreet statements." The officials in Shimoda even had large numbers of prostitutes brought to the town, in the hope that "those ladies by their charms would soften the hearts of foreign visitors and so make them less determined to exact political concessions from Japan!" (Sansom 1950, 289).

Harris, a gentleman of difficult temperament, barely had the patience to see this trying period through. He found himself in almost constant conflict and dispute with the Japanese. He seemed almost perverse and certainly petty in his arguments and demands—he wanted the guards at his gate removed; insisted that the fish and vegetable peddlers call and sell to him and that the Japanese interpreters sit on the floor when they visited his house (though the floor was filthy by Japanese standards and people walked through it in their shoes); he claimed the treaty provisions were broken by local shopkeepers refusing to sell sweet bean-cakes to his cook; he repeatedly charged that every price he paid was padded, and so on. At one stage, citing these and other problems, Harris accused the Japanese of trying to drive him out of Japan. He threatened that he would leave as soon as possible, and that a war would follow, in which Japan would be totally defeated. In meetings he repeatedly lost his temper, and he used the threat of war constantly. In most cases, the standard Japanese reply was that they were waiting for directions from Edo (Tokyo). Harris was convinced that he was dealing with "the greatest liars on earth," although, as Statler (1980) points out, "when it came to lying, Harris had a few blemishes on his own record." He was bluffing about his threats of war, and his demands were often in contravention of the treaty he had agreed to. Statler comments on Harris's determination to contravene the seven-*ri* (one *ri* = 2.44 miles) travel limit:

"From now on he would go freely where he chose when he chose . . . he would go to Edo . . . he would go wherever the situation demanded. And if he were prevented, it would mean war. Harris had completely lost his temper. His words were ugly. His actions were uglier still. . . ." (p. 293).

One matter that never found its way into Harris's diary or official correspondence was the arrangement, secretly schemed for almost from the time of their arrival, to supply Harris and his interpreter with two "ladies." The Japanese authorities eventually arranged for two bar girls, Okichi and Ofuku, to become their servants. Okichi was later to be glamorized and immortalized as "Madam Butterfly" in Puccini's opera.

Part of the explanation for Harris's temperamental behavior may be found in his poor health—he certainly suffered from severe peptic ulcers—but the sheer fact of dealing with local officials in an alien world of radically different values meant that he was, as with so many of us who have lived for long periods in Japan in daily contact with the Japanese, subject to repeated cultural shocks and unpleasant surprises. The local officials were then, as now, timid, cautious, and terrified of taking the initiative, and would avoid making any decisions themselves, even in trivial matters.

Nonetheless, as Sansom (1950) reminds us, Japan at that time "was not lacking in sensible statesmen and officials who could read the signs of the time." Certainly some of these sensible statesmen were in the first diplomatic party to visit the United States in 1860, headed by the then foreign minister, Muragaki Awajimori. In the diaries he left behind, there are some amusing comments, revealing the vast gap between the two cultures. When Muragaki went to the White House to present his formal documents of accreditation, he had a shocking experience:

"In spite of the fact that he is the President, he received us dressed in the same stovepipe trousers that were worn by merchants [and so regarded by the Japanese as demeaning for a president], devoid of any decoration, and without a sword. These barbarians make no distinction between upper or lower, and have no idea about proper ceremony!"

A little later, after visiting a sitting of the Congress, he confided to his diary:

"In spite of discussing matters of weighty importance to the nation, one man stood, dressed again in stovepipe trousers, shouting abuse in a loud voice like a maniac. As soon as that one finished, another would take his place and continue on in the same abusive manner" (reported in Sofue, 1989).

During the 1860s, as the number of foreigners increased, so did Japanese distrust and hostility, with many foreigners threatened by sword-wielding samurai and a few assassinated. With the restoration of Imperial rule in 1868, the country quickly normalized, and the life of foreigners in Japan became secure. Now the Japanese and Westerners could begin to see each other and muse over the apparent differences. Yokohama, at that time called the Wild West of the Orient, was a major site of these encounters:

"Both the foreigners and the Japanese of that period were rather queer," wrote one historian of the cross-cultural scene in nineteenth-century Japan. "The customs and habits of both were a source of never-ending amusement to the other. The foreigners laughed loud and long at the Japanese, but as few of them moved in Japanese circles they could not hear the Japanese laughing at them. For example, the management of the Grand Hotel in Yokohama . . . made a feature of the front verandah from which visitors could view the quaint customs of the natives on the Bund below. . . . There they sat drinking stone ginger beer or sarsaparilla, whilst they gazed and laughed at the Japanese, quite oblivious, however, that among the throngs there were often organised tour parties from the country, who had been brought along by their guides especially to see the queer *gaijin* (foreigners)—the curious bewhiskered men from the West with their wives who wore hats almost as large as umbrellas" (Williams 1958, 187–188).

Nor was it only mutual amusement. Early foreign travellers and residents were shocked at the near nudity of the Japanese, in summer or winter, at the way both sexes bathed together, and at the habit of bathing right on the sidewalk. The Japanese were shocked at the Western custom of wearing a coat at all times, even at the height of a Japanese summer, and were not surprised that a number died of heatstroke, no doubt abetted by the quantity of whisky they consumed. To illustrate his lecture on "Japanese Dress," a Western professor introduced a semi-naked Japanese coolie whose body was almost completely tattooed. The learned Western audience, though, were instantly faint with horror at the sight, and immediately carried a motion that "the specimen . . . be relegated to the exterior of the premises, where . . . anyone [who] desired might examine him critically" (reported in Williams 1963).

WESTERNERS IN THE MODERNIZATION OF JAPAN

More seriously, one of the earliest acts of the Emperor on the restoration of Imperial rule was to issue a "Five Articles Oath." The final article of the oath provided the basic philosophy for modern Japan:

"Knowledge shall be sought throughout the world so as to strengthen the foundation of Imperial rule."

Amongst other things, this meant the repudiation of the "expel the barbarian" policy (joi-ron), and a determination to build a modern and powerful Japan through the use of Western knowledge. The next decade saw the influx of large numbers of Westerners, whom the Japanese called *yatoi* (employee).

"The yatoi helped the Meiji period modernizers open the Pandora's box of modernization. They worked at the very cutting edge of technical innovation . . . they set examples . . . were teachers. . . ." (Beauchamp and Iriye 1987, 10).

The yatoi were very much a mixed bunch. Some were eminent scholars. The entire medical faculty of what was to become Tokyo Imperial University in the 1870s was composed of foreigners. Yatoi developed history, art, and applied scientific studies, as well as establishing the army, the navy, and many government ministries. Others were, frankly, confidence men, for it was easy enough in those early days for the Japanese to accept anyone Western at face value. As one authoritative writer of the time put it:

"The majority of the 'Professors' in the schools of Tokei [the original name for Tokyo] were graduates of the dry-goods counter, the forecastle, the camp, and the shambles, or belonged to that vast array of unclassified humanity that floats like waifs in every seaport. Coming directly from the barroom, the brothel, the gambling saloon . . . they brought the graces, the language, and the manners of those places into the schoolroom . . . Japanese pride revolted after a report that one of the professors was a butcher by trade" (F.V. Dickins, quoted in Williams 1963, 84).

Even the legitimate yatoi, most of whom had been sponsored by their governments, caused resentment amongst some Japanese. In the 1870s they were associated in the Japanese mind with the unequal treaties, extraterritoriality, and exclusive trade arrangements that the Japanese had unwillingly agreed upon. Their manner was often arrogant, for they recognized that they were more or less indispensable to the Japanese, and with their high incomes and culturally alien lifestyle, they played out a colonial master role.

"There is nothing picturesque in the foreign employee," wrote the Japanologist Basil Hall Chamberlain. "With his club, and his tennis ground, and his brick house, and his wife's piano, and the European entourage which he strives to create around him in order sometimes to forget his exile, he strikes a false note. . . . He was a sojourner in Lotus-land" (quoted in Jones 1980).

The 1870s were the heyday of the yatoi. By the 1880s Japanese had begun to replace them in most significant positions, such as heads of university departments. But that decade had been one of momentous growth. The great novelist Natsume Soseki describes it thus:

"We had to achieve in ten years something which took European countries a century, and to do so in such a way as would make it appear genuinely self-motivated, not hollow. This entailed serious consequences [for] we had to expend our energy at ten times the rate of Europeans. . . . At the same time however, this exertion would necessarily reduce the people involved to a state of complete exhaustion. . . ." (quoted in Jones 1980, 26).

Soseki's observation reminds us of the enormous effort the Japanese expended on rebuilding their country after the Second World War. We know today that the cost has been great—the deaths from overwork (*karoshi* in Japanese) and the widespread sense among the Japanese that they are constantly tired, that they can never get enough rest, are well documented in official surveys. So it is provocative to read that many of the yatoi of the 1870s felt that "everywhere was tension, fatigue, and a cry for relief" (quoted in Jones 1980, 27), indicating that the Japanese in the 1870s had as much driving commitment and self-sacrificing zeal as they were to show eighty years later.

THREE CASE STUDIES OF YATOI EMPLOYED BY THE KAITAKUSHI IN HOKKAIDO

Introduction

Concerned about the threat of a possible Russian invasion of the northern island of Hokkaido and hopeful about the island's potential resources, the Japanese government in 1869 set up a Hokkaido development commission called *Kaitakushi*, and subsequently asked the US government to assist in recruiting skilled advisers. At that time the American press was praising the Japanese as, for instance, "the most intelligent and practical of Oriental nations, the Yankees of Asia," and were, not surprisingly, flattered that the Japanese looked to them as a country "representative of the most advanced civilization." Additionally, Americans were predicting that, as a result of the assistance they could give through the Kaitakushi, America would directly benefit through greatly increased trade and enlarged manufacturing. Stemming from this background of images and expectations, President Grant dispatched his commissioner for agriculture, Horace Capron, to be commissioner of the Kaitakushi, with these words:

"I look upon the Department of Agriculture as a very important one. . . . But with all its importance it is not equal in value to your country to your new mission. From it I expect to see early evidence of increased commerce and friendly relations with a hitherto exclusive people, alike beneficial to both" (quoted by Fujita, in Jones 1980, 90)

1. The Case of Horace Capron

Capron went to Japan with high ideals and strong commitments to help Japan emerge "from a state of barbarism to a state of highest civilization," and considered himself to be a messenger of "the light of the most advanced civilization."

In spite of their "semi-barbarous" state, Capron quickly developed admiration and respect for many aspects of Japan and the Japanese people. He described their temples and shrines as "superb" and "beyond description," their sculpture as having "such composure, such majesty." Of the people he said: "Truly these are a happy people having few wants and these easily supplied. . . . Truly a wonderful people," he concluded, echoing very much the tone of the Jesuit priests 300 years earlier. And he wondered how much their happiness would be augmented by their intercourse with "outside barbarians."

He was convinced too of the future potential of Japan, since its enormous drive for modernization was coupled with an almost total lack of everything "from a cambric needle to a steam engine, every kind and description of farming implement and machine, from the hoe up . . . every description of wearing apparel, from a shirt collar, to the most elaborate toggery" (Fujita, op. cit., 98).

At the same time Capron found much to annoy and irritate him. The heavy weight of supernumerary officials within the Kaitakushi organization especially annoyed him. Inspecting salmon fisheries, he found "one official for every hundred fish taken. . . ." At one farm, he found spacious buildings erected for the accommodation of eighteen officials whose duty it was to supervise eighteen laborers. When a blacksmiths' forge was set up, requiring one smith and two coolies as strikers, Capron was astounded to see an office opened up with two or three officials to supervise the operation. Capron was constantly frustrated by the Japanese failure to consult with him, and by "the want of candor on the part of the officials of this Department, and entire exclusion from [him] of all information touching the designs or plans of operations. . . ." While he was constantly being interviewed on a great range of American topics, he found that when he thought his turn had come to ask questions, the interview was terminated, and information was hidden from him. He was shocked by his subordinates' refusal in so many public works projects to admit their ignorance or incompetence, and by their frequent attempts to deceive him. He concluded that these problems stemmed, not from their intention to interfere with his plans, but from "the great defect in the Japanese character . . . that is, overbearing confidence in their own judgment, and overweening vanity, which pushes them forward to cover up an error in their judgment when their attention is brought to it and to squirm out of it in some way at whatever cost." Most exasperating of all to Capron was that he himself ended up being made the scapegoat, especially in the press in Japan and the USA, for these many failures.

In spite of these troubles, in his later years back in the USA, Capron was to praise the Japanese as "the most industrious [people] known," "incomparably frugal," possessing "ambition . . . in an eminent degree," and skilled in "all works of art requiring delicate manipulation."

Capron's encounter with the Japanese reveals him as a man of great balance, pursuing his goals unswervingly while respecting and working effectively with the Japanese, and sharply perceptive about their strengths and weaknesses.

2. The Case of Benjamin Smith Lyman

Lyman was a well-regarded geologist and topographer when he joined the Kaitakushi in 1873. He was thirty-six years old, a bachelor and vegetarian, and one of his referees had written of him that "he has complete sympathy with the poor, and cordial benevolence to their suffering," which would exert an exemplary influence upon the Japanese.

In his first year in Japan Lyman had a positive and optimistic attitude toward Japan and the Japanese. His Japanese assistants, whom it was his responsibility to train, were, he wrote, "so bright, so anxious to learn, so quick at understanding outlandish things, so good humored, so polite." Lyman enjoyed this period greatly, and, with his studious nature, also spent much time studying the language and culture. He also came to view Japan as "the Sleeping Beauty that the young Prince [America] came to awaken to fresh life and renewed loveliness."

From his second year onward, however, the fairy-story feeling disappeared. Lyman began a running feud with the administration of the Kaitakushi that continued until he resigned in 1879. This feud reveals more about Lyman's personality than anything else, and it is a clear illustration of a clash caused by a certain perverse interpretation of Western principles of liberty and individualism that one still finds among foreign employees in Japan to the present day.

Lyman's complaints against the Kaitakushi began with his insistence that the order for Japanese students (at the Kaitakushi school) to serve the Kaitakushi for a number of years after graduation be abolished on the grounds that it was "oppressive" and "virtually an irksome slavery." He was demanding a "jealous regard for the personal liberty of the individual." When this appeal to Kuroda, the Japanese deputy commissioner of the Kaitakushi, failed, he turned on Kuroda, accusing him of wasteful expenditure, stating that Kuroda "has either connived at robbery of the government or . . . has through intellectual incapacity been unable to prevent it." In other words, said Lyman, "he is either a knave or a fool; and on either account is wholly unfit to act as head of a department." Next, Lyman attacked the regulations of the school, which among other things required a girl student to marry a male graduate of the school and work together with him for the development of Hokkaido. There was a perfectly simple reason for Lyman's seemingly principled attack on the regulations. He wanted to marry, and had proposed to a girl student, but the school head had refused permission. In attempting to have the regulation changed, Lyman attacked the character and fitness of the school head and raised other charges against him, such as "gross rudeness" by the headmaster to a Dutch teacher.

One can only be surprised by the long-suffering attitude of the senior Japanese people in Kaitakushi towards the overprincipled and troublemaking Lyman. For instance, Lyman next complained about the refusal of his interpreter to go with him to a party organized by another American. Lyman demanded "undisputed control" of his assistants as a universally acceptable right, but Kuroda pointed out that his employment contract made clear that all orders were to come from the authorities of the Kaitakushi. This appeared to make the inestimable Mr. Lyman determined to be released from his contract, "so ruinous [was this event] to my reputation." For good measure, he also demanded heavy damages, plus complete compensation of salary for the whole contract term.

Capron finally stepped in at this point and was able to get the problem resolved.

Lyman continued to fight with and bitterly criticize the Kaitakushi until he left in 1879, when he joined the Japanese Interior Department and Public Works Department for a further two and a half years before returning to the USA. He still found occasions for friction with his new employer and came finally to the conclusion that the Japanese were, after all, "so ignorant of modern methods of business, and so different to Anglo-Saxons in temperament." To a friend who was himself interested in working for the Japanese, Lyman, the lifelong bachelor, observed: "Serving them is like being subjected to a lot of girls—ignorant, arbitrary, fickle, vain, wilful, faithless."

Lyman's views of the Japanese remained essentially critical for the rest of his life. In a long article written later in life, entitled "The Character of the Japanese," he opined that their most outstanding characteristic was that, while they were "remarkably quick [in] external perception," which made them master imitators, they were "unreflective and not deep in reasoning and originality." As for their behavior, their ruling principle was "regard for others rather than self-respect," although their "genuine readiness to comply with the will of others" made them easier to deal with than Anglo-Saxons. They were able "to get along together without disagreeable friction," but it was their very respect for others and avoidance of friction that carried with it a dangerous tendency for them "to be subjects of despotic power." As well, "their politeness could turn to rude and overbearing, and even 'treacherous' behavior if they had no respect for others."

3. The Case of Edwin Dun.

Edwin Dun was an experienced cattle breeder leading a lordly life of chivalry and paternalism, who had grown up in a well-to-do Southern family. In 1873, when he was twenty-five, he was approached by Capron's son about a job with the Kaitakushi, and, it being the middle of a depression, he immediately signed a one-year contract as a fill-in job until the depression was over.

Dun fitted in well from the start. He was soon on "the best

terms" with his students at the school, and explained to Capron: "I have learned to take a personal interest in the success of the great undertaking which is the object of the department to carry through." When his contract expired, he immediately renewed for a further year and eventually stayed for seven years, until the Kaitakushi was abolished in 1881. He was particularly good at dealing with questions, unlike many of the foreigners with the Kaitakushi, he was quick to point out. Moreover, as his remarks in later life were to illustrate, his rural, aristocratic background gave him a strong sense of affinity with the young sons of samurai who were his students.

Dun returned to the US in February 1883 but quickly felt out of place. He was not the man of ten years earlier, and he felt a stranger in the midst of his family (an experience that has since come to be called reverse culture shock). Through a family connection, he was at length able to secure the newly created position of second secretary to the US legation in Japan. He took up that post in 1884, and in 1894 was appointed US minister to Japan by President Cleveland. He left that post in 1897 after which he worked for International Standard Oil Company in Niigata, and for a salvage company in Nagasaki, before retiring and spending his last days in Tokyo.

The man who had come to Japan just to spend a year waiting out an economic depression became, like others, a thoroughgoing Japanophile, in some ways more Japanese than the Japanese themselves. His respect and affection for Japan and its ancient culture shines through in his memoirs, published in 1919, entitled *Reminiscences of Nearly Half a Century in Japan*. He was particularly concerned that Japan develop its own modern character, not be a plastic imitation of Europe or America. He was not only highly critical of those Japanese who showed an "excessive craze for everything foreign"—he was equally critical of those Americans who urged Japan to hasten its emergence from "barbarism."

"The Japanese of today was a civilized being three thousand years ago and the teachings, traditions, and gradual development of thirty centuries has made him what he is today. . . . He must advance as a Japanese . . . in time develop along Japanese lines into a great people and nation."

In spite of his American origins, Dun was not tempted to recommend Western values of individualism to Japan. The main features of Japanese society, he pointed out, were hierarchy, paternalism, and the absence of individualism. Though he loved his country of birth to the end, he was deeply critical of its lack of "human brotherhood." Pointing specifically to public servants in America, he wrote, "one is ruthlessly cast out as a worn-out shoe is discarded without care or thought for the suffering of one who has spent his life in the service of his country." In contrast, he pointed to the paternalism that permeated the whole of Japanese society. Relations between employer and employee were "entirely different from those prevailing in the West." Feelings of mutual respect and esteem he saw as characteristic of Japanese firms. They gave their staff security for life, with health insurance and pension plans that were almost unknown in the West. In turn, the employee devoted himself to his firm, feeling he was a part of it, said Dun.

THE DIVERSITY OF YATOI EXPERIENCES

These three cases give a good feeling for the diversity of experiences and views formed about Japan by well-educated non-Japanese who spent long periods there. On the one hand, Capron and Lyman present an interpretation of Japan and their own experiences heavily influenced by their assumptions about the superiority of the West, and the but-recent emergence of Japan from "barbarism" (whatever that might mean to us today at the end of the twentieth century). Their impatience, and lack of perception and experience of social and industrial change, prevented them from understanding and being sensitive to Japanese sensibilities and needs. They were typical colonial-master types, one might say. Lyman spent much of his life studying the Japanese language and its culture, but he remained a superior-minded, self-righteous individual to the end, unable to truly identify with Japan.

In contrast, Dun (like Adams 300 years earlier) found a second home in Japan. He developed profound affinities for Japan and the Japanese with the kind of enthusiasm for the country and the preservation of its "best values" that one can find in religious converts. One commentator (Fujita, op. cit., p.114) has observed that Dun's "preoccupation with the uniqueness of Japanese culture tended to prevent him from perceiving other aspects of Japanese culture which contained receptivity to change." Perhaps that is so. One might also suspect that Dun ended up in a somewhat intellectually lonely situation in which he felt obliged to spend more energy on responding to and correcting the philistines who downgraded Japan than reflecting upon the opportunities for growth and development that lay before it. Certainly this is a condition and situation that many "old Japan hands," those who spend most of their life in the country, are very familiar with. Whereas "representatives of superior cultures" like Capron and Lyman retained this orientation to the end of their lives, Dun was representative of those who were deeply influenced and irreversibly changed by their close encounters with Japan.

CHAPTER
2
CROSS-CULTURAL RELATIONS AND THE JAPANESE PSYCHE

We can see from the last chapter that the Japanese historical experience of Westerners has been limited, and that their perceptions and judgments tend to be stereotyped and unrealistic. The author Kenichi Takemura (1981), in explaining why the Japanese do not regard foreigners as fully human, says it is because "the Japanese have never intermarried." They have no direct experience of foreigners in their lives, no imperative to think concretely about or be concerned about people living elsewhere. Foreigners therefore are rather like characters in a fairy story or a myth.

Curiously enough, the awkwardness that many Japanese feel on meeting foreigners—they use the word *iwakan* (meaning sense of incompatibility) to describe their feelings at such times—seems to be based on a general suspicion and apprehension of strangers as well as foreigners, and is most notable in Tokyo. Certainly in my experience (quite apart from travel all over Japan, I have lived for extended periods in four provincial cities—Fujinomiya, Hiroshima, Nishinomiya, and Matsuyama—as well as in Tokyo), far fewer Japanese in the provinces experience iwakan—their reactions to foreigners are far more natural and spontaneous, with little suspicion or awkwardness. This difference is attributable in part to the greater exposure of Tokyo people to ideas, judgments, and beliefs comparing Japan with the West. In the countryside, Japanese people are not so concerned about international comparisons. (The Japanese cultural anthropologist, Sofue Takao, makes the same point [1989, 17]).

In the capital, which is after all the key point of interface with the outside world, consciousness of foreigners and their countries seems almost forced upon people, and foreign news and issues are more prominent and more intrusive in everyday life. At different times in the past Tokyoites have been informed (rather than learning from direct experience) that the distant Western world is more advanced, wealthier, more glamorous and powerful, etc., than Japan; that Westerners are bigger, stronger, wealthier, more cosmopolitan and self-assured; and that the West differs from Japan both in culture and in the way of thinking. Given this sense of difference, acquired by a people never encouraged to make friends easily, should it be any wonder that many feel frozen by a sense of incompatibility when face to face with people physically different from them in so many ways, that is, Westerners? Among the Japanese, the problems of discomfort and awkwardness with foreigners have been so widespread in the postwar period that the Japanese have given the condition a special name: "gaijin (foreigner) complex".

GAIJIN COMPLEX

To the Japanese, a gaijin has traditionally been a white Caucasian, and it is only since 1987 that gaijin has taken on a wider meaning. Today, gaijin has a more truly international meaning, including blacks as well as whites, other Asians, and Arabs. Nonetheless, when using the term "gaijin complex" to mean an awkward orientation to non-Japanese others, gaijin still means white Caucasian to most Japanese.

How many Japanese can be said to have a "gaijin complex"? I have undertaken two surveys of Tokyo Japanese on this subject, one in 1983, and again in 1987, surveying a total of 270 Japanese. Six out of ten people said they personally had a complex about foreigners and this percentage was higher among those who had actually had the experience of speaking to a foreigner! Overall, these Japanese believed that up to three-quarters of the Japanese people had a gaijin complex. It is clear then that we are talking about a social dilemma of considerable magnitude, even though its causes seem simple enough.

When asked why they felt this complex toward foreigners the single biggest reason given was that "they speak a foreign language." This reflects a frank envy of the ability of foreigners to speak English and therefore to feel more at home in other countries, regardless of whether the foreigner in question is in fact a native speaker. The other main reason given for the gaijin complex is the belief that foreigners (again it is white Caucasians they have most in mind) have better-proportioned bodies, are better-looking and more sexually attractive. This brings us to the self-image of the Japanese—many regret their small stature and slight build, their shorter limbs and relatively longer spines as compared with Westerners. Ultimately, Hollywood has to take some responsibility for providing a glamorous norm of physique that the Japanese feel condemns them to permanent physical mediocrity.

WHAT CROSS-CULTURAL ENCOUNTERS ARE MOST TRYING FOR THE JAPANESE?

One of the most fascinating aspects of our gaijin complex surveys concerned the questions about how Japanese men and women feel about same-sex and cross-sex encounters. We wanted to know how they think Japanese young men and women would react to an encounter with a gaijin man or woman, and what they thought would be going through the minds of those Japanese. Here are the results for each of the four pairings:

A JAPANESE MALE WITH A FOREIGN MALE

The reactions here were uniformly negative. The feelings a Japanese male would have meeting a foreign male are described variously as: "stress . . . wants to escape . . . fear . . . he feels overpowered . . . he has a complex about his body or looks or strength . . . he feels inferior, envious . . . he feels competitive . . . he feels a sense of rivalry, opposition."

A JAPANESE MALE WITH A FOREIGN FEMALE

Reactions here were, overall, ambivalent. Some felt the Japanese male would be sexually aroused, yearning, envious; others had him seeing before him "her beautiful body, face, tall slender figure, blonde hair." This fits in well with a commonly heard "dream" of young Japanese bachelors, especially those posted overseas, to have a blonde, blue-eyed girl friend. But there were also those who felt only "stress, nervousness, fear, and a desire to escape." Very likely, these negative feelings are related to a perception of foreign women as taller than Japanese men and/or to self-perceptions of being homely, uninteresting, and boring.

JAPANESE FEMALE AND FOREIGN MALE

As with the previous cross-sex encounter, ambivalence is shown in the responses. On the positive side, the Japanese woman was seen as attracted and wanting a romantic relationship, perceiving the foreign man as good-looking, tall, or as a nice, kind gentleman. Instructively, and more manipulative in its underlying psychology, some Japanese respondents pointed to the perception, on the part of the Japanese female, of her foreign male partner as a cute "pet" whom she would like to display to others and have serve her (by carrying her shopping parcels, opening doors for her, etc.). This touches on the image held by many Japanese of the "Western gentleman" who, unlike the Japanese male accustomed to being served by the woman, is in every way attentive, helpful, and cooperative. Regarding negative responses, the Japanese female was also seen as under stress, "nervous, fearful, wanting to escape."

JAPANESE FEMALE AND FOREIGN FEMALE

Although there was again ambivalence here, this was the most restrained and least tense encounter. There was some perception that the Japanese female would feel stress, fear, and nervousness, but none that she would want to escape. On the positive side, there was a feeling that they could be friends in a normal and equal relationship, even though the Japanese female would be admiring and envying the good looks and nice figure of the foreign female.

COMMENTS

It is extraordinary, but true, that many clever, decent, affluent, well-educated Japanese are burdened by a complex about foreigners that stands obviously as a barrier to effective, clean interpersonal relationships. Every Japanese is aware of and has some understanding of what a gaijin complex is, even if she or he does not have one. Every Japanese is also aware that it is genuinely disabling, and under the right circumstances he or she will be honest enough to say so. Every non-Asian-looking foreigner in Japan has had regular experiences of Japanese refusing to sit in a vacant seat next to them. Just occasionally, I have struck up a conversation with a group of friendly Japanese men in a railway carriage at night, usually a little inebriated, to find one or more ingenuously admitting, "I couldn't sit next to you. I've got a gaijin complex!" We all know that it is amusing, for we all smile at his remark (though he doesn't), but we all also know that it is true!

To summarize, our two surveys found ample evidence of a broad consensus among Tokyo Japanese that the gaijin complex is widespread in Japan. It stems, for these particular people, from beliefs that foreigners (particularly Caucasians) have some superior skills—especially language and communication skills—and are more physically attractive. But for many Japanese, these beliefs coexist with negative, even painful, feelings aroused by an actual or anticipated interaction or encounter with foreigners. Clearly, these encounters are not universally welcome.

The surveys also indicate what ought in any case to be a commonsense conclusion, that the more the Japanese have encounters with foreigners, the more the gaijin complex emerges. This does not mean that every Japanese will have a gaijin complex, or will even experience negative feelings. But many, perhaps a majority, will, most frequently when it is a Japanese male meeting with a foreign male. Then, there will be a very good chance that the Japanese will feel, along with his awkwardness and inferiority, a sense of rivalry and competitiveness. In fact, Japanese men have been well aware of this sense of rivalry since World War II days and acknowledge it among themselves, though never, as far as I know, to non-Japanese. I have certainly never come across this in the plethora of things written about the Japanese, nor have I ever heard any Western businessman (it is a male-male phenomenon; foreign *businesswomen* are unlikely to be perceived as rivals) provide an analysis of his Japanese opponents or partners that recognized their latent, but hugely powerful, sense of rivalry with Westerners, especially Americans.

I think the evidence about mixed-sex encounters between Japanese and foreigners provides another cautionary tale. There is a romantic and stereotyped element in the attitudes of Japanese women to foreign men that, to me, bespeaks the fairy story of courteous English gentlemen or knights, and has very little relevance to modern-day Western men. The encounter between Japanese men and foreign women is perceived as less romantic, but has a good measure of sexual attraction along with stereotyping from the Japanese side.

The gaijin complex also reveals two other factors about the Japanese people. One, they have a very keen sense, as individuals, of their ethnic identity. "I am Japanese, and she is non-Japanese, and we are definitely different in many ways." Those whose consciousness of always being Japanese, in these intercultural relationships or encounters, hardly ever leaves them are undoubtedly people who, consequently, have erected a barrier against a freer, more unconditional, relationship.

To help understand this better, you might recall your own teenage years of growing up and struggling to find the right mix of behaviors that permit an easy entry into the adult world. In those days, as we experiment with proper, acceptable behaviors, we can also be on our guard with strangers, afraid that people might make fun of our immaturity and social awkwardness, might ridicule us for some social blemish that we have been unable to conceal. The only difference is that the Japanese, unlike advanced Western societies, are not forced at puberty to start becoming socially independent. Everyone in their society is supportive of the view that they should be enjoying their "golden school days" without threats to break the deep bonds with parents, so permitting a deep sense of identification with home and family and family-type figures throughout their life.

The other factor that analysis of the gaijin complex reveals is how exclusive-minded many Japanese are. The tipsy man in the railway carriage who declined to sit next to me was not just fearful, he was also exclusive-minded. The exclusive-minded person picks and chooses the people in his life he will trust or be open with, probably according to a complex agenda of conditions and demands that could only be met by extended interaction, and assurances and reassurances, over a period of years. The Japanese themselves recognize, accept, and are not unwilling to speak frankly about, this common tendency among them to be exclusive-minded. It means, in common parlance in Japan, that you "don't mix with just anyone," your affection or allegiance cannot be bought, that you "just don't buy any old product," etc. It means, more abstractly, having high, demanding standards—and being prepared to go without something or someone (if you are looking for a business or marriage partner, for instance) for as long as necessary, rather than lowering your standards. This has similarities to the snobbish class-consciousness one still finds in many countries amongst educated people, although the Japanese have learnt to affect a more polite and democratic air in their dealings with those "socially" or "culturally" beneath them.

GAIJIN COMPLEX AND INTERPERSONAL FEAR

Japanese psychologists long ago created a special domain of psychology which they called *taijin kyofu*, or "interpersonal fear." There was a very good reason for this—the Japanese, even among themselves, in expressing their fears of others in a rich variety of neurotic or pathological ways, often end up in the consulting rooms of doctors, psychologists, or less reputable "quacks." The predominant interpersonal fear of the Japanese comes out as "shyness," but in Japan there are many varieties of shyness.

Among children, that shyness which, in all cultures, often leads to their unabated crying in terror in the proximity or presence of a stranger is called *hitomishiri*, with the implication of fear of strangers being clear. When shyness among adults is discussed, the usual word is *hazukashigari*. Actually, the Japanese are rather proud to tell you that they are, as a people, hazukashigari, for this is a quality that bespeaks a certain unaffected naturalness of temperament. They see the shy person as someone still with his or her youthful personality unsullied by the world. This starts to make sense when you understand that the Japanese actually idealize adolescence as the best, most carefree days of one's life. The English metaphor "the springtime of life" is close to the word they use to describe the quality of this period of life. It is *seishun*, which literally means "green spring." Seishun also has connotations of innocence, ignorance of the sullied ways of the world—and many young Japanese, and their parents, still make valiant efforts to somehow preserve at least the appearance of innocence in an increasingly knowing society. But again this can have a cost in intercultural encounters. As we have seen, cross-sex encounters with foreigners can have a high degree of tension (and sometimes challenge) for Japanese. Puberty brings with it the development of gender awareness, of what it means to be male or female, and of what sexuality is. Among the Japanese, however, there is a special problem: Not only does puberty, and the institutions that facilitate its passage, not entail or demand the learning of techniques for initiating conversations or relationships with opposite gender strangers, but the schools and clubs that are young Japanese adolescents' primary groups actually reinforce in-group solidarity, fighting spirit, and competitiveness, resulting in an increasing social distance from non-group members.

Interpersonal fear and the gaijin complex both stem, in my view, from the proneness of many Japanese to a sense of shame. As a Japanese, you learn to feel ashamed to relate to someone who is "better" than you in some ways. The presence of something "better," for the shame-directed person, serves as a goad to longterm determination to improve oneself, but shame itself is psychologically crippling. As Nathanson (1990) has pointed out, shame often arises from feeling weak, frail, dirty or messy, from awareness of our mental and physical defects, from lost control over our body or feelings. What might trigger shame in an encounter with a foreigner? It may be some real behavior by that person—ridicule, contempt, disdain—but it can also be an imagined invasion of privacy by another. This fits the Japanese-Westerner case.

I shouldn't end this discussion of interpersonal fears among the Japanese without indicating some of the other types of fears and symptoms not uncommon in Japan, and documented in the psychological literature. Most familiar to non-Japanese is blushing, but there are also less familiar varieties—fear of looking others directly in the eye; fear of showing facial expression of feelings or emotions; interpersonal fears such as writer's cramp occurring only when writing in the presence of others; fear of swallowing if the sound of it will offend others; fear of sweating in front of others; fear of mouth or body odors or farting being detected by others; fear that one's imagined unusual body structure (such as having an unusually short or long spine or nose or other feature) is perceived disagreeably by others. These are not ailments that the sufferers wish to admit to or talk about to anyone, let alone foreigners. They are ailments that some Japanese carry throughout their working life, with fellow workers seeing the symptoms only as the result of stress, rather than the result of close encounters with others. Foreigners who have encounters with Japanese need to tread carefully with their Japanese opposite numbers, though by no means do all Japanese suffer from these complaints.

CHAPTER
3
FIRST ENCOUNTERS: PLEASURE AND PAIN

First encounters between Japanese and Westerners can, as I noted in chapter 1, be fuelled by a romantic, positive, excited interest in the other country, or they can be treated as something to be painfully endured. Under the heading of "first encounters," I want to discuss some examples of each type.

The "romantic" predisposition is common among nonbusiness people, such as Japanese visiting overseas as researchers or exchange students, or on a home-stay, or Westerners doing the same in Japan. There are a number of differences between these types of people and business people. They are more likely to have made the choice to visit the country themselves, whereas business people are unlikely to have personally selected the target country (this is particularly true for Japanese business people). Business people have objectives, tasks, deadlines, and so on, and they have to fit into a pre-existing business organization and work through local people in achieving their goals. Making friends, or knowing about and understanding the target country, are not usually high priorities on the businessperson's agenda. Those people with nonbusiness objectives are more likely to be interested in the people and their culture, and to be able to achieve their objectives without coordination and cooperation with local people or organizations.

Simply speaking, the businessperson has less time to deal with people as people or to enjoy informal experiences of the local people and culture, and is subject in the multicultural workplace to more pressure and stress in managing in, and communicating with, a different culture, so there is a tendency for the businessperson to enter the painful endurance category of sojourners abroad. This is true for both Westerners in Japan and Japanese abroad, as later chapters will show.

"ROMANTIC" EARLY ENCOUNTERS

Over the years in Japan, I have undertaken surveys of the crosscultural attitudes of Japanese and American exchange and graduate students toward each other, in the International Studies Schools of two Japanese universities. The American students had, on average, been in Japan about three months but had had a prior interest in Japan, quite often including language study. The Japanese students all spoke good English and had, in many cases, spent time in the USA as exchange students or, in a few cases, as residents. Certainly all were interested in the US. The first question they were asked was whether they liked or disliked the other nationality. Then they were requested to "explore this idea in writing below, being totally honest and not monitoring what comes up for you. Write out all the reasons you can think of for that opinion, then try and get at the reasons underlying those reasons." The responses discussed below come from composite samples of fifty of each group.

WHAT DO AMERICANS LIKE ABOUT THE JAPANESE?

The characteristics of the Japanese most liked by Americans were: politeness, their dedication to harmony/getting along well with others, friendliness, generosity and hospitality, honesty, kindliness, sincerity, diligence, and ability to work hard. Other characteristics mentioned were: cleanliness, sensitivity, self-discipline, loyalty as friends, service-orientation, formality, aesthetic sense, shyness.

The following comments make clearer what they had in mind:

"I like Japanese people. Most are friendly, kind, and almost always polite . . . they try very hard to be kind and respectful to one another . . . they work hard in whatever job they hold, no matter how high or low their position."

"I like the Japanese friends I have made and their concern for one another, including their concern for me! They are great at gift-giving. They know exactly when you've 'had it' with the system, then delight you with a flower, candy . . . they are very honest."

"I admire their dedication in keeping a stable *wa* [harmony]. I perceive them as a clean, hardworking, intelligent people . . . they are efficient and make maximum use of limited resources. I can learn from them!"

"I like the warmth and constant humor within the home, the food, friendships that once formed will last, the sense of harmony, their nonconfrontational attitude. . . ."

"The Japanese have been very willing to help me adjust to their different culture. If I do something wrong, they laugh *with* me . . . they have been willing to give me a chance."

"In general the Japanese seem like friendly, courteous, respectable people, something that's difficult to find in America."

WHAT DO THE JAPANESE LIKE ABOUT AMERICANS?

The American characteristics most liked by Japanese were: independence, friendliness, open-mindedness, ease in making friends, individualistic character, lightheartedness, capacity to enjoy leisure, ability to speak their minds clearly, confidence, positive/optimistic attitudes. Other characteristics mentioned were: self-control/discipline, calmness, sense of gaiety, naturalness, lack of ostentation, active nature, use of initiative, positive self-esteem, logical mindedness, ability to live as they want to live.

Representative comments were:

"What I like is that they are individualistic. They may belong to a group but are not swayed by it (unlike the Japanese). Americans usually have strong solid opinions about an issue . . . which they are self-confident about. They are interested in what is going on and are never unconcerned about their environment, unlike the Japanese."

"I feel it is easier to make friends with Americans than with Japanese people because they are more open-minded and have more character."

"What I like most about Americans is that most of them are so independent and have positive self-esteem. They really know how to amuse themselves in their spare time."

"I like Americans because they speak frankly, are logical, live as they want to, like discussion, and are generally independent."

"Generally speaking, Americans are very active and make us very cheerful. They speak clearly about what they are thinking. I think it is much easier to communicate with Americans than Japanese. If only I could make myself understood in English!"

"They are friendly and kindly—sometimes too much, so that I don't get private time. I can see what they are thinking, they are open, even with strangers."

"I like Americans, their positive attitudes, gaiety and light-heartedness. They do things naturally and honestly, not ostentatiously."

COMPARISON OF MUTUAL ATTITUDES

These results and comments show up the extreme differences between Japanese and American culture that are so often commented on. In many ways, they complement (one might even say, complete) one another: what is noticeably different about the other is what, they discover, they are lacking or deficient in. It is this perception that makes for both the attraction and repulsion between Japanese and Americans generally. Look above at the last comment by an American and the first by a Japanese. The Japanese comment—that Americans are individualistic and concerned about the environment—makes clearest what these young people have done in perceiving and evaluating one another: they have admired characteristics in the other which they believe they, or their fellow countrymen, are weak in. The Japanese like the individualism, open-mindedness, independence, and spontaneity of the Americans—characteristics which they see themselves as deficient in. The Americans see the Japanese as polite, nonconfrontational, genuinely friendly for the long term, hospitable—as the last comment in the section on American opinions puts it, "friendly, courteous, respectable; something that is difficult to find in America."

WHAT DO AMERICANS DISLIKE ABOUT THE JAPANESE?

The most commonly mentioned traits of the Japanese that Americans disliked were: attitudes toward and treatment of women; rudeness and lack of consideration of others in public; being cliquish and too group-oriented; introversion and lack of assertiveness; being cold/reserved/reluctant to show physical affection; being threatened by or uncomfortable with foreigners. Others, less frequently mentioned, were: submissiveness; a childish tendency to praise; being overorganized; crude humor; rigidity and stubbornness.

Representative comments were:

"Japanese people can be too ambiguous and superficial; it would be refreshing to hear something expressed frankly and directly. As well, the Japanese can 'overdo' it sometimes—even leisure activities are organized without much room for individual spontaneity."

"I dislike the Japanese in trains, subways, sidewalks. They smash and tread on and brush my new clothes and shoes uncaringly. I dislike the male treatment of wives, or any woman . . . their lack of respect for women. . . ."

"They are pushy and rude in public."

"They do not confide deeply about their own feelings or ideas. It is frustrating to have a friend who will listen to you, but has nothing to say [confide] in return."

"I dislike their stereotyped expectations of me. I cannot break them, and it's frustrating. I also dislike their 'threatened attitude' with foreigners—I have come across lots of cases of 'gaijin complex.'"

"I dislike some Japanese ideals—like work at the company, knock yourself out, have a family, etc. It's almost too intense the way people act in the subway—I saw a man almost break his leg, and women falling on the floor in their hurry to get on the train. I think it's crazy."

"In Tokyo, it seems such a burden to stay alive. All the crowds get on my nerves. The *senpai-kohai* (senior-junior) system is another thing it is real difficult to understand. [This student was staying in a Japanese student dormitory. Though he was four to five years older than the Japanese students, because he was in his first year in the dormitory, he had to play the most junior role and serve every senior with rice and soup at each meal. Refusing to do this, he created much dissension within the dormitory. It is worth noting that dormitory norms are fundamentally the same as those of any hierarchical organization in Japan, and represent a learning experience of value for those entering such an organization.] In America, that kind of thing does not exist, so it seems entirely useless to me as an American."

"Before I left for Japan, I thought I would be able to overlook the areas I dislike, such as the roles of women in society. I've had to bite my lips and keep my opinions to myself since coming to Japan."

WHAT DO THE JAPANESE DISLIKE ABOUT AMERICANS?

Again, there were far fewer dislikes than likes. The most common dislikes were: arrogance, overconfidence, aggressiveness, coldness/lack of sympathy, insensitivity/inconsiderateness, bluntness, excessive individualism, critical attitudes.

Representative comments were:

"If only more Americans would try to understand other cultures besides their own, they would be much nicer."

"They are arrogant . . . they do not learn our language and expect us to speak theirs. . . . They are not sensitive compared to Japanese people; they rarely sympathize with a person. . . . They do not seem to understand the delicate way the Japanese handle people's feelings."

"Americans never use flowery words or modesty. But the Japanese always use them to get along with others."

"I expect them to have more consideration of others."

"I dislike Americans because they seem to think they can do anything. Once they are involved in any dispute they seem to think they can solve any difficulty. Arrogant Americans!"

COMMENTS

The mix of likes and dislikes indicates that there is repulsion as well as attraction between the oddly matched pairing of Japanese and Americans. While the likes relate to the sense of being complemented and enhanced, the dislikes seem related to the violation of norms that each side cherishes—public courtesy, personal openness, courtesy to women, independence, etc., for Americans; moderation, sensitivity, delicacy, avoidance of aggression, etc., for the Japanese. Overall, the picture presented by this pattern of likes and dislikes is consistent with the nature of the people themselves. They are, after all, a rather special group—well-educated young people with interest in and curiosity about the other side. The dislikes that some of them express reflect the culture shock normally experienced when living in another country. This is shown by the more caustic language used by some Americans about their lives in Japan—especially about public rudeness, treatment of women, and fitting into an hierarchical society. It is likely that analogous comments would be heard in any survey of Japanese problems of living in America.

AMERICAN WOMEN IN JAPAN: EARLY ENCOUNTERS

Karen Hansen (1986), in a survey of the experiences of young American women in Japan, found that all her respondents agreed that the position of women in Japanese society was very much lower than in the USA, and that it was a source of shock and anguish to them. Some commonly held views were:

"What I find particularly disturbing is the subservient, cutesy, and childish manner in which their society teaches them to behave."

"Japan is a very chauvinistic country. For example, women on TV are often belittled in front of men. This affects me as well, as when my boss asks me to perform menial jobs he would not ask a man to do."

On the other hand, some American women have a more positive view. For example:

"I feel that Japanese women are in general happy in their traditional role of dominating the domestic sphere. They are much happier with their roles as mothers, wives, and homemakers compared to women in the United States. If they're happier, why shouldn't they continue to do what they are doing?"

Hansen also inquired about the difficulties they had adjusting to Japanese society as women. The single biggest problem is with *chikan*, or gropers, in trains, they said. This is a well-known problem in Japan. In tightly packed commuter and subway trains, and some unfrequented walkways (these often having large signs in Japanese warning Beware of Chikan), Japanese women have long been subject to this kind of molestation by some Japanese men. It turns out to be a difficult problem for any woman to handle. In a crowded train, as one American woman points out, "being a woman, you don't have many choices. If you make a scene, it's you who looks bad, not the man." There is no tradition in Japan of going to the rescue of someone complaining or shouting—the Japanese prefer to act as though nothing is happening. A common perception of a woman being molested would be that she probably brought it on herself, anyway. American women in Japan, aware of the problem, sense that it is deeper—that they are seen as "free and easy" sex objects by some Japanese men. One of Hansen's respondents said that she found it hard to decide when and how to speak to a Japanese man just in a friendly way, because the fear of appearing to be enticing the man was aggravated by the fact that cross-sex (nonsexual) friendships are far easier to make in Japan.

The other major problem for American women qua women concerned their sex-role behavior. One exchange student, while spending a year in a home-stay with a Japanese family, was expected to "serve" her 26-year-old Japanese "brother" in the same way as the mother did. This "subservient" role upset her greatly. Another reported that:

"Men sometimes expect you to do things just because you are a woman, lighting cigarettes, pouring drinks. I was asked for a light in a restaurant once, so I lent the man my lighter. He was deeply insulted, thinking that I ought to do it for him."

In the office, sex-role problems persist for American women. One, who worked in a Japanese market research company which had a lot of Japanese women in quite senior positions, found that they also employed women to serve tea and take out the trash. On the other hand, there are American women working for major Japanese companies and undertaking responsible projects, who find no difficulty in adjusting to the sex roles required of them. As one pointed out:

"I regard the sex-role factors as just part of culture-learning in Japan, although there is an element of having to work harder to prove yourself if you are a woman. I know also that Japanese men often have to do even dirtier and more menial jobs in their training years, jobs no woman would be expected to do."

A long-time senior American manager with Japanese companies in the US told me:

"In the 15 years that I've been closely involved with Japanese companies, most of the 'career moves' I've seen women make are to graduate from tea servers to notetakers to administrative assistants."

The biggest problem for many Western women in Japan occurs not in the workplace, however, nor in common interest groups, but in crowded, impersonal, or isolated settings where some Japanese men indulge in sexually bizarre, immature, and fantasy-based (because it can lead only to fantasy, not to orgasm or even penetration) behavior. Most of the other complaints are about Japanese role expectations of women or about the perceived subservience of Japanese women. These complaints seem to stem from a sense of intimidation, not social demand, but by no means do all non-Japanese women make such complaints. For many Western Women, indeed, the positive points of life in Japan outweigh the negative.

As far as Western women working in Japanese companies abroad are concerned, I have heard only very occasional reports, often at third and fourth hand, of anything remotely like sexual harassment by Japanese male executives. At worst, I was told of fleeting touches to the arms or shoulders, feeble attempts to steal a kiss from a secretary in an elevator, cloudy invitations to spend a weekend together. It sounds adolescent by Western standards, and if the reports are true, it is not surprising behavior by hardworking men far from home, who are often lonely and whose upbringing was never designed to make them socially poised with women.

COMMENTS

In the previous chapter, we saw how many Japanese inherit perceptions and stereotypes of foreigners which they call the gaijin complex, and that this is associated with social awkwardness in first or early encounters with foreigners. In this chapter, we have looked at early encounters, during which time those initial complexes and stereotypes about foreigners would be expected to be somewhat modified by actual experience. The Japanese and Americans in my samples were people with a special interest in and experience of each other, so we can accept that their views of the attractive and not-so-attractive aspects of each other are realistically grounded. Equally, we can expect that early encounters between Japanese and Americans lacking a special interest in each other will be less two-sided and less perceptive. This should lead us to predict that early encounters between business people from the two cultures, in the more formal, task-related, and stressful context of business, will be somewhat cooler and less friendly than those we have considered in this chapter.

PART 2

FOREIGNERS INSIDE THE JAPANESE COMPANY

INTRODUCTION
TO PART 2

In this particular piece of work, most of analysis will be concentrating on management styles.

When any company invests abroad, establishes offices or factories in another country, employs local staff or local man agers, it is entitled to be called a multinational company, that is, one which does business in and earns income in two or more countries. Apart from the challenges of manufacturing and marketing abroad, however, the novice multinational company will also be at the start of a cultural/organizational learning cycle. This learning process includes both management technique and human relations and communications skills. The former is concerned with how to create policies, business strategies, and practices that fit with both local realities (local laws, customs, infrastructure, etc.) and the demands of head office (for profit and growth); the latter with how to attract, recruit, train, manage, and motivate local staff. In the chapters that follow, we will examine, through a study of the experiences of foreign employees both abroad and in Japan, how far Japanese companies abroad have gone in learning how to manage these two processes.

In the early stages of any company's existence as a multinational, this learning process is all trial and error—trying something that is good, proven practice at home, and seeing how it works.

There is a simple reason for this. No one at head office understands or has had any experience of the foreign environment or its special needs. On the ground in the foreign country, the expatriate manager will soon discover that the foreign country is not like home, that people behave differently, and that many business and human relations practices that were effective at home are not appropriate abroad. But a head office without international experience is likely to be suspicious and critical of requests for different policies and practices. It only feels comfortable with its own traditional policies and practices, which it "knows" work (albeit at home), and doesn't want to experiment. Only when traditional ways fail will thought be given to seemingly riskier, more innovative ways of doing business and managing people.

Over time, multinational companies learn to balance their control over what the overseas subsidiary does by giving the subsidiary a degree of autonomy and freedom to adjust to the local environment and culture. In high-technology industries such as automobiles and advanced electronics, a very high degree of worldwide control is demanded in order to coordinate production, development, and marketing in the major markets of the world. More and more people in head office come to have overseas experience, enabling them gradually to understand both what is really different abroad and thus calls for novel practices or policies, and what is not so different and can be done much as it is at home. Japanese companies which, compared to US and European multinationals, were late to become international are still in the trial-and-error period of learning what the best balance is between head office control and local autonomy.

What makes the workplace different in the multinational company abroad? A multinational company abroad is a *multicultural* organization, unlike the monocultural organization back home (or at least this is the case in Japan, although many other countries have multicultural workplaces in their home country). A multicultural organization is always more unstable than a monocultural one. Language and communication problems and suspicion of people who differ from us (aliens, foreigners) are standard features of multicultural organizations, and are intensified when one racial group or nationality seems to have a monopoly on power or positions of authority. What we are learning about multicultural organizations is that these problems are minimal when there are few representatives of the head office (home country) culture in the organization abroad, though I believe that, since racial prejudice to some degree is endemic to all societies, we should regard problems in such cases as merely latent or dormant.

Once the number of expatriates from the home country of the organization who are in positions of power and authority starts to grow (from say four or five), cross-cultural problems of communication and human relations, such as misunderstanding, misperception, miscommunication, and suspicion of motives, become commonplace. It is from this base of everyday cross-cultural problems that secondary and more chronic and corrosive problems of factionalism, group conflict, and racial polarization emerge. These are also intensified by the tendency of expatriates to find exclusive community in one another's company—a trend that becomes more marked when relationships with the local people begin to sour.

CRITERIA THE JAPANESE USE TO RECRUIT FOREIGN STAFF

It is national policy in Japan to remain monocultural, monolingual, monoracial—the Japanese can see the problems that arise in polyglot societies and want no part of them. So it is a natural extension of national commonsense to be sensitive to and cautious about the problems that arise in multicultural organizations. It is not so easy to identify and recruit people possessing the kinds of cultural skills and the personal and social flexibility necessary to fit into an alien society like Japan. One hundred years ago, as we saw in the chapter 1 case studies from the Meiji period of foreign workers in Japan, it was most important that a foreign employee possess special skills, but in perhaps every second case, the foreigner had the right skills but the "wrong" attitude. This kind of success ratio probably persists today among foreign white-collar employees of Japanese companies, either in Japan or abroad. It is true that more white collar non-specialist staff abroad are now selected for having the right attitude and flexibility (so that they will be ready to turn their hand to many different tasks as the situation requires). Many foreign employees are, for instance, inherited (i.e., not recruited) from foreign firms acquired by or merged with Japanese companies. However, some workers—such as systems analysts, laboratory scientists, scientific translators—have skills that are so rare and in such demand that the Japanese accept them with little or no evaluation of their personal attributes or "attitude."

We can thus see that many of the foreigners who work for the Japanese abroad are not the product of a Japanese-style recruitment. Furthermore, even those who have been recruited and selected by Japanese managers are often "random" selections. The reason is that, just as is the case with Western managers trying to evaluate Japanese people, Japanese managers frequently find it difficult to "read" the personalities of Westerners. They tend to make more "mistakes" in selecting Western personnel abroad than they do in selecting Japanese in Japan, and there is evidence (Van Dyck 1987) that they spend less time on the evaluation and selection process for Western employees than for Japanese employees. The recruitment of Western employees in Japan is probably more systematic and perceptive, since Japanese companies can attract non-Japanese who have both special work or professional skills and the language and human relations skills to work with the Japanese. But even in such cases foreign employees are all too often employed in the hope—rarely fulfilled—that they will eventually return to their native country and work for the Japanese subsidiary there.

This "hope" is, however, important to understand. The Japanese realize that the cultural knowledge and language skills acquired by long-term foreign sojourners in Japan is of enormous importance in fitting a non-Japanese into a Japanese organization. It is not a matter of book learning nor even of advanced language skills. It is a matter of being comfortable with little things in everyday behavior: things which are almost impossible to explain to the culturally inexperienced. It is a matter of trusting your Japanese colleagues and bosses, even when you don't know what is going on: these are marks of the truly culturally acclimatized foreign employee.

Few foreign employees recruited for overseas subsidiaries will ever achieve this degree of cultural acclimatization. The majority have only a limited interest in Japan; a limited tolerance for the different "ways" of the Japanese; and a limited capacity or motivation to understand why they behave the way they do. Few foreign white-collar employees of Japanese companies abroad have ever been to Japan, or will ever do so. For most, home is where their hearts lie, and alien ways are at best endured or kept at arm's length. After all, they might say, home ways are the right and proper ways, and alien ones are not. And, whatever their noble sentiments about the importance of cross-cultural understanding, even the most cosmopolitan of people go through times when they misunderstand, feel confused, and think in a bigoted manner, times when for the sake of self-preservation, they know they must flee the prejudice of the "alien" and take refuge in the cosy familiarity of home and home's people.

So the Japanese hope that the culturally acclimatized foreigner recruited in Japan will eventually return to the home country subsidiary is very understandable. What a pity it is that so few stay long enough to realize the hopes and dreams of their Japanese seniors!

THE STRUCTURE OF CHAPTERS 4 THROUGH 9

In chapter 3 we looked at Japanese-Western cross-cultural relations in nonwork settings. In the next six chapters, we will look at the work setting and the experiences of foreigners working for Japanese companies from two broad viewpoints: one, the human relations and interpersonal communications dimension; the other, the conditions of work, employment, and management. In each case, there are two situations to consider—working for the company in Japan, and working for it abroad. If you work in Japan, Japanese values will usually dominate human relations, as will Japanese ways in work and management. Foreigners usually have little option but to fit in (though, as we will see, some recruited for their special skills can bargain or bully their way to compromise positions while larger numbers of foreigners can make for greater hostility and polarization, even in Japan). In contrast, those who work for the Japanese abroad tend to expect human relations to be determined by the local prevailing culture and values (so setting up potential conflict), and expect that the company's management and work practices and values will be a hybrid of local and Japanese.

In organizing the material of this key part of the book, I begin from an ideal model of what conditions would be needed in order for the organizational climate of a multicultural company (of which the Japanese company employing foreigners is an example) to operate effectively from all points of view. These conditions would be:

Good Human Relations
Effective Communications
Equitable Employment and Status
Equitable Work Conditions and Control
Equitable Management Involvement
Intercultural Harmony

Do Japanese companies satisfy these conditions? The goal of Part 2 is to answer this question by devoting a chapter to each factor. Thus, chapter 4 examines human relationships between foreign employees and their Japanese colleagues and bosses, asking, for example, how well they get along with each other; how much at home the foreigner feels, and how much at home he is made to feel. Chapter 5 examines the world of company communications, face to face as well as written. Chapter 6 looks at the employment, recruitment, and status of the foreigner, asking if they are equitable. Chapter 7 deals with the work conditions and control of the foreign employee, his or her roles in the company, and the demands placed upon him or her to adapt to the work environment of the Japanese company. Chapter 8 moves the examination into the managerial and decision-making area, looking at whether foreigners are able to become managers—if so, what is the cost to them, and if not, why not? Chapter 9 looks at those Japanese companies where everyday problems of imperfect human relations and communications, of dissatisfactions with work conditions and level of responsibility, become so aggravated that organizational harmony is lost, the house becomes chronically divided, and acrimony and overt hostility are daily fare.

A final chapter in this section puts the shoe on the other foot, giving the perspective of Japanese managers assigned to work as expatriates outside Japan.

CHAPTER
4
GETTING ALONG WITH COLLEAGUES AND BOSSES

We already know many things about human relationships between Japanese and Westerners from chapters 2 and 3. These showed the Japanese as a generally shy people who prefer to avoid, or have no contact experience with, foreigners (or other strangers). Only a very small number of Japanese, who speak English confidently and are university-educated, demonstrate the interest or motivation to relate positively to and create friendships with Westerners. This can be expected to be the situation also among those Japanese business people who become colleagues or bosses of foreigners entering Japanese companies—for the great majority, the ability to communicate effectively in English will not be a highly valued skill, even if they find themselves in the same work group as a foreigner in Japan; and may not be valued even after they have been placed in a foreign business environment. As for sociability with foreigners, we can generally expect the Japanese to be shyer than are Westerners in getting to know foreigners, and to take much longer to become overtly friendly. The findings in chapter 2 also remind us that they are likely to be somewhat repelled by any foreigner activity that seems to violate Japanese norms relating to moderate behavior, sensitivity and delicacy, and avoidance of aggression.

The new part of the cross-cultural context we are now to examine is the company itself; in particular the sort of work situation the foreign employees are assigned to and how they are supervised. In Japan, there are situations where foreigners in Japanese companies are located in their own foreigners-only section, having little connection with Japanese staff. This can minimize both cross-cultural friendships and communication problems. In stark contrast, there are individual foreigners who work as a part of a predominantly Japanese section—usually of six to ten people—and who quickly become close to their Japanese work colleagues. Obviously, in the former case, Japanese language proficiency is not nearly as critical to doing the job as in the latter, and the lack of proficiency will often be a major reason for separating the foreign from the Japanese staff.

The tables are turned when the company is abroad; we find either local employees working with and reporting to other locals and having little or no regular contact with Japanese expatriates; or, less frequently, the entire work section of local employees reporting to a Japanese expatriate manager. What is very rare abroad is to find a section where Japanese expatriates and local employees work together as equals, and cases where they all report jointly to a local manager are even rarer.

What this discussion leads to is the recognition that not every foreigner working in a Japanese company works in an immediate work environment that has anything specifically Japanese about it, or relates or reports to anyone Japanese. In many large overseas subsidiaries, in fact, most of the local office and managerial staff I have spoken to say that their immediate work-place looks like any other local company's office, and that their contacts with Japanese expatriates is minimal. In the United States, you would be hard pressed to see a Japanese face in the general offices of Sony, TDK, Sharp, Panasonic, Fujitsu, any of the Japanese full-service banks, and so on, where the vast majority of local personnel report to local, not expatriate managers. This means that for a sizeable proportion of local staff abroad, there is not much chance to develop friendships with expatriate Japanese, or indeed to experience much more than the exchange of casual greetings at the water cooler.

This is not to say that the locals cannot develop perceptions and expectations of expatriate staff—indeed they do. They form judgments about their friendliness or otherwise, about the quality of their communication skills, about their "inscrutability," and so on. They draw conclusions (valid or otherwise) about how expatriates view local staff, especially women and minorities, and about their willingness to recognize skills and recommend promotions. They can react emotionally to stories that circulate around the office about the expatriate staff, develop resentments, and feel unfairly treated or looked down on. For it is true that wherever there are expatriates (whatever their nationality), there are stories about the excessive privileges and benefits they receive, about coming to the office late, playing golf instead of being at the office, being rude or condescending to locals, etc.

WORK NEIGHBORS OR NOT?

It is obvious then that we can talk about two different levels of relationship between foreign and Japanese staff—one in which they are closely connected on an everyday basis and are working jointly on common tasks; the other in which only a superficial business relationship exists, and there is no direct task-oriented connection between foreign staff and Japanese. In the latter relationship, though the foreigners may have negative perceptions and emotions and express occasional animosity towards the Japanese, the problems of cross-cultural relationships or interpersonal communication will be marginal—we would expect these people to get along as well with their Japanese colleagues or bosses as they would with neighbors living down the street. In this book, therefore, I will concentrate on relationships and communications between Japanese and foreigners who work closely with each other in Japanese companies, either in Japan or abroad.

FITTING INTO THE JAPANESE COMPANY

How well do foreign employees fit into the Japanese company? Do they get along well with Japanese employees? In answering this question through the experiences of foreigners in Japan and abroad, we have to keep in mind that non-Japanese do not usually have the same "regular employee" (*sei shain*) or lifetime status in the company that the Japanese have. They are more often given the status of a contract employee (*shokutaku*). Does this affect personal relationships or mutual perceptions?

PATERNALISM AND FAMILY ATMOSPHERE

"Each employee feeling himself or herself a member of the company family" is a basic goal of many Japanese companies. Japanese managers in larger companies maintain paternalistic or avuncular relationships with younger staff members, giving advice and guidance, encouraging and challenging, and overall showing a kindly concern for their development as business people and as human beings. Not every young Japanese is fortunate enough to attract such patrons, but those who do feel gratitude for care that will usually last a lifetime.

Alfredo Villarante, a Philippine-born member of one of Japan's major computer companies, owes much of his career success to the ongoing avuncular concern of a senior Japanese manager. When Villarante joined the company in 1973, it was on the invitation of the manager. Whenever problems arose, especially as a result of his nonacceptance by some Japanese, a word to his patron helped resolve the problem. Today, Villarante occupies a middle management position in the company's US subsidiary, although he retains his status as a member of Tokyo head office. This has been maintained, among other things, to permit his patron, now a director of the company, to continue to claim Villarante as one of "his [the director's] men." It is important, this means, for the long-standing relationship to be maintained and to appear to be maintained.

With occasional exceptions, foreign employees are welcomed into the family-like atmosphere of most major companies in Japan as warmly as the Japanese themselves are. Carlton Patrick, a Canadian finance specialist, has this to say about his time as a regular employee with the head office of M Bank, one of the largest in Japan:

"M Bank is like your family away from home because of the

psychological dependence it encourages in employees. Everything is taken care of—your health care, meals, everything. I had a taste of that even as a foreigner. Whatever problems I had, they were able to help. In fact, I just had to tell outsiders that I worked for a Japanese bank, and their attitudes changed dramatically. "Oh," they would say in a servile, ingratiating way, "you are an eminent person (*erai desu ne*). . . .

"People treat you very nicely at M Bank. There's no hostility, no fighting or loud arguments in front of others. They don't tear people down to score points. Very civilized. They really make an effort to create harmony in office relationships."

This is a typical picture of what the Japanese would call an "elite" company. (Banks like this one, or major trading companies or manufacturers, attract the very highest quality male and female staff from the top public and private universities.) Such an atmosphere—democratic, fostering self-regulation of behavior and showing an absence of overt authoritarianism—reflects what are best thought of as elite culture values in Japan. Patrick has this to say about the costs as well as the benefits of sustaining this kind of atmosphere:

"They never tell you specifically—Do this! do that! They leave it up to you to decide what is right or wrong. On the other hand, it makes people more cautious and timid. They have exaggerated fears that they may be doing something wrong. I sensed a lot of underlying tension, with people constantly worrying: Is this right? Is this wrong? The Japanese spend so much time trying to be sensitive to what others think and feel that they can quite exhaust themselves. But overall the people are good and decent, and they do care about others' feelings. I'm quite impressed by that."

This fussy preoccupation with correct behavior, described by Patrick, is typical among Japanese staff members in their twenties and is not restricted to the leading companies. In the long term, such gnawing concern leads to knowledge of what behaviors are adaptive within the organization—that is, it leads to good understanding of one's work colleagues, their needs and interests, to office and administrative practices that promote harmony and cooperation, and generally to the avoidance of behaviors that might offend others.

THE OFFICE AS HOME

If the company is family, it is also true for the Japanese that the office is home. The long hours spent there, the frequency of overtime or weekend work, plus the intimacies and mutual understanding and knowledge that develop between workmates are parts of the way that the Japanese treat the office as home. But there is more to it than that. Foreign employees in every country have mentioned how their bosses make themselves at home in their office, in ways undreamt of by locals. The Japanese take their shoes off, walk around in slippers, pare their nails, read the latest sports and general news from home in a Japanese newspaper, and go to sleep on the office couch (thoughtful secretaries close the office door for expatriates prone to snore). Although they can penalize local staff for arriving late, some Japanese managers themselves arrive late, making no explanation, and from the locals' viewpoint, setting a bad example. Because many play golf during the week with customers, local staff have developed sarcastic comments in some companies. " Where is Tanaka-san?" someone asks. "Oh, he's at the green office," comes the knowing reply. Other expatriates feel freer to confide their real feelings to local staff. "I'm doing so much drinking, playing so much golf, doing so much entertaining, that I'm tired all the time." They dream of an early night at home but have to settle for a quick catnap at their desks before heading off for the bar district.

JAPANESE "CLUBBINESS"

Another part of the good family atmosphere in some Japanese companies comes from what we can call Japanese "clubbiness." This clubbiness is part and parcel of the paternalistic, family atmosphere in the firm. When you are a member of a regular work group in a Japanese company, you will be expected to spend not only most of your lunch hour with your group but some of your regular evenings off as well. You become like family. If you make a trip away, you are expected to bring presents back for everyone in your section. Foreign group members in Japan are incorporated into this set of relationships as a matter of course, and it would be out of the question for them to be treated in any way other than as a full group member.

From a Western viewpoint, this "clubbiness" can seem extreme, as Carlton Patrick points out regarding M Bank:

"You've got to go through this ritual where everyone has lunch together. Now and then I have things to do, but the obligation is so strong, I often give in and go to lunch with them. The feeling is, 'We've got to stick together.' In my section, ten of us would set off from the fourth floor to have lunch together on the tenth floor. If all ten of us couldn't get in the elevator, we would all wait for the next one, or the next! Unbelievable!"

This sticking-together is regarded as typically Japanese by the Japanese themselves. To go off on your own regularly and have lunch would be regarded as hurtful and even insulting to one's fellows, unless the reasons why were carefully explained and it was done infrequently. Fitting in with lunch and other group activities is one of the ways one demonstrates sensitivity to others in Japan.

Clubbiness, however, works best in top companies where all the group members are regularly in the office and work together cooperatively. Other work situations can be quite different. Englishman Paul Grove was one of the first foreigners employed by Seibu Department Store, and like the other foreigners there, he worked almost entirely alone. His first year was spent in familiarizing himself with the company, without being assigned to a specific work group. When he asked the personnel department to assign him somewhere, he was sent to a ham and sausage factory in Kawagoe, in Saitama Prefecture, to learn the business. He stayed six months doing everything from sweeping floors to assisting on the production line, as well as writing a weekly report for the personnel department. With that experience, he became a sausage maker and demonstrator at sausage boutiques in the group's department stores. Dressed in an immaculate chef's outfit, he would set up his sausage maker, put in casings and mince, and out would come fresh sausages to sell to suburban housewives.

Grove's experience is in total contrast to Patrick's but is no less

"Japanese" for that. He worked alone at a project assigned to him by the company. Clubbiness was nonexistent and unimportant.

"CLUBBINESS" ABROAD

With very few exceptions, Japanese expatriate managers do not socialize with their local staff in the "clubby" way we have seen often occurs in Japan. Language problems, the lack of common interests, and a lack of feelings of affinity are the principal reasons for the limited socializing—they rarely have lunch or evenings out together. Rather, Japanese expatriates spend their evening hours with other Japanese expatriates, either clients or colleagues, or friends they have made in the expatriate community. After having attempted to use English all day, most younger Japanese are likely to be stressed and in urgent need of speaking their own language. This is not normally a problem with more senior Japanese, but it is they who will be spending more time with clients, particularly as they will have the expense accounts to do that.

The lack of common interests is a very significant difference that is not recognized enough. Apart from the international game of golf, there is little of common interest as far as sport is concerned; the Japanese tend not to learn about local sports, so they will be locked out of office conversations about important games or news about sports-people. Apart from economic news, few Japanese business-people keep up with international affairs. If some international news is not reported in the day-old copies of national newspapers they receive each morning, they are unlikely to be aware or even informed of it. Again, there are those Japanese who resist socializing with their local colleagues because they think they are better than them, and that it would be demeaning to be socializing with people who are inferior. While there are many Japanese who take a serious interest in their host country, there are others who in private with other Japanese do not hesitate to make their criticisms known.

The experiences of Grove and Patrick can be taken as representative of those of foreigners who have regular employee status in the company, which gives them full equality with their Japanese peers. Many foreigners working for Japanese companies in Japan, however, are not regular employees, but special or contract employees. In some cases, their lot can be difficult. American Robert Klineberg worked for a leading construction company for five years (on renewable yearly contracts) as an English language and communication skills instructor. He recounts some of his experiences:

"My immediate superior in the construction company was younger than me and had overseas experience [unusual for a young Japanese]. He had honed his skills supervising Korean, Pakistani, and Bangladeshi construction laborers in Saudi Arabia, and he carried those skills [he said sarcastically] over to the supervision of the three foreigners in his education and training department. His was a feudal mentality. We were just tools to be used and discarded when no longer useful. He was arrogant and talked down to us, making sure we understood from his manner that we were inferior outsiders. So many times he treated us like dogs. For instance, we were located in a separate room outside the office of the Japanese staff in the department. Whenever we were there, one of the Japanese staff was there as well. We were not trusted. It was degrading. It was only when I left and went to work in another Japanese organization that I experienced total trust from my Japanese managers. It restored my faith in the Japanese."

This type of discriminatory treatment is relatively exceptional in Japan but somewhat more common in Japanese subsidiaries abroad. This manager probably shared prejudices with many other Japanese against foreigners who teach English in Japan. English teachers tend to be seen (not always unrealistically) as itinerants with useful but low-grade skills, easily replaceable, and likely to be in Japan for a short period only.

Alfredo Villarante, mentioned earlier, had a very different kind of experience. After five years of graduate studies in Japan—first in the Japanese language, then in electronic engineering—he joined a company as a contract (*shokutaku*) employee, which gave him a somewhat higher salary than the regular employees but prevented him joining the company union or the pension fund.

How was he accepted into the company? Villarante told me his situation had its good and not-so-good aspects.

"I was regarded as a showpiece, an experiment. The company had very little overseas experience, so everyone wanted to be exposed to foreigners. For the first four years it seemed like game playing. They would try to utilize me to learn English or meet foreigners. I was unhappy when they would try and push translation work onto me. In that early period, the only other thing in their minds was that I would eventually go back to the Philippines and be their man there. And they wanted to learn. In a way, I was their guide, everyone wanted to talk to me, people were friendly, I didn't threaten anyone because I was just a contract employee, so I was very well accepted. Speaking Japanese and looking Asian probably helped too."

The feelings of being treated as a novelty, as an informal English teacher, or, as others have said, of having been employed to promote the company's internationalist image, are very common among foreign employees in Japan but rare in overseas subsidiaries. The widespread Japanese hope and expectation that the foreigner will eventually return to his home country and work for the subsidiary there is a major factor in this kind of treatment. Typically, the foreigner stands apart from the rest of the staff, being perceived as closer to an honored guest than as another regular employee.

In most cases, few Japanese company men (even today in the 1990s) think of the foreigner as someone who has the same status and opportunities in the company as his Japanese peers. In Nagoya in 1991, I was speaking with a Japanese company president about the problems his company was experiencing in attracting high-quality people to work for his company. I somewhat innocently suggested that he could draw upon the foreign managers who worked for his subsidiaries abroad, but he merely looked incredulously at me. The subsequent conversation made clear that he had never thought of the foreign staff of his company as real employees. At best, it seemed, he viewed them as temporary workers hired as needed by his Japanese managers abroad. I am convinced that his attitudes are still typical of Japanese companies.

Even among the handful of companies in Japan that are today, as a matter of policy, employing more foreigners as regular employees, it has not been an easy matter to achieve an internal climate that is accepting and supportive of that policy. Understanding Villarante's experience is valuable, because he was one of the pioneer foreigners to accept lifelong employment in a major Japanese company. Today (1992), with nineteen years' service and having earned promotion to middle management by successfully completing, entirely in Japanese, the demanding four-month course for promotion, he is probably as integrated into the company as any non-Japanese can be. Currently on longterm assignment from Japan head office to the US subsidiary, he has been there fourteen years to date, and in the process has taken US citizenship (an act which caused considerable commotion within the company at the time, and which I will discuss in the next chapter). Moreover, he is confident that if he had stayed in Japan and taken Japanese citizenship, he would have had a very good chance of being elected eventually to the board of directors. But that is not an option he was ever interested in following.

What were some of the barriers he had to overcome in order to achieve the successes he has had to date? He recalls his first years in the company:

"In the early years, as I was slowly becoming more senior, it became time to have someone working for me. I did in fact have someone working for me, you might say, but it was quite fuzzy whether in fact that person was working *under* me. The problem of course was that the Japanese felt it was very demeaning to be subordinate to a foreigner in a Japanese company, and this particular young man made it clear that he hadn't joined a top Japanese company just to become the subordinate of a non-Japanese. I never pushed the matter, and it remained fuzzy as long as I was in Japan. Then, in my first years here in the US, I behaved just as one member of a team, even though I was in fact the most senior [which in Japan means one automatically takes the team leader role]. Usually, if you act as the leader of the group for a longish time, say six months or more, then it is official. But in my case, my divisional manager here in the US didn't know what to do. He had never faced such a case. I heard later that he had talked to the other group members—all Japanese—asking them, 'Is he OK?' They apparently said yes, so he made it official that I was the group leader."

This case ought to be taken as an indicator of the limits to the integration of foreigners into the Japanese company, at least as far as the more conservative members of the company are concerned. The fact that Villarante has gone as far in the company as he has should also be taken as a remarkable personal achievement, in his being able to work effectively in an ambiguous situation, without intimidating or offending his Japanese work colleagues. As we will also see in other such cases, the foreigner has to behave in an exceptionally sensitive and accommodating manner in order to achieve the support of his Japanese colleagues or eventual subordinates. Villarante's case also suggests that there would be strong internal limits or conditions to "clubbiness" between Japanese and foreigners who tried to press for their (Western-type) "rights" to a leadership position. Villarante's flexible, Japanese-like adapting to a difficult, ambiguous situation would not endear him to the many Westerners who believe that the only thing to do in such a situation is to be vocal in demanding your rights. Such Westerners would probably feel it was masochistic to persevere and be patient, in the ways that are called for in Japanese organizations.

There are some situations where foreign staff do behave more forthrightly than Villarante, because the Japanese businesses rely substantially on their skills. Tara Neilsen is a bilingual American, married to a Japanese, who is a specialist in Japanese consumer marketing. She spent many years working for Japanese companies before becoming an independent consultant, and it is her experiences in one—a cosmetics company in Osaka—that she speaks of here:

"The cosmetics company had me headhunted from a Japanese advertising agency, so I was in a strong position to begin with. They needed me to do a lot of work in English, as they wanted to start operating seriously in the United States. . . . While the Japanese in the company spoke little English, the English-related work was very important to them. When I first started there, they began by treating me just like a Japanese, but that changed swiftly, and I was put in a special category. After about two years, I started to hire a lot of foreigners. We ended up with six, and my job was real fun because they were there, and I was the buffer between them and the Japanese management."

In this strong position, Neilsen was able to resist the inevitable pressures to adapt to the ways of the Japanese company, which occasionally led to communication and relational troubles, of which the following is a rather extraordinary example.

"I never liked to have my lunch exactly at noon. I didn't like the way the buzzer goes off and everyone runs out and then comes back exactly at one. And in my case it didn't really matter. I was always working on special projects, close to the managing director, who was number two in the company. He approved whatever I did, and he approved my request to take my lunch hour at a time that suited me. One day, two of us went to lunch at one-thirty and got back at two-thirty. There was a note on my desk, written dramatically in red, saying, 'Go immediately to the vice president in charge of personnel.' I thought, 'Wow, what can it possibly be?' and we bounded up to the eighth floor. The vice president was waiting for us.

"Now I had never had a run-in with this man, but I didn't like him—a jerky old guy with an old-fashioned funky haircut. But here we were in front of him, in the middle of the personnel office. He was very, very angry, with his hands on his hips, and he was obviously going to give us a public bawling out.

"'Where have you been?' he shouted, and everyone in personnel tuned in.

"'At lunch,' I said.

"'What do you mean—lunch? It's two-thirty. You should have been back at one. The president wanted to see you. He had some guests for you to meet, but you weren't here, and this has caused great shame to the company.' He looked on the verge of a heart attack.

"By this time, I was just furious.

"I said, 'If the president has a problem, I'll talk directly to the president, but I'm not going to talk to you. It has nothing to do with you.' Now I was hopping mad, and my body was shaking.

"'No one talks to me like this.' I flung the words at him. 'This is the first time and the last time. I will tell the president. You do not behave this way with people. It's totally unacceptable,' I said. Now he was literally frothing at the mouth.

"I saw the president as soon as I could. He said, in quite a jolly way, 'I had some people here I wanted you to meet.'

"I said, 'I will be very happy to meet people, but please let me know in advance so I can change my lunch hour.' Then I went on to complain to him about the vice president, how he was not fit to be dealing with people."

The vice president of personnel genuinely believed, I am sure, that he had right on his side. Especially in Japanese companies, rules are made not to be broken but to be strictly observed and enforced without exception. Breaking rules is regarded as a sign of insincerity, a serious deficiency. Anyone permitted to vary rules would also fear that others would perceive it as favoritism and be concerned that they would be offended. The flexibility in lunch hours that Neilsen requested and received is unlikely to be requested by Japanese, unless they have made sure that everyone has been notified and has agreed. Japanese with similar ideas would be deterred from taking action by the extreme fear of being carpeted by a superior, in just the way that Neilsen was. What Japanese would do then would be the antithesis of her violent reaction. They would apologize, feel deeply ashamed, and want to escape from the situation and any discussion of it as soon as possible. Consequently, the vice president, clearly naive about cultural differences, expected that an American would respond in the same ashamed, crestfallen way. Instead, he experienced a very severe loss of face because he was berated in public by someone whom he was likely to have regared as inferior in many ways—female, a nonregular employee, junior in age and status, not to mention white and American. Furthermore, we can see that Neilsen behaved in a very direct, assertive way about her rights. How the more culturally adept Villarante would have behaved in a similar situation is an interesting question. Most probably, he would never have allowed himself to be put in such a situation—that is, he would have behaved in the Japanese way.

The end of the story is that the president's visitors came a few days later, and they turned out to be the *mama-san* (proprietor/manager) of a bar which the president patronized regularly, and one of her hostesses. They had come to ask if Neilsen would teach English to the hostess. Neilsen was offended, for she was a marketing specialist, not an English teacher.

"They came dressed to the nines, just to ask me that. It was really offensive. I just said dryly, 'There are lots of good English schools. Try those.'"

Requests to foreigners in Japan to teach English are commonplace. The Japanese see nothing wrong in making such a request—it seems commonsense, and many foreigners are pleased to be asked. Those foreigners offended by the request are usually professional people and managers like Villarante and Neilsen, who see English teaching as low-status work that is beneath their skills.

I have been writing about foreigners and the kinds of human relations and communications skills they use in the Japanese company in Japan. Villarante is representative of those few foreigners who aim to be lifelong employees, who recognize they must emulate Japanese human relations and communications skills, in most respects, if they are to survive and prosper and develop relationships of goodwill. In contrast, Neilsen is a business specialist who never intended to stay permanently in any Japanese company, seeing herself as a "hired gun." Her readiness to adapt to the culture of a Japanese company, or generally to that of Japan, was highly conditional. She has always said very forthrightly that she has rights to defend, that she is and always will be an American who happens to live abroad, even though she is married to a Japanese. She showed this very clearly in one story she told me about attending the morning pep-talks (*chorei*) in the cosmetics company, which were held daily at eight-thirty.

"In the chorei there is a certain way you are expected to stand, with your feet together, hands folded demurely in front. But I always stood loose, like this. [She demonstrated, with her body weight angled to one side, left hand on hip, and head inclined to the right.] I soon had people telling me how to stand, and I said, 'Well, isn't that fascinating?' But I never changed. It is one of those things that is culturally taboo for Americans."

If Villarante and Neilsen represent extremes of foreign adjust-ment to the Japanese company in Japan, New Zealander Robert Gage occupies the middle position. Gage, now a freelance writer and translator in Japan, originally worked as a writer for Novatech, a highly successful Japanese-owned communications and translation company in Tokyo, then spent several years over-seas. On returning to Japan, he was soon approached by the pres-ident of Novatech, Shuji Shinagawa, who asked him to come back and work for Novatech again. Shinagawa regarded Gage as the best all-round employee he had ever had—a first-rate organizer and people manager as well as a fine writer, who (unlike most of the foreigners he had experience of) fitted into a Japanese com-pany without any problems. This time, however, Shinagawa wanted him to take a management position and be a regular em-ployee. The position required him to be the coordinator of all translation, writing, and training in English, managing the flow of work (as well as its quality) in and out of the office to the many general and specialist translators they used, as well as developing course materials for and coordinating the instructors and the many different training programs they conducted in English.

Gage explained the background to his appointment:

"It was obvious that Shinagawa had become completely fed up with managing foreigners. He had nothing but trouble with them, and I must say that the foreigners felt the same way about Shinagawa, because he was too sharp for his own good, a very clever negotiator able to put himself in a position of power and get the most out of people for the minimum acceptable wage. Feeling that he was always trying to take advantage of them, they had de-veloped an entirely cavalier attitude towards Novatech.

"My job was to deal with these foreigners in his place. He was quite upfront about it. I wasn't thrilled about dealing with those people, but the work was interesting to me, so I said yes, and be-came a regular employee and a manager in the company, the first foreigner ever. As time went by, with Shinagawa now freed from having to deal with his detested foreigners, he started to use me as his spokesman, to do his dirty work. For example, there was one translator who had always refused to wear a tie to the office. This infuriated the president, but as the man was our only medical translator, he had a strong position, knowing he wouldn't be summarily fired. Shinagawa now felt that I might be more successful in getting the guy to wear a tie, so he told me that it was part of my job to convince him to wear a tie and fit in with office requirements. Naively, in retrospect, I went dutifully to the translator and said, 'The president insists that you wear a tie to work everyday.' Until this point, the translator and I had been friends, but he suddenly changed, accused me of being the president's stooge and mouthpiece, of having no soul of my own, of being antiforeigner and pro-Japanese. The reality was, I then discovered, that the company had long had this split in it, with the Japanese and foreigners being very conscious that they were on opposing sides.

"As the translator still refused to wear a tie, Shinagawa started to exert other pressures on him—delaying salary increases, and such like. Finally, he did start to wear a tie, but this only intensified resentment against me. I came more and was more under attack and subject to backbiting.

"So there I was in the middle. I could see the Japanese approach and the president's tactics and his attachment to maintaining control through insistence on truly minor points like tie-wearing or being extremely punctual. I could see the foreigners, too, and I have to say that the quality of the foreigners we got in to do translation, teaching, and rewriting was low—a lot of riffraff really. I was sandwiched between a rather ruthless, extremely astute businessman on the one hand, and a bunch of surly, opinionated, culturally maladjusted Westerners on the other hand. Eventually I became the enemy of most of the foreigners we employed, certainly all the Americans. The only people I retained good relationships with were some Brits and Australians, who understood where I was coming from."

Gage's experience is ironic. In striving for a better cultural adjustment to his Japanese boss and company, he only succeeded (according to him) in worsening his relationships with another group of foreigners—this time Americans. This is not an isolated case. In the USA and Australia, I heard similar stories from

Japanese expatriates, trying to manage a multicultural work force. In one case, the more the Japanese manager tried to coordinate co-operation between sections—one with a Filipino head, the other with an Italian who were at loggerheads with one another—the more antipathy both parties showed toward him. Such cases, however, carry us beyond the limits of the present book.

ISOLATION IN THE JAPANESE COMPANY

Foreigners working in general business departments in Japanese companies in Japan seem to participate in the company's social life, socializing with their Japanese colleagues and bosses. It is foreigners who are specialists—and who have been recruited into the organization directly from abroad—who seem prone to experience isolation and loneliness. Academics, research scientists, engineers, and others with special intellectual skills are typical. However, two factors at least ward off isolation and loneliness. One, most seem to go to Japan in groups—relatively few are alone. Two, most are able to find in Japan fellow expatriates and people from their own country to provide important social support in the early, difficult days of adjusting to an alien culture like Japan's.

A 1990 survey of mostly single expatriate scientists working in Japan (STAG 1990) found many complaints about the lack of social life, possibly due to the remoteness of some of the locations. One researcher with a larger company commented, "The most important thing to say about social life is that there is not much of it." It is very likely that, if you are recruited as a specialist for a Japanese organization, you will be left not only to your own devices as far as work is concerned, but will not be admitted into whatever friendship groups exist.

CONCLUDING COMMENTS

Westerners working for Japanese companies in Japan generally fit in well, and enjoy good human relations with their Japanese colleagues, and bosses. They are treated equitably by their employers, especially when they are regular employees, work for a major company, and have a senior Japanese manager who watches over and advises them on their careers within the company.

In such companies, Japanese-type paternalism is an important factor in facilitating good human relations between all regular employees, Japanese or otherwise. The foreign employee's relationships with his or her company peers, workplace colleagues, and seniors are "clubby" and fraternal, with great care normally taken by the Japanese to fit in with others, promote office harmony, and avoid giving offense. At the same time, many foreigners claim they are employed more to promote the company's international image, or for their future value working for the company's subsidiary in their home country, than for what they can concretely contribute to the Japanese company in the here and now.

In smaller companies in Japan, or when the foreigner is employed on contract (and not on a regular, "lifetime" basis), paternalism does not seem as strong and in some cases may be discriminatory—witness the treatment of Klineberg by his young manager—or rigidly authoritarian, as in Neilsen's clash with the personnel director.

Overseas, however, it seems fair to conclude that human relations are much less family-like than in Japan. There seems to be far less socializing between Japanese expatriates and local staff than there is in Japan between Japanese and foreign employees, and there seems to be less paternal or avuncular guidance of local employees by Japanese expatriate managers. This seemingly lower frequency, I believe, is due to the high incidence of younger (under 35) expatriates, who even in Japan would still be too young and immature to play the avuncular role well. Certainly, my impression overall is that many senior (over 45 years) Japanese managers abroad generously strive to encourage their more talented local managers (male and female). I see this difference as due to their greater personal maturity (Japanese businessmen mature more slowly than their Western counterparts) and better communication skills—that is, better English, better expressive and socializing skills, and greater self-confidence.

One twist in the human relationships between Japanese and Westerners is the involvement of third or fourth cultures in the workplace, both abroad and in Japan. For example, Gage's experiences at Novatech seem to include culture or value conflicts and differences with highly individual-rights-conscious Americans and British Commonwealth citizens (British, Australians, New Zealanders), who seemed more ready to fit into the more formal, less "principled" mores of a Japanese office workplace. Overseas, we noted cross-cultural problems within Japanese companies that involved representatives of three or more nationalities—not just the locals versus the Japanese. I believe that the emergence of these secondary cross-cultural conflicts test the cultural knowledge, understanding, and sensitivity of the Japanese. In Gage's case, his Japanese president had no understanding at all of the cultural differences between the different nationalities of Westerners. Abroad, Japanese managers do recognize that, for instance, Filipinos and Caucasian Americans come from very different cultures, but they rarely have the intellectual curiosity to search out what the value differences are that lead to workplace conflicts.

In summary, human relationships in the Japanese company between Japanese and Westerners do not allow any simplistic generalizations, although they are clearly less intimate and less involved when two conditions apply. Firstly, when the Japanese company is abroad, and therefore in unfamiliar territory for its younger expatriates. And secondly, when the foreign employee is a contracted and not a regular member of the home office. In a recent study of Japanese companies in the USA (Global Industry Culture Research Institute 1990), some expatriate managers reportedly claimed that the reason why American employees are treated differently than Japanese employees is because Japanese companies and managers assume that Americans have no interest in lifelong employment. In my experience, this assumption is generally correct, but I believe the Japanese should draw conclusions about individuals (in this and other respects) on the basis of their judgment of each individual, not on the basis of a sweeping generalization. In the selection of their own staff in Japan, they are highly discriminatory about who will fit in and succeed. Regrettably, they do not seem able to be as prudent or selective with foreign applicants.

I suspect that these two conditions affecting human relations are connected, as my story about the Nagoya company president, who could not contemplate foreign managers in Japan, suggested. The connection is this: Local employees cannot at present be regular members of the mother company; only expatriates are regular members. This splits employees of the subsidiary abroad into two classes; the locals, and the expatriates who tend to see themselves as superior to the locals (this is especially true of younger expatriates). This inhibits their willingness to socialize or even to become involved in discussion with local employees. We will see the other aspects of this "two-class" system in the next few chapters.

CHAPTER
5

COMMUNICATING
WITHIN THE COMPANY

C ross-cultural communication is a minefield of problems in private or business life, the seriousness of which should never be underrated. Even at its best, cross-cultural communication remains occasionally flawed with the incomprehensible or the incommunicable. Managers in Japanese companies employing foreigners know that this is so, having learned from their own experiences, or from the mass media in Japan, for whom cross-cultural communication problems—such as trade friction, lack of mutual understanding, negotiation conflicts—have long been a favorite topic.

Talk to Japanese managers, at home or abroad, about what they do to solve their cross-cultural communication problems, and you discover the usual human diversity of reactions to the problems. A few managers work hard at improving communications with their foreign staff, energetically encouraging language study and socializing on and off the job, as well as organizing frequent meetings including both Japanese and foreign employees. Most managers recognize the variety of problems but are less active in leading their staff to positive counterstrategies to improve communications. And there are a few others who either ignore, downplay, or fail to recognize that problems exist or need addressing. Finally, there are those Japanese companies which, because the number of expatriates abroad or foreign staff at home is so small, can truthfully claim to have few cross-cultural communication problems.

What do we mean by cross-cultural communication problems? Of course, we especially have in mind occasions when one party fails to communicate his or her intended message to the other—these include occasions of misunderstanding, non-understanding, and confusion. While few multicultural workplaces can expect to be free of communication problems, the London subsidiary of Japan Couriers Overseas is one of the better ones, a small company with a local staff of fifty and two expatriates. Leonard Bright, the general manager, explains:

"I'm surprised how well it has gone. Although we have a real mix of nationalities, everyone gets on very well. So much depends on communication, and the Japanese girl handling subscriptions speaks excellent English. The managing director's English is pretty good, but there are some points of difficulty. For instance, his English is good enough for people to think it is better than it is, and they take liberties with him, speaking far too volubly, much too quickly.

"The main point of conflict is the young expatriate Japanese. His English and his communication skills are not good. These things, plus the fact that he is not in a position of authority, lead to conflicts. For example, a Japanese client telephones and says, 'I don't have my *Asahi Shimbun* and it's three o'clock in the afternoon. I normally get it at eleven to read with my coffee.'

"The young expatriate then goes to a staff member to explain the problem, but it comes across as blunt and dictatorial. The response might be, 'For God's sake! The driver's sick, man.' There is immediate conflict. Fortunately this happens rarely.

"Some Japanese have a somewhat excessive pride in their English ability and don't want to show that they don't understand. The managing director's predecessor was like that. We found it difficult to work out when he was understanding and when he wasn't. The present man has the good sense to make it plain when he doesn't understand."

Misunderstandings occur easily with the culturally inexperienced, and this comment from Robert Klineberg is another illustration:

"A lot of times Americans dealing with Japanese don't even recognize that they aren't communicating. They presume they are communicating, they assume they have explained the problem. I always find that amazing. I'll ask them: Have you discussed this with the Japanese? 'Oh sure, no problem there,' they'll say, 'Watanabe thinks it's good.' But when I talk to Watanabe, he's not happy at all. It is really amazing how Americans perceive things. If the Japanese does not openly complain, he will be perceived as agreeing."

This could alternatively be called misperception—when the absence of overt complaint is taken as positive endorsement. This also happens as a result of other characteristically Japanese types of behavior (which in Japan would not be negatively interpreted) such as—being silent in a situation in which a Westerner would respond, and be expected to respond; giving a seemingly perverse response, for example, responding "perhaps" or "it's possible" rather than giving an explicit "yes," "no," or "I don't know"; giving responses which are culturally ambiguous, and thus misunderstood, such as saying (as the Japanese frequently do) that something is "difficult" when what is really meant is "impossible, out of the question"; or changing the subject without notice, especially when orally challenged. Understanding that Japanese culture promotes harmony and uses avoidance, silence, denial, and even perversity to achieve that, thus preventing aggression and hostility from coloring interpersonal communications, it is easy to see why this kind of behavior is not taken "the wrong way" by other Japanese. In Western society, however, such behavior tends to be socially unacceptable and confusing or offensive to others. Unlike for the Japanese, the normative, expected responses in our culture will usually be unambiguous, and instead of indirect communication or avoidance, we will use oral explanation, lateral humor, put-down remarks, or even remonstration. None of these ways of communicating would be contemplated by the Japanese.

These examples make clear that interpersonal communication is more than language. The cultural meaning of value-driven behavior like silence or avoidance must be recognized if communication is to be effective. Here are some other examples from the context of in-company behavior: Leaving the office promptly at five is regarded as disloyal and coldly rational in Japan. When Japanese overseas first see local managers and staff leaving at five, the reaction is suspicion and scorn. "What kind of person is this?" they typically think, and in some cases reported to me, Japanese expatriates have queried local managers whom they trust as to what sort of people they are to be leaving precisely at the official finishing time. Again, Japanese wives rarely socialize with company people, and even less with foreigners. But abroad, the failure of Japanese wives to appear at couples-only parties—which seems perfectly acceptable to the Japanese—is regarded as offensive and mildly insulting to Westerners.

Other misunderstandings do stem from language use. In one American-Japanese joint venture negotiation, I reported (March 1989) that:

"One constant irritation for senior Americans (from the American Mannheim company) was the habit of younger Japanese (from the Japanese Mansha company) of saying, regarding a proposal prepared by a senior American, that this or that point was a 'problem' (in Japanese, *mondai*). Actually the nuance of the word 'problem' in English is stronger than the Japanese word mondai, which means 'something that needs looking at further,' whereas 'problem' means more like 'something that is going to be difficult' (March 1989, 41)."

The connotations of a number of words and phrases translated from Japanese into English can vary greatly and lead to misunderstandings and worse. Many words and phrases do not have exact equivalents in the other language, thus making 100 percent interpretation or translation an impossibility.

Moreover, although the Japanese may speak English, it is still a Japanized English, and their knowledge of local idioms or slang is likely to be minimal, especially in countries like the USA and Australia, where everyday male business speech is replete with local color. This makes for enormous strain on expatriates trying to understand their local subordinates. Here is one typical example, where communication problems in the cross-cultural workplace stem from limited ability to comprehend spoken English and are aggravated by differences in non-linguistic communication patterns.

Hal (Harunobu) Kawasaki is a director of an overseas subsidiary of Canon Inc., the camera and office automation products giant. Four local English-speaking managers report to Hal, and because his English is by no means perfect, he has daily problems of communication in the process of managing effectively. Some of his problems are very understandable. For instance, a manager who promised to finish a certain project by a specific date doesn't meet the deadline. Hal has promised it in turn to his president—and now he has been let down. "Why wasn't the project finished on time?" Hal asks. The local manager launches into a long explanation, and soon Hal loses his grasp of what is being said. The manager's speech is too quick and too colloquial. But Hal keeps nodding as though he understands. When Hal finally ends the meeting, the local manager still doesn't know that Hal hasn't understood.

If Hal had been dealing with another Japanese in this situation, he would have assumed that the Japanese really knew what was in his, Hal's, mind, i.e., that he wasn't understanding what was being said. A Japanese who didn't intuitively understand what Hal was really thinking would, in fact, be regarded by Hal and most other Japanese managers as "an unpromotable fool." On the face of it, that is, and looking solely at the words used, one can see that people behaving like Hal might be thought to be agreeing to something, or at least indicating "non-denial." But words in themselves in Japan are not "the message." It is a society in which, in the office or the coffee shop or the bar, communication is indirect, built upon hints and nonverbal cues. If, in spite of signs, obvious to Japanese people, of what one was thinking or feeling—especially the absence of élan or enthusiasm, and the choice of neutrally toned words—a subordinate did not "cotton on" to the real message, he or she would surely fail to survive as an effective member of the work group.

The problems of Hal Kawasaki in comprehending his subordinate's extended statements are commonplace for Japanese managers abroad, and are made worse by the failure of Japanese managers to make local staff aware of their limited grasp of colloquial speech. Moreover, once the Japanese listener loses track of what he is being told, he will inevitably listen less intently, signalling by facial expression or gesture that he has in fact largely tuned-out. It may be a familiar human situation, but it is also both a waste of effort and a sign of the diverse impediments to improved cross-cultural communication.

LANGUAGE COMPETENCE AND SOCIAL DISTANCE

Language competency problems also lead to increased social distance and hostility between Japanese and non-Japanese. Criticisms by local staff of the Japanese on this point include: Japanese speaking loudly to one another in Japanese in the middle of the offic, (Australia and USA); holding weekly meetings for senior staff in Japanese (UK, USA, and Australia); refusing to permit local managers to sign their names to internal memos—only department names are permitted when local managers write memos, but expatriates may sign their own names; control over the tone of memos extending to the rewriting of those of even senior local managers to eliminate any personalizing or warmth of expression; expatriates deliberately blocking efforts by local staff members to learn the Japanese language (USA and Australia); prohibition against the use of Japanese in several US trading company subsidiaries where many American staff speak fluent Japanese.

Japanese lack of English competency is probably behind some of this behavior. In cases where use of Japanese was prohibited, I have to assume that younger Japanese complained that they were not getting the opportunities they needed to practice English. Knowing how many foreign students of Japanese in Japan complain about the refusal of many Japanese to converse in Japanese, I can sympathize with the plight of the younger Japanese expatriates. But a blanket prohibition, made in these cases without explanation or discussion, is an authoritarian act that does nothing to foster organizational goodwill and seems to confirm the problems that Japanese expatriates are said to have in managing non-Japanese effectively abroad. As one English manager in a Japanese bank told me, "Few Japanese can be called competent English speakers. They struggle to express anything complex, and soon give up. The large number of daily aborted attempts at communication is a good indicator of how little we are in touch with one another."

Lack of English competency also lies behind other complaints, for instance, that Japanese managers are far less "hands-on" overseas, monitor staff work or contribute to on-the-job training, avoid details, are ignorant of the local environment, do not form out-of-office relationships with the staff, socialize with locals only on a formal basis such as for quarterly social club or sports club events, are bad-mannered in the office, poor listeners, often ignore or stare right through others or do not respond to greetings, remaining poker-faced (*shirankao*). Japanese explanations of their distance from local people and society that point to their heavy involvement in socializing with local Japanese customers and colleagues and visitors from Japan are certainly true in a literal sense, but are as much rationalizations as explanations. Local staff are not avoided nearly as much by Japanese expatriates who speak the local language well, and have outgoing personalities and a genuine interest in the local society and people.

A COMPLEX ABOUT MASTERING ENGLISH

In chapter 2, I wrote about the Japanese "foreigner complex" and showed that it is partly due to the foreigner's English fluency. The Japanese are most ambivalent about mastering the English language. In Japan, many Japanese businessmen are openly critical of those of their fellows who speak English well, and the resentment is such that the shrewder of them do everything they can to avoid speaking English in the presence of their colleagues. It is hard to avoid the conclusion that simple envy lies behind the criticisms of those who speak English well.

A hard-to-believe but true illustration of this occurred just after Kiichi Miyazawa was elected prime minister in 1991. Miyazawa differs from past prime ministers—and most of his political party colleagues—in speaking fluent, educated English. US Secretary of State James Baker was about to visit Japan, and the Liberal Democratic Party was making preparations. Clearly afraid that non-English speakers in the party would not be able to follow the exchanges between Miyazawa and Baker, the party arrived at the following consensus: Miyazawa was to speak to Baker only in Japanese when others were present, and Baker had to wait for English language interpretation. No one knows what Baker or Miyazawa thought about this odd shadow-play. The only consolation for Miyazawa was that he understood Baker's response at once—but what was Baker's "consolation"? At most, that he was already accustomed to communicating through interpreters in other countries.

If it is true that many Japanese businessmen feel envy and jealousy over the superior English language skills of others (Japanese or foreign), it makes their abbreviated conversations in the office, social distancing, lack of socializing, avoidance of dependence on subordinates for local information, etc., sadly understandable as behavior to control others. The occasional perverse efforts to impede the use or learning of Japanese by local staff abroad can also be viewed as attempts to control in-company communications. It could be a serious loss of face and a matter of shame if one's local (and subordinate) staff were to become bilingual, while you the Japanese were still struggling to express yourself in a foreign language you had been studying since first entering high school.

INDIRECT COMMUNICATION

Contrary to the West, Japanese culture places much more emphasis on indirect and economical communication. The following story is a startling example of this. Carlton Patrick, the Canadian financial specialist, told it to me.

"There was a Japanese guy, Uchida, aged about 28, who worked right next to me. He had just come back from Stanford with an MBA. I don't know what he was like before he went to the US, but now he was different to Japanese eyes. Very outspoken, he would get on the phone to his buddies back in the States and talk in a loud voice. His biggest crime was to argue with the assistant manager, who happened to be the most powerful guy in the division, and something of a peacock who thought very highly of himself. Uchida would stand in front of the assistant manager's desk and give forth with his opinions in a loud voice, so everyone in the division knew what was happening. After a couple of months he was reassigned, and I later heard rumors that they had tried to sack him on psychological grounds so they wouldn't have to pay his pension. Then I stopped hearing about him.

"One day, I got a phone call from a foreigner in Tokyo asking for Uchida. So I asked the secretary, where's Uchida-san? She said, '*Nakunarimashita.*' I thought, hello, I know what that means, it means he's dead. How strange, I thought. Or was it really a euphemism for 'he's fired' that I wasn't familiar with? No, on further reflection I decided it could only mean 'he's dead.' But I couldn't believe it. I said to her, 'You mean he's dead?' and she said 'Yes.' I felt suddenly drained. 'What am I going to say to this guy on the phone?' I picked it up and finally said, 'Sorry, I don't know how to get hold of him.'

"I went back to the secretary and asked, 'What happened to him? Did he commit suicide?' She looked surprised. 'How did you know?' How did I know? I said to myself. A healthy, robust guy like that doesn't just drop dead. Later I went to lunch and sought out the nicest guy in the division. If I was going to get a straight answer, he would be the best bet. I said, 'Something I want to know. Is Uchida-san dead?' He said, 'Yes,' and that was it. It suddenly struck me how incredibly cold the Japanese are. Once you are out of the group, that's it. Something like the Russians who erased people's names from the history books—that is exactly what happened with Uchida. If you work for a Japanese company, they are always sending notices around about the death of someone's father or mother, with funeral details. But about Uchida— nothing. His name was never mentioned again, although the names of people who had passed through the division over the years would crop up every now and then. Not Uchida's. He had never existed. It was quite an eye opener."

One cannot be sure of the background to this story. Most likely

Uchida, before his suicide, had worked himself, by his extreme and un-Japanese behavior, into a situation of near ostracism by other members of the bank: enough perhaps to make him a non-person in their eyes, and to devastate himself psychologically.

The Uchida suicide case is an extreme example of a Japanese cultural and communication difference. Patrick was horrified in particular by the lack of emotional expressiveness among the Japanese concerning the suicide of this outspoken and lively young man. There were no words, no expressions of sorrow or of shock—just a guarded and restrained neutrality. How should we outsiders evaluate the whole situation? Clearly, the Japanese were behaving in a culturally approved way. We cannot know what their real feelings were—they may have been as horrified as he— but we would be justified in suspecting that their restraint and apparent absence of feeling was not just skin-deep.

NO PRAISE, NO FEEDBACK

Japanese self-suppression is, in one form or other, understood by foreign staff in Japanese companies. They discover that the Japanese are most reluctant to give praise. It smacks of toadying or insincerity to them. They see individual projects as enmeshed in the flux of company activity. One finishes, another begins. It seems frivolous and lightweight to say more than an occasional "not bad" (warukunai) or a rare "well done" (yoku yatta). Often, however, nothing will be said.

Westerners are accustomed to and expect praise for a job well done, or constructive feedback when their ideas or work need improvement. Many local staff of Japanese companies abroad complain that they get neither. For instance, I hear complaints in every country that Japanese bosses are indifferent to proposals for new initiatives. The boss seems to sit interminably on a proposal, saying nothing. For instance, John E. Rehfeld, a thoughtful observer of the Japanese as well as former vice-president of Toshiba America and currently president of Seiko Instruments USA, has this to say about his experiences:

"My managers and I really knocked ourselves out during the early years at Toshiba . . . I was under a lot of pressure to make the goals. We started to achieve the budget in the third year, and we continued to make it for something like nine periods in a row . . . I kept waiting for my efforts to be acknowledged. But I never got a thank you. . . . I was frustrated by this. . . . My staff was discouraged too and complained to me, 'We do this great job, but we never get a thank you. Do the Japanese think we're their slaves?'"

Rehfeld believes he knows why the Japanese do not give praise: "They continuously strive for perfection," and never stop to rest on their laurels just because one target has been achieved. Apart from interest in the result, he says, "they are equally interested in how they can do it better next time." These factors mean that the Japanese, even if all other things are equal, will always outperform others. Nonetheless, he says, understanding as he did, there were still "times when positive feedback would have boosted my enthusiasm and morale at Toshiba" (*Harvard Business Review* 1990, 170).

Rehfeld is only partly correct about why the Japanese do not give praise. A more basic, more ancient cultural reason is that, according to traditional male (warrior) values, words are not completely to be trusted. In the Japanese ethos, giving praise does sound "phony," even hypocritical. The Japanese have a host of sayings and proverbs that are still current which warn against trusting words or the wordy—for example, "silence is golden," or "the mouth is the root of all trouble."

A more serious and frequently mentioned concern among foreign employees is the lack of feedback and information-sharing by Japanese managers and co-workers. Peter Banting, manager in a Japanese subsidiary in the US, points to this problem (Hayashi 1989). Simon (1991) surveyed local employees in Japanese subsidiaries in the US and found this to be the biggest problem, after faulty communication. Among my own respondents, many cited the refusal of the Japanese to share information. And it was not just the Japanese refusing to share information with foreign employees—many also refused to share with other Japanese. For instance, I was given two separate incidents of outgoing managers clearing their files completely, leaving nothing whatsoever—not even correspondence on pending matters—for their successors. Carlton Patrick had two related experiences at a Japanese securities company he worked for. First, his Japanese predecessor emptied the personal computer of every file and program, forcing Patrick to start from scratch. Later, Patrick offered a compound interest calculation program he developed to the Japanese co-worker next to him. That was refused, but his neighbor stayed late a number of nights to create an identical program for himself.

Lack of enthusiasm is a related complaint. A number of local executives in the USA, the UK, and Australia complained that their proposals, on which they had spent much time and whose merit they had checked on with others, were treated negatively by Japanese superiors—merely criticized on small details or treated sceptically, with no broad appreciation of what was being presented. In part, this is a communication problem. The personnel director of a Japanese airline service industry company in the USA suggests:

"The Japanese can be taken as offensive, a bit blunt, a bit direct. We, on the other hand, feel that we have to preface our remarks with 'I'd appreciate it if you would.' Most of them have a language problem and we don't understand what they are trying to do. It comes over to us as directive, one-way communication. They can't explain fully in English. For me, for instance, when I was putting together a new promotional proposal recently, there were a lot of points they didn't like. I changed them, but they were still unhappy. They had difficulty in understanding what I was explaining to them, and I had difficulty understanding what they wanted. In this case, they only grasped it when I wrote it out in detail."

This statement gives a realistic appreciation of how far-reaching communication problems can be, when English is used. It is a tedious process, not necessarily because the Japanese are legalistic or jesuitical and want to query the meaning of words and phrases, but because their grasp of English for communication at this level is superficial and shaky. So many foreigners report interminable discussions about the meaning of specific words. For instance, one reported such a discussion about the word "director" in a draft agreement, meaning, member of the board of directors. The Japanese believed that it had a much looser meaning—as in executive director, activities director, traffic director, etc. After the discussion had finally ended, and the Japanese accepted that the word had the precise meaning intended, the foreign lawyer said privately that in his view the scepticism and repeated questioning of the Japanese was grounded in their suspicions of foreigners in business.

Feeling emotionally secure with non-Japanese is a very major factor for Japanese in effective business communication. Without this, the Japanese tend to think the worst of their local employees, even feeling intimidated by their local staff. They do not feel the security they do with staff in Japan, and tend to agree easily with one another that local staff members are lazy, devious, prone to complain, and ready to strike over trivial issues. Fear of unions is quite intense. The Japanese are unused to them, for in Japan all unions are enterprise unions, that is, the only members are company employees and junior managers, and strikes are rare and short-lived. In other countries, however, they are craft-based, so there is the possibility that strikes may be triggered by people unrelated to the company. Arthur Tomkins, personnel manager of a large Japanese company in London, says that the Japanese believe local staff, when unionized, cannot be motivated to work hard, and that this conclusion is used to justify their own inability to manage and motivate local staff. Marcus Frew, administration manager of a trading company subsidiary in the USA, makes virtually the same point, saying that expatriates are ready to use the local staff as a scapegoat if anything goes wrong.

When I returned to Australia in 1988 after 15 years in Japan, I was asked to speak, in Japanese, to a lunchtime meeting of the Japanese Chamber of Commerce in Sydney, on the subject (which the chamber requested), "How to Use Your Australian Staff More Effectively" (subsequently published, March 1989). Ninety-three expatriates attended the lunch, the largest number ever, indicating how widespread concern was on this issue. I was already convinced that the human relations and communications were satisfactory to neither side, but I could not in a public lecture come out and say who was to blame bluntly. So, after pointing out some basics for effective cross-cultural adaptation (learn to manage stress, accept and understand the local culture and local people, develop the business skills needed in the foreign situation), I had to create a device for saying some tough things without giving offence to my audience.

The device used was a fictional character, Tom Brown, an Australian senior manager in a Japanese company who, over 20 years, had seen both expatriate and local staff come and go and knew the thoughts and feelings of both sides intimately. First, Brown reported how Japanese expatriates perceived their local staff—slow and lazy, aggressive to their seniors, insincere, incapable of apology for mistakes, lacking in flexibility, loyalty to the company, and business skills. "It would have been better if they had never been employed," many Japanese feel (according to Brown), "and I hope they leave soon." On the other hand, I continued, local Australian staff had strong views on the Japanese expatriates (from this point on in my talk, the audience became eerily quiet)—they were curt and abrupt when they gave orders, gave no explanations of why they wanted something in a hurry, were rude and lacking in basic good manners, were unfriendly, and showed no interest in "us" (the locals), with no words of praise for jobs well done. Cliquish to an extreme, they were uneasy in their relationships to "us," did not promote locals to positions of responsibility, and treated them in an insensitive and demeaning way. They were deficient in both management and communication ability and had no interest in training or motivating "us." "We" wish they had never come to Australia and just hope they return to Japan as quickly as possible.

Tom Brown device or not, I was tough on the Japanese, and some may think it is an anti-Japanese bias coming out. However, seven years earlier, in a talk to the American Chamber of Commerce in Japan, I had used the same device to tell Americans very similar unpalatable truths in a palatable way. This time a Tanaka-san was the medium to tell the Americans that their Japanese staff thought they were poor communicators, used a coercive management style, were ethnocentric and racially arrogant, and had serious inadequacies both as people developers and trainers.

"Nothing in our Japanese experience," said Tanaka, "has really prepared us for people like him. It quickly becomes no pleasure to work for him, and we start to avoid him whenever we can. Is it any surprise that he starts to feel more and more isolated?" (March 1983, 31).

In other words, management for the culturally inexperienced is situational and does not transplant: and this, I am confident, is true universally. In the context of the present book, and in view of the worldwide spread of Japanese businesses and bosses, the spotlight is upon them, showing up their shortcomings and pockmarks as managers and bosses.

EFFORTS AT IMPROVING CROSS-CULTURAL COMMUNICATIONS IN JAPANESE COMPANIES IN THE USA

In a recent survey of Japanese subsidiaries in the USA, CSBK (1991), a division of the Japanese Ministry of International Trade & Industry, reported on strategies being used to improve communication with local staff and managers. Not every company answered the questionnaire, and some answers that were given seemed unsophisticated, hardly addressing the problems. The answers included: "We are building a real family spirit"; "We are not a Japanese-type hierarchical organization, for we fit into the American (egalitarian) way"; "We pair Japanese and American managers together"; "Expatriates are permitted to use Japanese with one another during the lunch hour but at no other time." Having regular meetings or morning pep-talks was regarded as beneficial for communication by a number of companies. A few, however, were sceptical about the value of formal meetings in the US. One Japanese manager, resident in the US for nine years, wrote:

"We have few meetings of a formal nature. I believe that Americans don't like those sorts of meetings. As our policy is to leave the practical affairs of the business as much as possible to the Americans, I want to avoid any meetings that suggest they are being 'summoned.' But we do have frequent meetings that are informal sit-ins, and communication then is one hundred percent. We do have formal management-level meetings twice a year, which discuss company progress. The first one is always attended by the president from Japan and divisional general managers. We send our American senior managers to Japan every year for a week, where they do a training course on Japanese culture, and management methods and principles. Our American middle management go to the Japanese factory to study production techniques."

"Senior managers, with their wives, have two to three dinner parties a year, but unfortunately senior managers are not yet inviting one another to their homes.

"We have a number of expatriates who speak good English and they have their section or department meetings in English. Almost all communications with Japan are in English, and information flows freely throughout the company. Our warehouse people are able to communicate directly with the Japanese factory, which contributes much to the internationalization of our company" (CSBK 1991, 85–6).

I have quoted this manager's report at length because it is exceptional in its comprehensiveness. He and his company set standards that few Japanese subsidiaries can yet claim to have achieved, including meeting practices adjusted to the overseas culture, senior managers socializing between cultures, and written communication with Japan in English. This last practice is still almost unheard of in Japanese companies. More usually, American managers in Japanese companies criticize both head office and the expatriates for continuing to write faxes in Japanese. As a result, when expatriates are out of the office, nothing can be done on urgent projects until the expatriate returns and translates the fax.

Other ways that cross-cultural communication is encouraged by the companies in this survey include: Christmas parties, birthday parties (only in companies with twenty staff members or fewer), "after five" relaxation, parties at Japanese homes, occasional picnics, and education about Japan for the local staff, including trips to Japan in one case.

COMMUNICATION BETWEEN EXPATRIATES AND LOCAL FEMALE STAFF

Japanese expatriates are obviously uncomfortable with Western female staff members, according to my Western manager respondents. I was told this, or heard or read reports of this problem, in every country. Complaints included: expatriates failing to greet or respond to greetings from female staff on arriving at or departing from the office; expatriates avoiding meetings or discussions with female managers or supervisory staff; exclusion of female staff members from the company golf club. Remembering our survey results from chapter 2 on Japanese male/Western woman interaction, this is no surprise.

THE DIFFICULTIES OF MUTUAL UNDERSTANDING

The initiatives taken in some Japanese subsidiaries abroad to improve communication usually stem from one experience common to all such companies, namely, that there are times when the members of each side find it impossible to understand one another. Many of the problems I have reported so far have arisen in simple communication exchanges, but the counter-measures established, or proposed, to mitigate the problems have been diverse and mainly long term in nature: educational and training programs, regular meetings, parties and socializing, study trips to Japan, pairing Japanese and Western managers in the workplace, written communications in English rather than Japanese, etc. Much to my surprise, I found no company or manager seriously proposing language skills improvements (either English or Japanese) as a means to solving communication problems. A few expatriate Japanese take refresher classes in English conversation but this seems aimed only at smoothing everyday life. It seems a just conclusion that most Japanese managers abroad, faced with complex communication problems, see, not language but the cultural aspect as the key. They believe that only when foreigners learn more about the culture of the Japanese nation, of its business world, and of the company itself, will cross-cultural communication become smoother and problems be minimized.

How should we evaluate this tendency to emphasize the

foreigner learning Japanese culture as a prime means to solving problems? Factually, the Japanese are correct. They know the culture of their host country abroad far better than the host country people know that of Japan. Perceptually, however, they are treading on dangerous ground. Their request for foreigners to learn more about Japan looks one-sided, as though the Japanese are implying that Japan is more significant than the host country. Conducting seminars on doing business with the Japanese in many countries, I find that one of the commonest questions put to me is, "Do the Japanese try to learn about our country in the way that we do about theirs?" People abroad are suspicious and concerned that training and education courses about Japan are mere brainwashing to accept things Japanese more readily. Whenever I see evidence that the Japanese are not making a genuine effort to learn about, adjust to, and use the techniques of their host country, I share those concerns.

READING ONE ANOTHER'S MIND

Another factor behind communication problems is the apparent inability of many Japanese to read the personality of foreigners. People whose psychology and personality other Westerners can read simply and accurately often seem like a closed book to the Japanese managers. American personnel manager Brian Needle told me :

"The Japanese complain a lot to me about local staff. They ask my impression of them: 'Do you think this person is any good? What sort of person is he?'

"For example, one person is doing a certain job, but the Japanese feel uncomfortable with her. They say to me, 'We can't trust this person, she lies.' 'Why is that?' I ask. 'She told me she would do something but it is not being done.'

"Or they'll say, 'Do you think this person works hard, or is he lazy?' The reason for this will be that he leaves the office before 6, in spite of being in a senior position. My usual response to them is, 'Have you asked the persons directly why they do that?' That shocks them. 'Oh no, no, no!'

"If someone weren't performing, I'd have no problem talking

to them confidentially and finding out what was going on. But one thing I am is paternal, and the Japanese are not. I don't want to see people coming and going because that creates a really bad impression of the Japanese. They talk to me so often about staff turnover, but they never ever ask why they come and go. A lot of Americans are loyal to a company for the best part of their lives. Only a small portion are mobile.

"The problem is that we just have a few hundred employees and we can't rotate them to develop them and keep their interest up. In Tokyo, that's easy because there are 10,000. It's not so easy to keep people here. The Japanese expatriates find it hard to remember that we are a small company here, unlike Tokyo."

Needle enlarges our understanding of the difficulties the Japanese exhibit in dealing with local staff. Just as some Westerners might say, "All Japanese look alike," so there are many Japanese who will say, "All gaijin (foreigners) look alike." They may be inscrutable to us—but we are often inscrutable to them. Getting to the point where you can read the thinking and psychology of people alien to you is likely to be a lengthy process for business people when they are distanced, by work duties or rationalized choices, from the alien country they temporarily live in.

Westerners, too, find the Japanese hard to fathom. When we are unfamiliar with them, they also tend to look alike to us. Carlton Patrick, ever the perceptive observer, has this observation to make on trying to understand the Japanese:

"The Japanese are changing a lot on the surface but not inside. This is typified to me by one of the guys in project finance [a department of his present company in Tokyo]. A Tokyo University graduate, Rhodes scholar, Oxford graduate degree, vain, cosmopolitan, witty, eloquent English. You would meet him and then come away thinking—this is the new breed of Japanese, hardly any difference at all. He presents himself so well. But after I worked with him day in, day out, I discovered that, in reality, he can't stand foreigners! Now I'm inclined to think that the Japanese are very good at creating images, but the reality is something else, and that we are still a long way from getting close to them."

As I pointed out in *The Japanese Negotiator* (1988), patent dissembling and the disguising of real feelings or true intentions are very central to Japanese culture. Humility, self-effacement, the absence of pretension are cultivated social virtues. But the point that is easy for foreigners to gloss over is that the Japanese use dissembling and disguise just as much with other Japanese as they do with foreigners. They are also just as modest and reticent with other Japanese. This means that a Japanese can work side by side with another Japanese for years and not even know if the other is married or has children. I know many cases like this. Patrick's experience of this "new breed" of Japanese will serve him well in the future as a warning, especially pertinent in Japan, not to judge a book by its cover.

CONCLUDING COMMENTS

Like most cross-cultural communication, that between Japanese and Westerners in Japanese companies is frequently ineffective—meaning we don't convey the message we intend—and often counterproductive: relationships can become worse or more confused even when we are doing our best to make them better. If we wanted to lay blame or take sides, it would be fair to say that it is expatriate Japanese abroad who, notwithstanding that they have entered an alien culture that does not speak their tongue, fail to learn the new language or new culture sufficiently well to make a good attempt at everyday interpersonal communication.

A few Japanese companies and managers do try hard to adapt and be good communicators, they do change in-company practices so that regular cross-cultural communication is institutionalized and made to feel natural. But many more seem to be struggling—blaming the local staff for miscommunications and misunderstandings; fearing their laziness or their trickiness, or that of their trade unions. But both sides are trapped in the snare of culture. Not quite knowing how culture can warp our judgment of any culture save our own, many of us—Japanese or Westerners—see foreigners behave in a way that is impermissible at home and judge them as immoral or otherwise defective. Judging them so, misunderstandings and worse mistakes easily occur.

The importance of culture in a study of cross-cultural communication cannot be overstated. It is indeed more important than language. Some Japanese managers are expressly able to point this out, in order to explain why they cannot communicate. Why does the Japanese head office operate the way it does? he can be asked, but be unable to answer, partly because he doesn't have the language resources, and partly because there are some things that you must experience and see for yourself. Merely to explain or describe them may put too great a strain on the listener's credibility or imagination.

Most Japanese managers abroad, however, are more likely to be in a situation similar to that of Hal Kawasaki—decent people trying bravely but often ineffectively to manage in a foreign language/culture situation. It is the difficulties that they meet here that increase daily stress and drive them further into the sociable arms of their fellow expatriates, back into the greater use of Japanese in meetings and written communications. Afraid of getting into communication situations with the local staff that they cannot properly manage and where they easily lose the thread, they may fall back on relationship and communication control techniques that are permissible in Japan, such as avoidance, denial, poker-faced indifference, ambiguity, imperious orders, but abroad only serve to aggravate communication problems because they suppress the warmth, friendliness, the expressions of praise or respect or enthusiasm that are socially lubricative in Western countries.

Both sides, not just the Japanese, have problems in reading the personalities and real intentions of one another. The local staff abroad, for the most part ignorant of what is involved in cross-cultural communication, collides with the language and culture barriers between it and the Japanese expatriates. Something is being done in a few Japanese companies abroad to educate and train the foreign staff, but the problems are immense, not least because the Japanese managers, who ought to make decisions on matters like this, have no perspective on cross-cultural training and no guidance or support from the head office. There is thus much remaining that ought to be done, which we will look at more closely in the final chapter.

CHAPTER
6
RECRUITMENT AND STATUS
OF
THE FOREIGN EMPLOYEE

The world of the Japanese company which the foreign employee enters has, in a number of respects, long been misunderstood by the West and thus by the newly entering foreign employee as well. For example, Japanese employment is usually referred to as lifelong (*shushin koyo*), but in fact the Japanese Labor Standards Law prohibits employment contracts of more than one year. So, legally speaking, neither company nor employee are bound to each other in any permanent way. The Japanese lifelong employment that is written about so much is thus based on trust and mutual understanding: the employee commits him- or herself longterm to the company, and the company in turn commits itself to support and provide care for the employee. In the larger, consistently successful companies in Japan, regular employees (sei shain) customarily have no written employment contract but feel entirely secure that they will be employed until some mandatory retirement age. Even with an economic downturn, it is improbable that they will be laid off, though they may be asked to accept lower pay, take accrued leave, etc. In smaller or less successful companies, lifelong employment is not always possible or even implied. Bankruptcies are frequent among smaller companies, while family succession problems, illness, or business recession can mean the severance of workers.

Apart from regular employees, Japanese companies in Japan employ sizeable numbers of "nonregular" employees. According to the Japanese Statistics Bureau (quoted in Inohara 1990, 160), just over 10 percent of the Japanese work force is not regular, with 70 percent of that number being female. There are different varieties of nonregular employees in Japan, but the category under which foreign employees most often fall is *shokutaku*, usually translated as nonregular staff. Then there are *rinji yatoi* (temporarily employed), *kisetsu rodo-sha* (seasonal workers), and *hi yatoi* (daily workers). In addition to these workers, there are *arubaito* or part-time employees, for whom various labels are used: *jun shain* (associate employee), *teiji shain* (fixed hour employee), *kikan shain* (fixed period employee), and *paato* (occasional employee).

The shokutaku category is commonly used for employees who have reached the mandatory retiring age for regular employees, but continue to be employed on a nonregular basis.

"Their treatment varies: In some companies they are treated like full-time employees in terms of work hours, whereas in other companies they are part-time employees. Some companies pay, besides regular monthly earnings (usually, a basic salary 30–50 percent lower than their last one under regular employment, and a commuting allowance), seasonal allowances at a lower rate. . . . Other companies pay only a monthly salary. Usually no retirement benefit is paid when their employment is terminated. These terms of employment, in many cases, are not clearly stipulated in the contract" (Inohara, op. cit., p. 161).

It is important to understand shokutaku employment, because the foreign employees of Japanese companies abroad are employed, in the view of Japanese managers, as though they were shokutaku. Regular employees they are most certainly not, nor are they the equal in status of regular employees in the view of the Japanese (regular employees) themselves. Japanese managers, generally speaking, believe them unlikely to stay longterm with the company—the Japanese think Westerners are like "nomadic tribesmen" who fail to put down roots anywhere for long, in contrast to themselves, agricultural-type people who cling to and remain on their land.

Although there are virtually no foreign regular employees working for Japanese companies abroad, half of the foreigners employed by Japanese companies in Japan do have regular status (JOEA, 1988), putting them on the same level as Japanese employees with equivalent seniority. This means that their salaries follow company policy for regular staff, and they receive subsidized housing or a housing allowance and identical training to their Japanese colleagues. However, the same data show that even as regular employees there are constraints on foreigners. In only 80 percent of companies where the foreigners are regular employees do the companies say that it is "possible to become a senior executive," and in only 67 percent do the companies say "we definitely want to employ them [long term]." The remainder say that the "long term is not clear" (JOEA 1988, 132).

A recent survey (Roger March, 1990) of working conditions for foreigners in foreign companies in Tokyo provides more qualitative amplification of the conditions of foreign employees in Japanese companies. Replies were received from 20 foreigners working for Japanese companies. Four of the twenty were employed as regular employees (sei shain) and thus had no contract. Twelve had shokutaku status, and most of them had signed a one-year contract initially. Three had not subsequently renewed the one-year contract, so that they were working on an open-ended basis. Another had started out on an open-ended basis, but subsequently signed a one-year contract. A further two had entirely open-ended jobs with no contract, while the remaining two said they had two- or three-year contracts (notwithstanding that contracts longer than one year are in fact illegal).

Asked if their benefits differed from those of regular Japanese employees, the four regular employees said they received the same benefits as Japanese, including housing, recreational, and commuting allowances (typical allowances received by Japanese are for housing, commuting, family, pension, health plan, low-cost, vacations and sport facilities). Half of those on one-year contracts said their benefits were no different from the Japanese. One said vehemently, "absolutely none. Not even overtime," meaning that, like Japanese regular employees, they are not paid for overtime. Those saying their benefits differed from the Japanese had varied responses:

"My salary is higher and I get longer holidays, but I get no housing allowance. Otherwise everything is the same."

"I get a housing subsidy of 150,400 yen a month, which is about six times what the Japanese get. Everything else is the same."

"Foreigners are excluded from the pension plan. My housing subsidy is probably higher than that for Japanese."

"The company pays health insurance but no pension plan. I received a housing allowance from 1990 but my salary was reduced."

"Up to the age of 30, pay levels are higher for foreigners. Thereafter, the same as for the Japanese."

"I get the same as Japanese contract (shokutaku) employees. We only differ from sei shain (regular employees) in terms of housing and pension plan."

As for working hours, the average per month was 200 hours, ranging from 140 (for a proofreader of a newspaper) to over 300 hours for the respondent who reported that he or she was not paid overtime.

WHY ARE FOREIGNERS HIRED BY JAPANESE COMPANIES?

From the viewpoint of Japanese business, the employment of foreigners is essential to the enhancement of the internationalization of the enterprise that has been more or less forced upon Japanese companies by the strengthening of the yen and the consequent loss of competitiveness of goods produced in Japan, leading to the decision to invest, manufacture, and market overseas. One Japanese survey (JOEA, 1988) of the reasons why foreigners are hired by Japanese companies found that just over half hired them for their overseas activities, while one in five wanted them for their language skills—meaning three out of four hirings are international-related. As Japanese writers have pointed out, however, "It [hiring to help the company's internationalization] has led to repeated mistakes of trial and error in the employment of foreigners" (Shimada 1989, 34).

Foreigners employed by Japanese companies in Japan are the best source of information on what these mistakes are. Most generally, they complain that few Japanese seem to have any idea about how to effectively use foreign staff. They commonly complain that their duties seem limited to checking English texts for grammar, or English correspondence, which, if they do not read Japanese, they cannot be sure are accurate, and that this type of work leads to frustration. Or their biggest contribution may be entertaining foreign visitors. Japanese managers frequently find foreigners difficult to evaluate and may employ a foreigner because he or she speaks English or seems a flexible person who will fit in, without considering whether the person has skills or background in the industry. Japanese managers, foreigners say, fail so often to give any thought to what the foreigner will do once they have hired him or her, and in particular give no thought to what the foreigners must be taught about the particular line of business of the section they are attached to. Part of the problem is the common Japanese suspicion that foreigners will only stay for a few years before returning to their home country. This seems to narrow the range of possible contributions that the foreigner is perceived to be capable of, and can ultimately lead to the foreigner perceiving the company as an employment "dead end street." Another factor is that in a number of cases the foreigner does not speak Japanese adequately enough, which turns out to be a constraint on potential. And there also are cases where the foreigner does speak Japanese quite fluently but can neither read or write. In both these cases, many feel that such people would not be able to envisage working for a Japanese company over the long term.

ATTRACTIONS AND NEGATIVE PERCEPTIONS

This is not to say that employment in a Japanese company is unattractive. Job security is an outstanding attraction for foreigners working in Japanese companies abroad. There are other reasons, too, why they seem attractive: many of them are the leading firms in their industry and seem destined to grow more rapidly than foreign firms, perhaps to become market leaders abroad as well. They are seen as successful and well managed, in contrast to local companies, so many young people believe they have much to learn and understand through working for the Japanese. Not least, work experience in a Japanese company looks good on one's ré-sumé.

There are also negative perceptions of Japanese companies abroad as places to work. They are seen to reserve the top, decision-making positions in the company for Japanese. The ceiling of promotion is low compared to local companies. If you do get close to the top, you will still have to report daily to a Japanese shadow manager—and there are no decisions you can make on your own. Salaries are sometimes at or below the industry norm. If, because of these factors, the Japanese fail to promote or motivate their better local managerial staff, they end up being unable to retain quality people. As a result, local staff who remain long term with Japanese companies abroad tend to be seen as mediocre and lacking in initiative.

HOW INVOLVED CAN THE FOREIGN EMPLOYEE BECOME IN THE JAPANESE COMPANY?

We have already seen that local employees are generally treated like nonregular, contract employees of the Japanese company abroad, to which we can add that no expatriate Japanese seems to report to a local manager. A dual administrative structure—Japanese at the top, coordinating with Tokyo head office and making decisions, and local staff below responsible for operations—is typical in manufacturing and trading companies. In financial services and similar businesses, the local staff has more direct dealings with Tokyo to realize specific projects, but general management decision-making remains with the Japanese.

DISCRIMINATION AGAINST LOCAL EMPLOYEES

The second-class status of most local managers is clearly indicated in reports of recent findings against Japanese companies on discrimination (BRW Weekly, June 14, 1991). In December 1990, former US employees of Matsushita Electric's Qasar Co. won a

$2.5 million verdict. An Illinois federal judge found that Qasar had preserved the jobs of Japanese nationals during recent job cuts. In February 1991, Sumitomo Corp. of America was ordered to grant sizeable wage increases and make awards of back pay to 130 current and former American employees. Court papers said Sumitomo dispatched executives from Japan to head every department except the mail room. Many Japanese firms have at least one discrimination case pending in the US. For instance, a class action suit against Mitsubishi Bank charges it denied promotions to non-Orientals on the basis of race. Another pending case alleges that DCA New York, a subsidiary of Dentsu, the world's largest advertising agency, discriminated against non-Japanese staff in a 1991 lay-off.

The American public has heard much since 1988 about problems occurring in Japanese subsidiaries. One 1989 survey found that most Americans believe that "Japanese companies are more likely to discriminate against women, are less open to advancement by Americans, and provide less job security than American firms. . . . [and] that Americans are less willing to work for a Japanese company than for Canadian, British, or West German concerns" (quoted in JEI Report, May 4, 1990).

EQUAL EMPLOYMENT OPPORTUNITY AND JAPANESE FIRMS

In most of the interviews I have conducted with foreign personnel managers in Japanese companies abroad, a major complaint has been that Japanese managers have resisted adopting employment practices which differ from those which they were able, legally, to practice in Japan. Most Western countries today have legislation prohibiting and penalizing the use of race, sex, religion, age, etc., as criteria in hiring decisions. Japanese managers, with few apparent exceptions, are accustomed to hiring people in Japan on whatever basis they wish, so it goes against their "commonsense" to have to appear indifferent to, say, the sex of an applicant—certainly, in Japan, sex and even race would be highly relevant to an appointment. Moreover, even if the expatriate manager accepts the concept of equal employment and decides to appoint a female manager, it is not rare for head office personnel office to delay or block the appointment, on the assumption that a male would in principle be more effective.

Equal Employment Opportunity legislation and its active implementation are most advanced in the United States. There has been a surge of articles in the mass media since 1987 concerning the failures of Japanese companies in this area. Sumitomo Corp. finally settled a 12-year-old lawsuit in 1987 accusing it of favoring Japanese and American males over females. The settlement involved payment of $2.6 million and agreement to institute employment reforms, including providing Japanese language training for women employees. One commentator (JEI Report, May 4, 1990, 11) said, "This precedent-setting case generated a Supreme Court ruling that civil rights laws apply to US subsidiaries of foreign companies."

In 1988 Honda of America Manufacturing Inc. paid, by order of the Equal Employment Opportunity Commission (EEOC), $6 million in damages to 377 female and black employees (who were originally turned down on the basis of sex or color) for discrimination they had suffered in hiring and promotion. In addition to these payments, Honda agreed to expand its recruitment area to cover districts with a high black residence, change its promotion procedures, make a commitment to promote more black and female production workers, and set up a training program to teach Honda expatriate managers about the discrimination law. According to the *New York Times*, March 24, 1988, there had been another EEOC-Honda settlement less than a year earlier, when back pay of $461,610 was paid following an age discrimination investigation by the EEOC, and there was suspicion then that more discrimination investigations against Honda were pending.

In 1989 Nissan Motor Corporation agreed to accept the EEOC's direction to pay $605,600 in back pay to settle an age and race discrimination case involving 92 workers. Nissan also committed itself, said Clarence Thomas, then chairman of the EEOC (*NYT*, Feb, 4, 1989), "to providing increased opportunities in high-level sales and management positions for blacks, Hispanics, women and persons covered by age discrimination laws." Nissan was also reported as having agreed to revise recruitment and hiring procedures to assure nondiscriminatory treatment of potential employees; to eliminate college degree requirements for most sales and management positions; to conduct annual training for management on antidiscrimination laws; and to submit compliance reports to the commission.

Again, *Business Week*, Dec. 17, 1990 reported that three senior managers laid off by Fujitsu Systems of America were suing Fujitsu for discriminatory practices, namely, that they had been let go because of their age and race. Most telling of all, in 1989, the vice chairman of the EEOC charged two American subsidiaries of the Recruit Company of Japan with "blatant" employment discrimination based on race, sex, age, and national origin. Documents submitted at the time included a memorandum by one of the subsidiaries which detailed a code used by the company on job orders to indicate when a client wanted an employee of a specific age, race, or sex. The codes included "talk to Maria" which meant the client preferred Hispanic employees, "Mary" which meant Caucasians, "Mariko" which meant Japanese, "Adam" for men, "Eve" for women, and "Maryanne" for blacks.

Problems seem likely to continue in the USA. The *Wall Street Journal*, Aug. 29, 1989, reported that "57 percent of 331 Japanese companies operating in the US face possible worker lawsuits on race, color, religion, age, sex, and other equal-employment issues, a survey for the Japanese Labor Ministry showed. Over 70 percent of these Japanese companies urged their ministry to tell them how to avoid 'unnecessary' trouble" (front page). The *New York Times*, June 19, 1989, reported that "in New York and California, where the Japanese have the strongest presence, more than two dozen cases have been filed against subsidiaries, which include C. Itoh, Mitsubishi Bank, and Nikko Securities" (page D2). The year 1990 saw the growth of sexual harassment suits against companies in the US, and, reported *Shukan Gendai* (November 1991), of 5000 suits filed, forty were against Japanese companies.

Attempts to explain the extraordinary prevalence of discriminatory hiring in the United States by Japanese managers in Japanese companies have been, I feel, unduly lenient. The Japan Economic Institute, which is funded by the Japanese Foreign

Ministry, is most circumspect:

"Analysts attribute these difficulties to the Japanese discomfort with the heterogeneous nature of American society and general unfamiliarity with US business practices. . . . Japanese companies bring to their US companies their own values . . . [including] strong control from headquarters and a mentality that makes a clear distinction between insiders and outsiders—between Japanese at the core of the firm and foreigners at the periphery" (Report 18A, 11).

This is too insipid an analysis. Recruitment in Japan is explicitly discriminatory. Jobs are seen as suitable for males or for females. In the vast majority of cases, managers must be men, women will not be considered. Managers must be *Japanese* of "good" background. This means that non-Japanese born and educated in Japan, and especially Koreans, will be and are clearly discriminated against. The despised minority class, *burakumin*, are still identifiable, though no longer through the household registers, and the investigations routinely carried out on character and background prior to making employment offers frequently include a specific question about whether a person is of burakumin background or not. Books are available in Japan, and bought extensively by companies, which make it easier to identify someone of burakumin origins. Eurasian children, even with Japanese nationality, if they do not *look* Japanese, are also discriminated against. The Recruit Company's use of codes to indicate preference is perfectly consistent with the attitudes and approach that many Japanese businessmen can be expected to adopt in the US. In the UK and Australia, where equal employment legislation exists but is weakly enforced, Japanese expatriate managers make their preferences very clear to recruitment and executive search companies. Although discriminatory phrasing is omitted from job ads, discrimination is still widely practiced.

Japanese businessmen are raised in a society where discrimination is thought to make perfect common sense. The fears of foreigners (gaijin complex) and of strangers (*taijin kyofu*) that I wrote of in chapter 2 are no doubt also related to Japanese discrimination. From the viewpoint of Western cultural values, the Japanese are clearly unfair, condescending and nonegalitarian, and they take their values directly into the foreign workplace. The somewhat pathetic appeal contained in the finding that Japanese companies want their Labor Ministry to tell them how to avoid "unnecessary trouble" in hiring Americans suggests that they hope there may be some useful tactics they can employ, but that they have little drive or concern to adapt to the values of American society.

THE RECRUITMENT OF LOCAL STAFF

We have already seen much evidence of racially based and other discrimination used by Japanese companies in the USA. Looking more specifically at recruiting abroad, I have found that it is common everywhere for Japanese managers to tell personnel recruiters that the most important quality they want in administrative or junior executive staff members is a "good attitude." Both Inohara (1990), reporting on research on Japanese companies in Europe, and Marshall (1990) on those in Australia, say the same thing. As soon as expatriates become involved, as they invariably do, in recruitment interviews, evaluation criteria are changed from "experience" or "skills" to "attitude"—which means flexibility and a readiness to pitch in on whatever has to be done without resistance or complaint. There is no doubt in my mind that good "attitude" is uppermost in the minds of Japanese managers wherever they are recruiting. Assertive people are fine as sales representatives, but office and project cooperation, Japanese-style, needs something close to meekness (*sunao-sa*), a quality much admired among the Japanese.

However, an interesting and curious factor has been noticed by my colleague Judith Van Dyck of Oregon State University. In a 1987 paper, "Problems in Multicultural Organizations," she noted that Japanese companies do a far less thorough evaluation of foreign job candidates than of Japanese candidates. Foreigners were interviewed fewer times, for shorter periods, and little or no background checking with referees was done. After this was pointed out to me, I suddenly recalled many similar cases in my own experience. Is it the "foreigner complex" at work again? Do Japanese managers simply feel incompetent to make the shrewd judgments they do make of Japanese job candidates? It may well be so. It may be a transitory phenomenon. The Japanese may feel impelled to hire "inscrutable" foreigners in the name of the current fashion concept, "internationalization." Another related problem with some of these foreign "hires" has been the special fringe benefits offered them, including occasionally ludicrously high salaries for people in their twenties. Van Dyck reports that, while Japanese co-workers were resentful of the salaries, etc. of the foreigners, the foreigners felt guilty when they discovered how overpaid they were. There are points of similarity to the nineteenth-century yatoi here, but our contemporary young people seem to be much more "decent chaps" in their sense of fair play.

FINAL COMMENTS

The discussion of unfair or discriminatory practices by Japanese companies against foreign employees has drawn largely on the US experience, where Equal Employment Opportunity legislation is most advanced and most severely applied. However, discrimination against minorities (women, blacks, colored, Jews, etc.) is a fact of life wherever the Japanese do business, though they themselves may balk at the use of the word.

As to my equation of nonregular or shokutaku employment status with the employment of local people in overseas companies, this does represent a great watering-down of the reputed job security and equality of employment in the Japanese company. However, job security in the Japanese company abroad is still very much better than what will be found in most non-Japanese firms.

UNEQUAL TREATMENT
OR
A DIFFERENCE OF
PERCEPTION?

FIRST DAYS IN THE JAPANESE COMPANY FAMILY

Every foreigner interviewed in Japan, and most abroad, reported the same initial orientation upon entering a Japanese company for the first time. Instead of formal training, they were told merely to "soak up the atmosphere," "get the feel of the place," etc., and then to come up with ideas on what they would like to do.

Grove reports:

"On the first day, I was assigned to the Import Department of Seiyu supermarkets, a part of the Seibu Group. My boss was a senior manager then waiting for reassignment. He said to me '*asonde mo ii*' (literal meaning: it's OK to play) and so for months I just soaked up the atmosphere."

Villarante put it this way:

"The first thing a Japanese wants of you when you join is for you to sit on your own and just absorb the atmosphere. They don't give you any real job. I was told I could attend any courses I wanted to, but there was no special training for me."

Similarly, Neilsen said of her cosmetics company job:

"The first six months I was training and becoming familiar

with the company, the industry, competitors. They more or less left me on my own. I went to some Japanese training courses, but really I was just studying what and how they think, and the company image. After that I got a lot more responsibility."

Klineberg reported:

"My job in the hotel [in Tokyo] was ill-defined at the start, but I thrived on that. . . . In the construction company [his previous job in Japan], their approach was—plop the baby in and wait for it to swim. It would be so un-Japanese to create a whole structure or plan in advance."

These examples demonstrate the importance Japanese place on intuitive understanding of and familiarization with situations, on tuning into and feeling at home in the workplace environment (or any other for that matter). It demonstrates what is sometimes called their high-context culture, meaning a culture where knowing the context is critical to evaluating and reacting to situations. The contrast is American low-context culture, where things or events are evaluated with more indifference to the context and with greater emphasis on principles, logic, and legal guidelines. This is brought out in the following charming story told by Robert Klineberg:

"It was a few nights before my last day at the hotel. At that point, being philosophical, I asked my Japanese boss and my colleagues if they believed in God, and what they thought about that. Then, moving on from there, I told them my own philosophy— that people have choice in their lives, that everyone is presented with a road map at birth, and we make our decisions about which route to choose; whether it is to be a rough road, or a smooth one, a fast one, or one that is beautiful along the way.

"This view seemed to captivate them. They were very interested in what I had to say, but when I asked them for their own thoughts and feelings about God, and choice, and about this map, they all said—We Japanese don't have a map! Neither do they have choices, they said. Now my boss was a cultivated person, a man I had learned much from. I respected him for all his efforts, trying to include me in the organization, and explaining things along the way. He tried very hard to understand the cultural differences that came up but said to me: basically, you just sit and wait for the organization to tap you, to give you an assignment, to take advantage of you as the raw material.

"He gave me some examples from his own career, how he had been assigned to the Osaka office to build it up in anticipation of the new hotel they were to build. He was to be in charge of everything, from start to finish. It was just dropped in his lap. That is how the Japanese do things."

WORK AND EMPLOYMENT CONDITIONS

One of the most common concerns of Westerners is the lack of a job specification or description, which they are accustomed to receiving when accepting employment by a Western company. This is not a practice of Japanese companies. Klineberg had worked for a Japanese company previously to his interview with the hotel, but in any case, he guilelessly asked them at the recruiting interview if they had a plan for his new job. "They looked quite frightened," he said. "A job description would mean a complete structure for an individual, and so a loss of flexibility. It just wasn't there, and with this sort of fear in their eyes, they answered sincerely 'no.'"

The lack of a job description is closely connected to the unstructured first months of employment, for Japanese and foreigners alike. As with new managerial appointments of foreigners in Japan, many locally hired appointees outside Japan have experienced the same lack of job description or definition, and the same expectation by their Japanese employees that they would learn to tune in and feel at home. Local staff, however, with little or no knowledge of Japan, do not seem to achieve the insights of the foreign employees in Japan. Peter Banting, director of administration for the US subsidiary of a Japanese electronic equipment manufacturer, had this to say of his first year with the company:

"In the US, both experience and academic qualifications are job prerequisites. In my case, I also brought the company an extra—my wide experience in organizational development. . . . In my first year, I tried to do what is just common sense in the US—work hard to show management that their decision to hire me was a clever one.

"So, in addition to my routine work in the first six months, I developed a plan for a better organizational structure and eventually presented it to my boss, a Japanese vice president. A few weeks went by, but I got no response. So, needing feedback to develop it further, I went and asked for his comments. Unfortunately, he didn't give me anything really clear. Meanwhile, I worked on another proposal and presented that. Again, no response. I started to feel that my ideas weren't on the same wavelength as the VP. I made some more approaches to him, but now it seemed I was wasting my time and was even being given the brush-off" (Hayashi 1989, 39).

Banting went into something of a slump, fearing that his future with the company was not bright and seeing ominous omens in the 30 percent plus turnover rate for local managers in this firm. Banting's Japanese vice president was interviewed separately about this, and commented:

"The first year is the time for settling in and adjustments. It never occurred to me that Americans would think the first year so critical in establishing one's self in the firm. In fact, if anyone at all brought me an innovative proposal, I wouldn't know what to do with it if careful groundwork (*nemawashi*), preparing the way for successful implementation, had not been done."

When told of the vice president's comments, Banting was exasperated:

"They might have told me what they expected in that case. The Japanese do things differently. Not only is it difficult for us to understand them, Japanese managers themselves show little willingness to explain these things. From an American viewpoint, there can only be two reasons for giving no explanation. Either the Japanese believe Americans are not bright enough to understand, even with an explanation, or the Japanese simply don't trust us."

It is hard not to sympathize with the American's exasperation and frustration, nor, I suppose, with the naivety of the Japanese, blithely assuming, as do so many people abroad, that things are much the same everywhere. I suspect that this problem occurs frequently, especially in the USA.

ROLE IN THE COMPANY AS CATALYST/INNOVATOR

We saw earlier that foreigners are often engaged by Japanese companies because they help to foster an international spirit among the Japanese employees. Others had more specific tasks. Many came to their posts already assigned to specialist jobs, while others were expected to be innovative and act as catalysts to Japanese personnel. In Robert Gage's case, his role at Novatech, the Japanese communications company, was not only to manage foreign staff in the company but to act as a buffer between those foreigners and the Japanese president, who found dealing with foreigners stressful and distasteful.

"It was obvious," Gage said, "that he [the president] had become thoroughly fed up dealing with foreigners. They didn't really give the company a fair go, while he was always projecting a stern and forbidding demeanor towards them, trying to get them to work as hard as possible for as little as he could get away with. As a result, he had endless problems with unreliable Westerners. . . . He wanted me to act as a buffer, so he wouldn't have to deal with them directly. He was quite up-front about this."

Klineberg described his role at the Tokyo hotel as follows:

"I was brought in to develop the banquet market in Tokyo among non-Japanese clients. At the same time, my boss looked to me to shake up the whole banquet organization, make it more internationalized. Systems were inadequate, staff were untrained, few people spoke English."

"The president looked to me as a catalyst," reported Tara Neilsen of her cosmetics company, "someone who could stir things up. They could get pretty straight answers from me. A lot of Japanese were so reluctant to say what they thought, especially to the president. So they would bounce it off me, saying, 'What do you think, honey?' I would give it a shot, and that would take the pressure off the Japanese for a while."

Nancy Haughton, at the *Yomi-Asa* newspaper, worked under a series of incompetent general managers until a watershed event in the paper's life. The paper, the *Yomi-Asa Daily News* (YDN), ran an embargoed obituary for the late Emperor Hirohito *before he died*. This faux pas was big news in Tokyo for a day or two, and seriously damaged the paper's reputation. Disgusted, Haughton resigned, but on the day she put in her resignation a new general manager took over, replacing the one who had resigned to take responsibility for the obituary. The new man, it turned out, proved to be the first really competent manager placed in that position for many years.

"I liked and respected him from our first meeting," says Haughton. "He was a man of vision, someone with managerial abilities, so I agreed to stay on and play a key role in putting YDN back on its feet. From that day I was centrally involved in designing, for the first time, a fair and proper system for the employment of foreign staff. Since then, I have continued to act as the person who puts the general manager's special editorial ideas into practice."

Most of the foreigners I interviewed in Japan, in fact, had been explicitly employed as leaders/catalysts/change agents. However, unlike the situation in Japan, the Western employee of an overseas Japanese company has no special cross-cultural role to play as an innovator or catalyst of Japanese staff, or any others. In the case of Peter Banting above, Japanese expectations were actually loaded against innovative proposals or behavior, in the short term at least.

Among the managers I interviewed or had reports on in the USA, UK, and Australia, there were a number of administrative managers, a typical Japanese position which involves personnel, legal, accounting, and office work responsibilities. Their feelings about their experiences range from very positive—a sense that their employees were highly creative and supportive of the Japanese expatriates, to negative—a sense of being intimidated and resentful. Brian Needle, employed by a Japanese airline branch in the US, with a staff of 200 including 5 Japanese managers, plays an important role in facilitating the frequently difficult communications between Japanese and locals. His skills are evident from his dual role as confidant to both sides. He is trusted and relied upon by the Japanese managers—for his opinions on the quality of local staff and for his patience in teasing out exactly what it is that his Japanese seniors and colleagues are telling him in imperfect English. He explains further:

"The Japanese say, 'Brian works so hard.' Their trust and respect has a lot to do with the work ethic. We were at a meeting recently with some state officials, and suddenly they said without
warning, 'Brian will now give you a presentation on this point!' I
stuttered and stammered at first, but everyone listened and took in
what I was saying. The Japanese managers were grateful because
it got them off the hook."

Needle shows that there are important roles for key local staff
members to play, as people who can handle difficult public communications or help smooth out problems with the local staff.
Needle certainly does that, a necessary role for the non-Japanese
employee in the overseas subsidiary. Local people also complain
to him a lot.

"For example, women tell me, 'The Japanese are very sexist.
They don't recognize women, don't promote us, except perhaps
for years of service—certainly not for work performance.'

"Again, people say, 'They don't listen to our ideas . . . they're
bossy, everything is one-way.' I do see that it seems blunt when
they are talking to each other and a Japanese manager, if he wants
someone, will just call out, and the person leaps out of his or her
chair and goes to his office. An American manager would be more
courteous."

ARE FOREIGN EMPLOYEES TREATED EQUITABLY?

The most important element of structure in a large Japanese organization is the *senpai-kohai* (senior-junior) system. It is the system
which dictates one's seniority, and thus one's income and one's
status. It is also peopled exclusively by what the Japanese will
identify as the regular employee (sei shain), and excludes all others such as full-time contract employees (the shokutaku) and part-
time or seasonal workers. (Only a few, if any, of these non-regular
employees will be non-Japanese in Japan.) How do non-Japanese
staff fit into the structure of Japanese companies, and how are they
treated by management, when compared to Japanese employees?

Foreigners with regular employee status are not only more secure than other foreigners, they are also less prone to discrimination within the company. Alfredo Villarante of Hitoba Computers

had to endure a lot of suspicion and distancing behavior from Japanese employees and from the company personnel department, but he was able to progress quite rapidly in a company that has now committed itself formally to making foreigners equal in every respect. Contract foreign employees, however, do not threaten regular Japanese employees in any way, so comparison between the treatment of the two types of foreign employment may not really be valid. In cases where all foreigners in the company are nonregulars, as for instance at Nancy Haughton's *Yomi-Asa Daily News*, we can expect that they will be treated as contracted hired hands, as Klineberg was at his construction company; or we can expect them to be interested only in contract employment, as with Tara Neilsen, the marketing specialist. Usually, it is the regular employees who have higher status within the company, not the hired hands, many of whom are English language teachers—and who, typically, are young people passing though Japan for two to three years, quite happy to be treated as hired hands (though not happy to be discriminated against or distrusted).

In the perceptions and expectations of Japanese managers, too, there are differences between foreign employees. A few expect foreign employees in Japan to fit into the Japanese organization completely and seamlessly, others only expect that they will become prepared for eventual posting overseas, while yet others have short-term expectations: that although the foreigner will eventually return to his or her own country or resign, he or she can make some useful contribution to the company's internationalization.

As to prospects for foreigners in Japanese companies in Japan, financial specialist Carlton Patrick has this to say:

"Working for a Japanese company is an interesting experience, as long as you go into it with the realization that you're not going to get anywhere! If you start getting frustrated and making noises, they may throw you a bone or two to try to keep you quiet. But the Japanese think of foreigners in terms of stereotypes, such as, 'they're going to leave anyway, as soon as someone offers them more, because that is what foreigners are like. They're only motivated by money'."

Robert Gage, the writer who had been with the Novatech communications company, takes a rather extreme view. If you want to succeed in a Japanese company, become as deferential and self-sacrificing as the Japanese, he advises.

"As a Westerner coming into a Japanese company, be aware of what is expected of you, that you are expected to surrender to virtually everything that is required of you. This might well be offensive to you, make you feel you are not being treated as an individual. But if you are here to live and work, you can't expect to be treated like a Westerner.

"If you are prepared to sacrifice some of your individualistic attachments, you will get tremendous benefits. You'll find that as much as you are loyal to the company and the other staff, they will be loyal to you in turn. You will be looked after, but there's an element of trust here. You have to surrender to the company first, prove yourself, and then you will find you will be looked after without having to actively struggle at getting everything yourself. At the same time, you have to be aware of the indisputable fact that the company owns you! If this is too irksome, then negotiate a contract right from the beginning."

Gage seems to be advocating a quasi-religious transformation—sacrifice of attachments, surrender to the company—which, though not realistic, acutely pinpoints the enormity of the task of discarding one culture conditioning for another, very different one. Although not a serious option for most Westerners, some degree of change in values and overt behavior is inevitable for those who stay in Japan long term. In contrast Neilsen, a bilingual marketing specialist, finds nothing attractive about working for a Japanese company as just another regular employee and is completely secure in her identity and behavior as an American. Having no interest in lifelong employment in a Japanese company, she expects to be valued for her special skills and to receive preferential conditions and treatment.

"In my experience there are lots of different ways in which Japanese companies employ foreigners. Some try to run things on a strict basis of equality, treating foreigners in exactly the same way as Japanese. I don't know what would get into a foreigner's mind to take a job like that. I wouldn't consider it myself. I remember once I was working for a Japanese marketing agency. They had other foreigners there but none of them spoke Japanese. Foreigners speaking Japanese in those sorts of businesses are really in such a special situation."

March: "You are talking about a situation where the Japanese also don't speak English?"

N: "Right. I haven't been in a situation where the Japanese spoke English, so I really don't know that side. In my situation the Japanese don't speak any English, but the English-related work is really important. So when I started there, it was on the basis of treating me as a Japanese, but that changed quickly. I was put into a special category. As you see—no one is going to mistake me for a Japanese, outside or inside."

In spite of Gage's views, I believe that the way Neilsen was treated is closer to the norm. Non-Japanese, especially Caucasians, may be treated in terms of employment conditions in the same way as Japanese employees, but their contribution to the organization will always reflect the special skills they bring with them. Villarante, who is Asian-looking, was used because of his special knowledge and understanding of the West. Paul Grove was used in sausage merchandising because, to the Japanese, sausage is a very European, non-Japanese product, and he is a classic Germanic type.

DO SOME FOREIGN EMPLOYEES DESERVE THE TREATMENT THEY GET?

Finance man Carlton Patrick's comments on his next job after M Bank are worth recording for their parallels with other cases. He is critical of the quality of the foreigners there, and their ignorance of and indifference to Japan. This time it seems it is the foreigners who are distant from and condescending to the Japanese. I might add that I have heard many similar stories about foreigners like these in Tokyo since the liberalization of the securities and financial services markets in 1987.

"Euro-Fin was a joint venture—85 percent Japanese, 15 percent American, with about 70 staff members, including 12 foreigners.

The foreigners were in a section off to the side, and there was very little interaction between the groups. The Euro part was basically Japanese-oriented, specializing in Forex (foreign exchange) deposits, whereas the Fin brokers were internationally stronger with a worldwide network. It was a good fit between the two strengths. . . .

"Few of the foreigners had any knowledge of Japan. Worse, they had no interest, and some of them were embarrassingly ignorant. Grossly overpaid, and just not nice people—'greed is good' types. Their boss was an Australian, of the crude, crass, beer-drinking, rugby player type. So it's not surprising that the Japanese didn't want much to do with the foreigners there. . . ."

The quality of foreign employees was also related to Robert Gage's experiences at Novatech. When he finally resigned, after the rigors of being in the middle of a cross-cultural war (see chapter 4), his Japanese president, Shinagawa, was beside himself in frustration.

"He ranted and raved about how I had betrayed him. 'You cannot trust a Westerner!' he shrieked. 'This is now absolutely clear to me, even you'."

What also was clear to Shinagawa was that he was losing the only person who had been able to handle dealings with the foreign staff, whom he detested deeply. We can recall the views of Gage about the (nonregular employee) foreigners he had had to supervise. "The majority are people I would never employ . . . a lot of riffraff," said Gage. Gage's words and Shinagawa's views remind me of the descriptions (cited in chapter 1) of the nineteenth-century yatoi—"those graduates of the dry-goods counter, the forecastle . . . coming directly from the barroom, the brothel, the gambling saloon."

DO JAPANESE KNOW HOW TO MANAGE FOREIGN EMPLOYEES?

A common complaint of foreign employees in Japan and abroad was that they were not given enough work, and that this had been the reason for them leaving the company. For instance, many of the foreigners in Japan who had been hired in the expectation that they would eventually return to their home country and work for the company complained that no real place for them had been created in the Japanese head office. Villarante experienced this earlier in his career with the computer company, as did Grove at Seibu. Carlton Patrick cites lack of work as the main reason for leaving M Bank:

"They certainly treated me very well, I'll give them credit for that. The main reason I left was that, unfortunately, they really didn't give foreigners enough to do. I think our manager's philosophy was to employ foreigners in the hope that they would go back to their own country or to other countries where M had branch offices, and become bridges with Tokyo. But it fell apart at the middle manager level. The bank was very dependent on the Japanese managers in the sections where foreigners were employed. They monopolized the work, so foreigners were fearfully underutilized. There's a lot of tokenism around. I recognized how underutilized I was when I was posted to the Chicago office of M and saw how the Americans worked there. They were doing high-level, highly responsible work, and now it was the Japanese who had to rely on them. Back in Tokyo again, it was very frustrating. That's when I decided to leave, and when they actually offered me more. They seem quite surprised, quite hurt, when foreigners leave, and they have to go through this ritual of throwing you a bone. 'Oh, we were going to promote you. If only you had stayed! You ought to have been here three years, strictly speaking, but we were thinking that, because of your superior performance, we would promote you after two years. . . .'"

The problem of not having enough to do stems from the reasons that many foreigners are employed in the first place. Whenever they are employed for "ideological" reasons—to promote company internationalization, to stimulate Japanese staff—and not for their specific skills or for a specific situation, they are likely to be underemployed. In its early days of recruiting foreigners to promote its internationalization, Seibu was said to have lost more than half of its recruits within twelve months, for this reason.

CONSTRAINTS ON FOREIGN MANAGERS: HOW SHADOW MANAGERS ARE USED

Japanese culture is richly endowed with many versions of people holding power behind the scenes. In medieval times, warrior leaders used doubles, called *kagemusha* or shadow warrior, to deceive their enemies. In the classic folk theaters of kabuki and bunraku, figures in black called *kuroko* either assist in clothing changes or, in the latter, are the puppeteers. Convention dictates that, being dressed in black, they are not to be thought of as truly present. The most commonly used word for "power behind the throne" or "wirepuller" is *kuromaku* (black curtain), which also has a kabuki origin and which refers to someone who waits in the shadows for his chance to use power. A common convention in business negotiations, especially with foreigners, is very similar to this. A middle-ranking manager acts as spokesman, while the top man sits inconspicuously to the side, but is ready to enter the discussions at the point at which he can have most impact. This is sometimes called the tactic of concealing the top man (*oyabun kakure*). In family life, the Japanese recognize a type of wife, called *kakaa denka*, who is meek and deferential to her husband in public but at home is domineering and controlling. Similarly, some males are called *uchi benkei*, which translates loosely as "A lion at home, a mouse abroad."

Given this rich heritage of shadow roles, it is entirely understandable that the Japanese have appointed locals to serve as public chiefs, while being privately controlled by Japanese expatriate managers. The Mazda US situation (Fucini & Fucini, 1990) is entirely typical. The American president had to discuss his daily program with his shadow, and all decisions, however trivial, had to be worked out in advance.

Alletzhauser (1990) tells the following story that gives deeper insight into the role of shadow managers. At the Nomura New York Christmas party of 1985, senior manager Andy Saito told the Christmas revellers a story. It was the tale of the success of Matsushita Electric Industrial, the world's leading consumer electronics company. Saito followed this with the story of Matsushita's competitor, Philips Electronics of Holland, which, he said, was a relative failure.

"The reason for Philips' poor performance is that it does not have a tight grip on its overseas offices. That is why Matsushita is a world leader; it rules its overseas offices and gives them little autonomy. Remember, Nomura will always be a Japanese firm run by Japanese."

Saito was heading back to the Tokyo headquarters and wanted to scare the Americans. He succeeded but not in the way he had hoped. Within two months five salesmen had left.

Shadow managers seem most common in manufacturing companies, with their meticulous monitoring role apparently aimed at zero-defects management, as well as at developing the foreign manager as manager. John E. Rehfeld, during his time as vice president of Toshiba America's computer business, worked with a shadow manager. Both of them reported to Tokyo as well as kept each other informed, but it was his shadow who maintained crucial informal contact with Tokyo.

"What it really means," says Rehfeld, "is informing Tokyo of what is going on and what requests will be made. It is much like a lobbying effort that precedes a formal plan or proposal. . . . But I've heard that other Japanese companies use shadow managers to relay what amounts to orders from Tokyo through the assistant general manager [Japanese] to the general manager [local] and then to the division, effectively depriving the non-Japanese executive of any real decision-making power" (p. 172).

Toyota and Nissan, according to Hayashi (1987, 55), also employ close monitoring methods. At Toyota, every important US line manager is paired with a Japanese coordinator, while Nissan USA is completely dominated by expatriate managers. We have to assume that the use of shadow managers (or, more extremely, blanket Japanization of the subsidiary's management) is the best choice to make for competitive and strategic reasons. But there are downsides. There are the resignations and disillusionment of the local managers who work under these "shadows"—their loss is costly and disturbing to the organization. There is also the political impact, especially in the USA: in what is currently a marked upswing in anti-Japanese mood, the anger of discontented former executives of Japanese companies benefits no one.

ORGANIZATIONAL CONTROL AND THE FOREIGN EMPLOYEE

Earlier, we reported Gage's opinion that Japanese companies are highly exploitative of their staff. For Westerners, this is linked to at least three other factors mentioned by interviewees: the mechanisms of staff control in Japanese companies, the use of the morning pep-talk (chorei) and the way it is connected to staff education, and the hours that employees are expected to work.

Control Mechanisms

Tara Neilsen, the American marketing specialist, has this to say about control in the Japanese cosmetics company she spent three years with:

"The control element was strong in the cosmetics company. Every day you had to write down how much time you had taken to do what, whom you had seen or had meetings with. Every person in the company, 1000 employees, did that, and those 1000 reports ended up daily on the president's desk. Of course, sometimes he would read them and sometimes he wouldn't. He had a rather large secretarial staff, but he would also thumb through them and pick up points here and there. That is pretty good control over people, although you have to remember that they were mostly young and female."

In my own direct experience, control through regular reporting by all staff members is not uncommon in Japan, particularly for sales staff, although this is the only case I know of that requires daily reports; weekly is more usual. This degree of control is a long way from the spirit of trust that William Ouchi (author of *Theory Z*) and others say is characteristic of Japanese companies; a long way too from radical Japanese companies like Idemitsu Petroleum or Wacoal Foundation Garments, which do not even use time clocks.

Morning Pep-Talks and Staff Education

The morning pep-talk seems as much a device to get people to work on (or before) time as to pep them up for the day ahead. Patrick, for instance, observes:

"Let me comment on the morning pep-talk (chorei), which I've experienced in two different companies. What people say about it building a better company and motivating everyone is rubbish. It's just another way to control people, to ensure they get to work on time. What managers and others say at chorei is generally meaningless. At Euro-Fin, they talked about the previous day's performance, which was just read off the board, or what the interest rates were, and at the end someone would always say, *'ganbatte kudasai'* (do your best). A total waste of time."

The president of the cosmetics company at which Neilsen worked used his company's chorei as a part of his comprehensive effort to train and mold his young staff (this is the same man who receives 1000 staff reports each day). Neilsen explains:

"The president was a powerful controlling personality. The way he handled the chorei was a good example. Once, he went around the whole group in the international department, criticizing everyone except me. Their appearance, clothes, hairstyles, manners, personality. He was very sarcastic, but also funny. Then he turned to me and said, 'Isn't that right, Tara?' as though I was the ultimate judge. I just mumbled something equivocal. Everything he did was so detailed, all designed to reinforce the senpai/kohai [senior/junior] system [where juniors learn to defer to seniors, and seniors learn to lead and take charge in an older brother/sister fashion. Even the language one uses is graded to be appropriate to the status of the person you are addressing.]. People were always trying to figure out how to speak to a person. If they know the status of the person, they know what the proper level of language should be. This was so much a part of their automatic everyday behavior. You'd see people speaking to one person on one level, then switch immediately to another level for another person.

"The president was always giving lessons on things like this to the staff. Sometimes it was a little chorei lecture, but other times he wrote short papers for distribution in the office. One time he wrote a book on manners which everyone was supposed to read. How to speak on the telephone, how to greet guests, how to behave in the office, what polite expressions to use when. You had to be sure to use the person's title. You had to say, for instance, Takeda Bucho [Department Manager Takeda], not 'Takeda-san' [Mr. Takeda]. I made some boo-boos. I once asked, '*Bucho, musume, o genki desuka?*' [Department Manager, how is your daughter?] I shouldn't have used the word *musume* for daughter—that is too informal. I should have used the honorific *ojosan*. As soon as I said it, I knew I'd slipped. Still he didn't blink when he answered. But a female secretary in our group freaked out as soon as the bucho had left. 'You don't speak to Bucho-san like that!' she shrieked, then told me what I should have said."

For all her experience of Japan and her excellent language skills, Neilsen didn't seem to have been aware that this emphasis on manner, etiquette, and proper language and expressions, is typical training for young women in Japanese companies. Some of the best-selling books in Japan are etiquette books for young ladies. Even the heavily ironic critiques offered by the president would be nothing new to most Japanese. From quite an early age, seniors can offer gratuitous and sometimes scalding advice, which is "gratefully" received by juniors.

The chorei is being cautiously tried out overseas, principally among managers, not ordinary staff. Provided that it is used wisely and fits in with local cultural values, it should contribute to better mutual understanding and teamwork.

Expected Hours of Work

Every company has set hours of work, and in most cases employees sign or clock in and out. There are often severe penalties for tardiness. Some companies penalize late comers up to 30 minutes' salary for each minute late, with five minutes earning a day's-wage penalty. Although there are official working hours in Japan, no one, according to a recent survey, leaves for at least 30 minutes after the official finishing time (even if they have no overtime to do), and most are at their desks at least 10 minutes before the official starting time. As Villarante, who has been a Japanese company man since 1973, puts it:

"You have to put in long hours. You don't necessarily work hard, but it must be long. If you didn't put in the hours, you'd probably be ostracized." Villarante then goes on to relate a case at odds with the usual strictness late comers encounter:

"When I joined the company, there was one guy about 50 years old. He was hopeless, always late at the office. All sorts of people would criticize him. He would just come and go in an entirely irresponsible way. I asked the manager why they let him behave in this way. He told me, 'He's not my responsibility.' So I asked him why they didn't retrain the old guy. The manager said, 'It's too late now.' They wouldn't fire him unless he did something immoral or illegal. So he just stayed there. I'm sure he wouldn't be tolerated in a Western company."

The most likely explanation for this exceptional treatment is that the individual concerned had been with the company so long that strictness, normally directed at younger employees, was tempered with respect for his long-term loyalty. Another aspect of Japanese work hours is the obligation to spend some evenings with work colleagues or customers, a part of the "clubbiness" that Patrick spoke of. Gage has this to say:

"There is a widely held perception that people working for Japanese companies are expected to go out drinking with the rest of the staff or customers, often up to five days a week, and are forced to roll home drunk at midnight. This is not true. While it is important to go out drinking occasionally with your colleagues just to cement personal relationships, or at times with customers, for the most part one can graciously decline the invitations without offending anyone."

Patrick brings up some different angles on work hours:

"When Japanese work for a foreign company they can take liberties that would be unbelievable in a Japanese company, especially arriving late and leaving early. I've talked to friends who run businesses in Tokyo and employ Japanese staff and they usually say the same thing: Japanese staff, especially the women, take the foreign employers for a ride. They seem to think that foreign work conditions mean you take every holiday and every hour you can, squeeze the boss on everything, giving as little as possible in return, because, they reason, 'that's the way foreigners work, isn't it?'

"The flipside of that is the myth that foreigners don't work hard. Certainly in Canada a lot of people work as many hours as do Japanese. The only difference with us is, if there's no real work to do, then we get the hell out of there. But the Japanese are often motivated to stay behind just because their colleagues are there. I saw plenty of that at M Bank in Chicago. The Americans would just work their shift, but the Japanese would stay at the office till midnight, come what may."

Patrick's view that "Japanese are often motivated to stay behind because their colleagues are there" may in part be true overseas, where the Japanese tend to see themselves as a lonely minority clinging to their own kind, but in Japan there is also fear of possible criticism—that they are not committed to their jobs—that motivates long hours in the office.

Initiative Comes from Above

Klineberg, a former employee of a major Tokyo hotel, pointed to another, very subtle control mechanism in some Japanese organizations, what we might call "the tap on the shoulder" method of project execution. He puts it this way:

"The Japanese wait around to be told what to do and otherwise are in waiting mode. They certainly aren't going to take up any particular initiative and wouldn't even feel a sense of frustration or desire to leave. For them that is the way things are. Perhaps you could say they are more like drones in the hive. It is still clearly a feudal system, feudal mentality and hierarchy. You are not there to upset or challenge the system, but to work. You are certainly not expected to have your own opinions or desires if they run counter to those of the 'greater organization.' Those who are ambitious and aggressive to become managers do work hard within the organization. I know people like that. They succeed or fail entirely on the basis of their personality. Their ambitions and aggressive character are recognized by others, and if they can work within the system and not ruffle feathers, they will be respected.

"There is no fast track as we know it in Western business. But you know if you are running smoothly on a track, or if you have been derailed. There are some who feel the train goes too slowly, and those who are bitterly frustrated because of the time it takes to get anywhere. That was my major problem, I think—and the problems of most Westerners in Japanese companies. Had I been able to hang in there for 10 or 15 years, I would have become a bucho (divisional general manager). But it was too feudal for me."

The involvement of foreign employees in management and decision-making in Japan seems conditional upon, first, their status—are they regular employees or not?; second, how long they stay with the company—do they demonstrate long-term commitment, as Villarante did, for instance, by taking exams for promotion?; and third, how much support there is in the organization at the top—are the top managers committed to seeing that the organization adjusts to having foreigners treated as fairly and as equitably as Japanese employees? Both Villarante's computer company and the Seibu Group have demonstrated all three conditions, with the computer company senior managers intervening to ensure fair treatment for Villarante over issues—such as overseas postings and change of nationality—that narrow-minded junior managers would otherwise have tried to penalize him over. The computer company, a pioneer in employing foreigners as regular employees, seems now well advanced in its internal internationalization and the establishment of precedents to open up career paths that do not depend on nationality. We should not, however, give corporate Japan high marks for one or two cases like this. The inertial and conservative character of Japanese organizations, such as Klineberg's hotel, is formidable. Junior and middle managers may possess little power to initiate change, but their power to resist the changes required to integrate foreigners is great. Their genius for bureaucratic-type punitive behavior—such as the move (unsuccessful) to have Villarante transferred to the US company and so become a shokutaku again, simply because he had changed his nationality—warns us that the path ahead for foreign employees in Japanese companies that have established no precedents for their employment and career development is hazardous. Only the continuing attention of top managers to the task of organizational structure, to ensure that non-Japanese employees receive equal opportunities and are fairly treated, without overt or covert discrimination from lower-ranking Japanese staff, can bring about the long-term goal of a more internationalized Japanese organization.

CONTROL AND DISCIPLINE ABROAD

Japanese management abroad exhibits a mixture of close control and reluctant hands-off laissez-faire. In overseas factories, Japanese management does preserve much of the style and method of the factory in Japan, such as just-in-time inventory control, Quality Control circles, and work group management. But the overseas office is less culturally "invaded." One sees little of the morning pep-talks (chorei), or staff education in manners or customer treatment, or of the "clubbiness" of fellow workers. Most effort at control of employees is put into emphasis on punctuality and work attendance, both of which are heavily emphasized in Japan as well. Days taken off for sickness are looked at suspiciously, more so than in Japan. The reason is clear. Japanese expatriates are suspicious that local employees will take advantage of them (as we saw earlier, Japanese employees may take advantage of foreign companies in Japan), by tardiness, days off, slacking on the job, or resigning after a short period of employment. Moreover, expatriates soon learn that they will not have their orders obeyed in the unquestioning fashion of Japanese subordinates. Fear and suspicion lead to distance from and coldness to local employees as means of control, and to rigid interpretation of work rules concerning working hours, although I have had no reports of the severe penalties for lateness that are meted out in some Japanese offices. Nonetheless, one British personnel director has this to say:

"The Japanese are neurotic about lateness and sickness. There are unappealing, highly regimented rules still prevalent in many Japanese companies. Here [at his bank in London] everyone must sign in before 9:00 A.M. Even if you are only a couple of minutes late, you are in big trouble and can be liable for dismissal. If a member of staff 'goes sick' regularly—as people often do in British [also American and Australian] companies—they could also find themselves out of a job without warning. The Japanese are also very critical of sloppy behavior in the office, such as eating sandwiches at your desk" (Jones 1991, 159).

In the US and Australia, rules used by Japanese companies seem to have become less strict. Dismissal for occasional lateness tends to run foul of legislation in many states. For persistent lateness, Japanese firms are now adopting the American practice of sending formal warning letters to offenders. In Australia, legislation favors employees and work rules are more flexible, while in both countries Japanese firms have also learnt through experience that they will soon lose good-quality staff if they apply strict, seemingly petty punctuality rules.

Compared to overseas, management in Japan has almost unlimited power to impose economic penalties for lateness, up to a day's pay for being a few minutes late. Again, in Japan, it is social pressure (that, if transgressed, would translate into economic threat) that keeps staff staying late, after "official" hours have ended. The loss of this control and thus of predictability in staff behavior is one of the most telling reasons for Japanese suspicion of local staff, and for the use of other means of control, such as reluctance to promote or to award titles to local staff, salaries kept at market average level or lower, disinclination to encourage new initiatives from local staff, exclusion from decision-making, as well as occasional sarcasm and heavy-handed criticism of the local people and their culture, as they are compared unfavorably to the Japanese.

Even the use of the Japanese language by local staff, especially when the locals become reasonably fluent, may be discouraged by expatriate staff, as I noted earlier. One local manager told me that, after he spent a few weeks taking lunchtime language lessons from a Japanese secretary, his expatriate manager told him to stop, since the secretary was not paying rent for the company office premises they were using for the language class. What is this, if not petty, controlling, and hostile behavior? Such behavior demonstrates the lengths to which a few overseas Japanese managers will go to assert their power over powerless local employees!

TERMINATION PRACTICE

The traditional Japanese preference for avoiding confrontation can appear as deviousness in a business situation. Two of my personnel manager informants told me that they had been instructed to fire various people whom the Japanese wanted to see off the payroll—some who were alcoholic and were drunk in the office, others they didn't trust. But the task given the personnel managers by their Japanese bosses was to "find some other reasons to fire them." The *Journal of Commerce* reported another case:

"Arthur Shebar gave notice to his boss at Sanyo Business Systems Corp. in North Bergen, New Jersey, that he intended to quit his job as national sales manager for the company's computer division to accept a position with Sony Corp. His immediate boss told Mr. Shebar that he was personally insulted, and the company's then president, a Mr. Yamazaki, persuaded him to stay with the company and tore up his resignation letter.

"Four months later the new company president, Mr. Tomochika, fired Mr. Shebar just as he was about to leave on a business trip. Mr. Shebar responded by suing. The case ultimately went to the New Jersey State Supreme Court, which remanded it to the lower court, where the parties reached a settlement before it went to a second trial" (March 1, 1989, p. 1).

Such cases do not make for a good press for the Japanese, and will make many question the claims that Japanese business is grounded in mutual trust and secure lifelong employment. An alternative viewpoint is that local employees like Mr. Shebar, are, as I've said earlier, not regarded as regular employees by their Japanese bosses, but as contract employees. This, even by Japanese practices, makes them "disposable" people.

SECOND-CLASS STATUS OF FOREIGN EMPLOYEES ABROAD

The overall picture to emerge from this chapter is that foreign employees have an implicitly second-class status in the Japanese company abroad, although in Japan, where occupational status is explicit, up to half of the foreigners employed in Japanese companies have the same status and conditions as Japanese employees. Abroad, almost no Japanese expatriate, in any country, reports to a local manager, despite the fact that the numbers of Japanese expatriates abroad are double or treble those of any other nation's multinational corporations. Local staffs seem to be perceived suspiciously and with distrust by many Japanese expatriate managers in all countries, who tend to believe that locals are lazy, may try to take advantage of the company, could strike on flimsy pretexts, and are unlikely to stay long with the company. One major upshot of this is that there is little training for local white-collar executive staff, with most Japanese expatriate managers seeming to believe that it would be money wasted.

With the possible exception of financial services businesses (banks, insurance and securities companies, etc.), very few local employees have substantive management responsibilities. Most of those with "manager" titles are functional or technical specialists, not generalist managers. Apparently, Japanese companies abroad are unable to attract, or retain for very long, genuine general managerial candidates, due to their failure to give the responsibility and decision-making autonomy these individuals were accustomed to receive in other major, non-Japanese, corporations. As far as financial services businesses are concerned, greater responsibility seems to be given to local staff, and there is some modest spending on training. Study and textbook allowances, Japanese culture short courses, and especially study trips to Japan, have also been reported.

In manufacturing subsidiaries also, courses at company induction and specialist training are offered to small numbers of overseas employees each year by major companies, often with emphasis on learning how to behave like a "good Japanese"—to stand when the lecturer enters the room, sit up straight in classes, etc. The thinking behind this is to Japanize the local employee and make him more profoundly into a long-term member of the Japanese corporate family. This is unlikely to work in white-collar, managerially oriented or merchant-oriented businesses, where expatriate Japanese show the least skills in managing foreign staff. There is also some evidence that while some Japanese companies abroad have been reducing their numbers of expatriates (presumably when the business is going well and confidence in local staff is high), others change course and revert to increased numbers and greater "re-Japanization" when the business encounters difficulties.

CHAPTER
8
THE FOREIGN EMPLOYEE
IN
A MANAGEMENT ROLE

For foreign employees to become involved in management and decisionmaking, it will have become clear that they must usually first move from non-regular employee (shoku-taku) status to regular employee (sei shain) status, and that they should stay long term with the company to acquire the seniority, experience, people-handling skills, and (as usually required) formal qualifications needed to be an effective manager in a major Japanese company.

FROM NONREGULAR TO REGULAR EMPLOYEE

First, I will examine how some Japanese companies have made the transition from employing foreigners as nonregular, contract employees to employing them as regulars.

Increasing interdependence of the company with customers and suppliers external to Japan is obviously one factor that makes foreign employees more valuable to the Japanese firm, not just in setting up branches or subsidiaries overseas, but also in increasing purchases of components or raw materials from abroad, or having more foreign clients visit Japan. After the strengthening of the yen in 1986, Japanese companies rapidly increased their purchases from overseas suppliers and found many difficulties in everyday dealings with foreign sellers. The recruitment of more foreigners into procurement departments as well as into overseas business departments became a virtual necessity for many Japanese companies as they struggled with both paperwork and extended business discussions and negotiations in English. Another factor promoting increased status for foreign employees is the strong desire of many Japanese companies to internationalize their Japanese staff through language and communication training, and through the stimulation of the mere daily presence of foreigners working side by side with the Japanese.

As we will see in the case of the *Yomi-Asa Daily News* (YDN) and Nancy Haughton, however, the establishment of an equitable system of employment and conditions for foreigners does not occur simply or smoothly, and any movement for change in their status or conditions means confrontation and collision with the inertia of the Japanese organization. As noted earlier, conditions at YDN improved only after the company changed management due to a scandal. This case is, I believe, very representative of the degree of inertia in many Japanese companies when facing demands for change.

Nancy Haughton's sense of belonging to and membership of the Yomi-Asa newspaper company (YA) was a long time coming. The *Yomi-Asa Daily News* had been established in 1922 by some forward-thinking members of the *Yomi-Asa Shimbun*, one of Japan's largest. When Haughton joined, the editorial staff was entirely Japanese, and foreigners were employed only to proofread or to rewrite into English, translations first done by Japanese. Haughton was the first bilingual foreigner they had employed, and she found herself working with resentful and maladjusted foreigners (reminiscent of Gage's experience) who felt they had always been treated patronizingly by the Japanese and had no say in newspaper management or policy. As Haughton put it, "The Japanese ran the show and the foreigners were just there to fix the English."

Five years before she joined YDN, the parent company, YA, had been declared bankrupt and was only kept in business by severe cost-cutting, which persisted into the time Haughton started. There had never been any management leadership or vision of what YDN might become, with many of the Japanese assigned to YDN being people who had failed elsewhere in YA.

After spending her first year as a translator and proofreader, Haughton was promoted to city news editor. This was the start of a process that eventually led to more equitable employment for foreigners. She relates the story:

"'City news editor' was a fancy name for someone who chose and edited all the news stories for our one 'soft' domestic news page—that is, everything except economics and politics. Little did I know that this was a position of slave labor with long arduous hours and small compensation. We were so poor at the time that I had also to translate everything that needed to be translated from the *Shakaimen* (social pages) of the Japanese language newspaper, as well as arrange for all the photos on the page. It was a horrifi- cally stressful job, requiring extreme concentration, high speed and accurate translation ability, and good judgment. In the beginning I was content to do the job because I knew it was a wonderful ex- perience for me, but I soon realized that I was working twice as hard as any other foreigner for the same money. The reason for this was that there were simply no conditions of employment for non-Japanese translator/editors. Nor did it seem that any Japanese manager would bother to improve matters. After a year of work- ing in this position, another bilingual foreigner started, and he was soon highly vocal about our miserable conditions of employment. Unlike me, however, he confronted management, asking point- blank if there would be an improvement in conditions. The gen- eral manager said 'no,' and he left."

A different perspective is brought out by examining Villarante's experience. There we see a very large Japanese com- pany in slow but effective transition from a point where foreign employees had hazy and indeterminate positions and rights, to- wards a situation where they are being integrated into the main- stream of the organization. As Villarante tells it, however, it was a transition that came about not as the result of new policy formula- tion, but by a series of small pragmatic adjustments that would permit foreigners to be increasingly integrated into the company.

"I went to Japan," says Villarante, "in 1968 on the [government-sponsored] Monbusho Scholarship Program, and spent a couple of years at Chiba University studying Japanese in a special course for foreign students. After that, we were farmed out to different universities. I went to Denkashi University in Aichi Prefecture, where they teach electronic engineering. I finished in 1973, then joined Hitoba Computers on an associate training scholarship for one year. During that year I became very friendly with a manager who was eventually to become my mentor. He said, 'Why don't you stay and join the company?' So I stayed and became a nonregular (shokutaku) employee in 1974. I wasn't in the labor union, but my salary was a bit higher than a regular employee. I was a special case, and in fact I only became a regular employee after I was promoted to a managerial position.

"Some years before that, something happened in the politics of the company and my mentor got pushed aside for a few years. As he saw me as one of his men and didn't want to leave me isolated while he was exiled, he steered me to the Systems Engineering Division (SE), with the understanding that he would pick me up again later. In SE, I got involved in special support work for government and other major users in the USA, and eventually in 1980 was sent to the US, where I have been ever since. What's special is that I was sent here as an employee of Hitoba Japan, not America, and I still am today. This is important for my mentor, who still feels I am just on assignment and that he controls my destiny. Today he is quite high in the company, a vice president."

March: "Were you regarded as an experiment in those early days?"

Villarante: "I guess I was—a showpiece. At that time the company was just beginning in foreign markets, and they wanted more exposure to foreigners. They wanted to learn."

March: "Did it seem clear to you that they had no real plan?"

V.: "There would have been two things in their mind. One, that I would eventually go back to the Philippines and be their guy there. That is probably what they expected. Then I was also to be their guide, and in fact everybody wanted to talk to me, to learn something from me or practice their English. People were generally friendly at that time. I was a bit unhappy when they tried to push translation work onto me. Even today, some people say, hey, this is Japanese—come here, can you translate this? I have to be careful, otherwise I'll end up as a translator."

The Hitoba case reveals a large, well-established and successful Japanese company that slowly digested foreigners like Villarante into its system. YDN was different, a culturally and administratively split organization with Japanese in charge and foreigners as subordinates, similar to the Novatech company reported on by Robert Gage. From the viewpoint of the non-Japanese employees, these organizations demonstrate a high degree of inertia when facing demands for change, especially from people as powerless as foreigners. And, as noted earlier, around 20 percent of foreign employees in Japanese companies are either English teachers or otherwise involved in correspondence, translation, or rewriting. These may be in the least powerful position of all foreign employees, in terms of effecting organizational change.

Villarante has made this inertial tendency clear in the way he has related his own, path-breaking adaptation to Hitoba Computers. Initially, he was expected to return eventually to the Philippines. Later there were problems about his leadership role. That the organization had no clear-cut policies for handling foreigners is made clear by two more stories from Villarante:

"Some Hitoba people have funny ideas. When I first came to the USA, I technically came as an immigrant. I took US citizenship a couple of years ago. Anyway, this upset the personnel department in Japan. They started to say, for the first time, this guy is different, he has an odd way of thinking. They felt it was OK for me to be a Filipino, but when I took American citizenship without telling them beforehand, they were offended. They felt I ought to be forced to leave Hitoba Japan and become a local employee of Hitoba America. They actually created a *ringi* (a circulating proposal) asking that this be done."

March: "Assign you to Hitoba America?"

V: "Let's terminate his employment and all connections with Hitoba Japan and make him a local employee. But when my mentor got wind of it, he said, no way, he's one of my Japan-side guys. There was a bit of commotion there and they talked to me about it too. But I had no problem—it's my right to take whatever nationality I want. It doesn't affect my job performance. Eventually they dropped it, but not before another personnel guy tried to get me to leave the company because I was disloyal!"

March: "I suppose from a narrow viewpoint it could have looked like betrayal or desertion."

V: "Yes, this particular guy felt that—very narrow-minded. . . . Then there was the case of my younger brother, who also studied in Japan. After he got his masters from the University of Tokyo, he had some discussions with Hitoba. This personnel department is very conservative. The personnel manager talked to me and said, 'Why are you and your brother both in Japan? (I'm the older brother). Isn't it your duty to go back to the Philippines and help your father in the store?' I was insulted."

Villarante's experiences with the Hitoba personnel department were varied and often strained, but they also point to an underlying process of change and improvement that benefited those foreigners who joined the company after him. Also, the experience of Japanese managers and personnel people in dealing with him contributed to their education about the world beyond Japan, that is, to their "internationalization." It even helped to shed doubt on some of the myths that the Japanese hold about themselves, as the following dialogue shows:

"Before I was assigned to the USA, there was some trouble. A young guy from the personnel department said, 'How come they have decided to send you, of all people?' He was very surprised."

March: "Since you are a foreigner, you don't really have a place in the company, is that it? A Japanese company, by definition, is only Japanese? Maybe some jealousy there, too."

V: "Traditionally, that was so, although it is slowly changing. These days, we are hiring some 15 to 20 foreigners a year as regular employees, compared to the 2 or 3 in the first year when I was hired. It's a very significant shift in the company."

March: "Could it still happen that somebody was being sent overseas, and a personnel man says, why are you being sent, you're a foreigner?"

V: "No, it won't happen again. My case set a precedent. . . . A precedent is very important in Japanese companies."

March: "Were you the first?"

V: "Yes. Life is orderly and systematic in the Japanese world. Anything that is an exception or is appearing for the first time—people simply don't know how to handle it. Once you have a precedent, there is no problem. They know who to talk to and they look at what happened in the past. However, the manager who actually made the decision to assign me here told me before I left that I must come back because, 'if you don't, I'll lose face'. So he was sticking his neck out for me, because his mind was saying, 'This is a foreigner and he's going to escape. Japanese are different. They always come back.'"

March: "Those fears are in the past now, I suppose."

V: "His fears are past, that's true. But guess what? The old myth about the Japanese always coming back home is also gone. The Japanese guy that I succeeded, he escaped! Resigned, joined IBM, and never went back to Japan. He created a lot of problems, let me tell you. The Japanese myth is not valid any more."

Villarante's transition from nonregular to regular employee to manager can be seen as the establishment of a series of groundbreaking precedents, for which he was a true pioneer. Klineberg's experience is different. He finally concluded that the precedents needed to integrate him into the organization would not be realized. He comments:

"Things are not easy in an organization where there is a fixed way to do everything. When a foreign company or embassy asked for something special or personalized, problems arose. Usually the first answer was 'no.' So I had to do lots of nemawashi [behind-the-scenes negotiation] to get them to understand, gain their support, and only then would we move forward."

March: "Could you give some examples of these special things that required nemawashi?"

K: "Well, menus for a banquet. A Middle Eastern embassy had a prince visiting. They wanted to have a special banquet. This was not just an expensive banquet with Middle East-type foods. This was to be an event, the flowers were to be carefully chosen, even the colors of the tablecloths, the music, the entertainment, and highly elaborate decorations. In planning, we had tasting sessions to try out the recipes, but the immediate response from the Japanese was, 'no, it cannot be done.' I had to orchestrate repeated meetings, and detailed organizing had to be done by someone from the banquet reservation department of the hotel. At the meetings, we had someone from the company supplying the orchestra, from the florist, from the entertainment company. The chefs would present different ideas for the meal, including special breads native to the country, with the symbol of the country on top of everything. The dessert would also have a symbol of the country designed into it. At first, everything seemed impossible or too expensive, but eventually we achieved everything through these meetings, and through spending lots of time with the chefs. We'd go to the kitchen and talk to them individually, to each chef, in the appetizer section, pastry section, bread section, not to the executive chef's office."

March: "The initial 'no' came from whom?"

K: "Everybody!"

March: "What resistance was there when you went to talk to them, one on one?"

K: "That was a different story. I was able to play on their sense of service. In Japan there is a saying which is very meaningful in the hospitality industry—'O kyaku san wa kami san' [The customer is a god]. That is ingrained here and I was able to play on that. Then I would ask them why we couldn't achieve something that the customer wanted. My sincerity was also important. They sensed the project was important to me personally, and that made it a person-to-person thing. I think this is what made the difference. There were times when requests seemed impossible to me too, and I would tell the ambassador, 'Sorry, but it can't be done.' But they would insist, 'On the contrary, it can be done.' They had become so accustomed to the Japanese saying 'no' in the past that they suspected that I was just giving them the same line. I learnt eventually just to ignore those of our people who said 'no' and go ahead with discussions with clients. Sometimes discussions would reach such a point that an obligation was created in the minds of some of the Japanese staff. Now the project had its own momentum, so they simply had to get aboard. Put another way, no Japanese wants to be seen to be dragging behind or saying 'no' when everyone else is saying 'yes.' This is the power of consensus in Japan."

LIMITS TO ORGANIZATIONAL INNOVATION

Klineberg's story is instructive for what it tells us about the limits to which a foreigner can fit into a traditional Japanese organization like a hotel or to the ability of the organization to incorporate an alien subsystem. When he decided to resign, he felt that "the situation had become intolerable":

"The main reason I decided to leave was that I had standards that I wanted to uphold, and I felt that because of staffing deficiencies, because of the incredible success I had [he tripled banquet sales in his first year, and thereafter increased them by 40 percent a year], the hotel eventually was unable to cope with what I was doing or the methods of management that were essential to handling that level of business with foreign clients. . . . My complaints about an inadequate support system came as my own job responsibilities started to dig deeper and cover more client companies. For instance, I needed a typist, and a secretary who could think, make decisions, and take messages in English. I needed an English-language word processor, and more foreign salespeople. . . . This was all unprecedented. Not even vice presidents have secretaries in Japanese companies. So this posed a huge difficulty for the entire organization. And of course, nothing happened, and I think in the end they were glad to see me go."

It is fascinating to see the real dilemma posed for the Japanese organization by Klineberg's success. Underlying this would be, I am certain, understandably strong human emotions on the Japanese side: jealousy at his success, and resentment at the idea of a young foreigner having such a staff and controlling a business (within a business) that was virtually autonomous, that none of them felt any control over. It is no wonder then, as he says, that they were not concerned about his departure, that they made no attempt to have him stay, and that they failed to appoint anyone to succeed him. They had discovered that in banquet sales at least, internationalization was not going to work for them.

MANAGEMENT DECISION-MAKING AND THE FOREIGN EMPLOYEE

It is one thing for isolated Japanese-speaking, non-Japanese like Villarante to make their way up the Japanese corporate ladder. It is quite another for foreigners abroad, with neither language nor cultural skills, to do so. When we look at the major, globally-integrated Japanese multinationals in automobiles, computers, electronics, we find a style of management that prevents any individual abroad, Japanese or local, from managing or making decisions autonomously. Decision-making power is ultimately located back in Japan, with the senior expatriate Japanese responsible for recommendations and final negotiations with head office while the senior local managers are responsible for communicating decisions to the local organization at large and seeing them implemented. With just a very few, albeit striking, exceptions—Sony America, Toshiba USA, Pilot Company America and some others—the Japanese style of running a multinational corporation leaves no room at the top for local managers.

WHY SHOULD JAPANESE EXPATRIATES BE SO PREFERRED?

Even when a local employee is given the title of president or chief executive officer, almost invariably he has a shadow (Japanese) manager to whom he reports or with whom he consults on a daily basis. In short, expatriate Japanese are the real bosses of Japanese companies abroad, whatever their titles. Why should this be so?

Expatriates are seen as committed to the parent company for life, locally hired managers are not. Moreover, local managers do not and cannot, currently, fit into the Japanese decision-making style. Discussions on hard issues flow over into after-hours and weekend socializing, all of which are conducted in Japanese. Even when local senior managers are given major responsibilities in building a business, they find that their Japanese senior, or the president, or their adviser, changes every few years, and that they have to train and learn to live with another new expatriate. After this is done once or twice, the local manager may start to lose his enthusiasm for training someone who stands in the way of any further promotion—it seems so unfair. In other cases, they find the new appointees to be more difficult to get along with, or more autocratic, or less effective as communicators, and lose heart.

The Japanese view is usually that they nurture and support the local manager, give him a good salary and bonus, buy him country club memberships, and then he resigns, proving that foreigners are neither loyal nor to be trusted. This is clearly going to be a serious problem for Japanese companies well into the future, first, because few top companies are as yet committed to "localizing" by replacing the expatriates overseas with locals. An American management consultant colleague who does human resource development training all over the world for a very large Japanese company tells me that the Japanese managers still firmly believe that local staff will only stay a few years, and consequently they refuse to approve staff training, study trips to Japan, or even transfer assignments to Japan, as a sheer waste of money. The second ongoing problem for Japanese companies is that their failure to appoint locals as responsible senior managers is now a political issue and public relations concern that is constantly simmering in the USA and will inevitably intensify in other countries, especially in the post-1992 European community.

In a special report in 1987, *Electronic Business*, a US trade magazine, interviewed many Americans and Japanese on the issue of Americanization. Hostility and resentment were expressed because Americans were being given ample responsibility but no autonomous decision-making power. One frustrated American finance manager of a Japanese company was not even able to sign checks. A vice president of Hitachi US's Telecom Division was unable to grant promotions, raises, or job changes. His Japanese senior did all these autonomously. Others complained that, when they attempted to make decisions in areas where it would seem entirely natural for them to have ultimate authority, the Japanese would respond with "we should study this further before making the final decision."

The *New York Times*, Jan. 25, 1988, reported the following case: "In lawsuits filed last year, Thomas McDannold and Edward A. Neubauer, once the highest-ranking American managers at NEC Electronics Inc., tell a tale of frustration and broken promises. Both men . . . say they were given assurances that they would have wide latitude to run the corporation's American operations. Those promises were soon dashed, Mr. Neubauer said, when the company, over his objections, began to send more and more Japanese-born executives to fill management positions. . . . The men contend that nearly every facet of the business here . . . is run with a dictatorial and arrogant hand from afar by its parent company. . . .

"'The Japanese,' Neubauer was reported as saying, 'essentially don't trust anyone who doesn't speak the language, who is not of the same race, or has been out of Japan too long'. . . . He once heard a very high-level Japanese accuse a Japanese colleague of 'no longer being Japanese' because 'he had been out of Japan too long.'"

The *Washington Times* (June 13, 1990) reported a Nissan US directive to its American staffers that, in future, only a select few would be permitted to communicate directly with the head office. And everyone was required to consult with a Japanese staff member before any "important telephone conversations" with Japan. This staff memo was widely leaked to the US media at the time and reinforced the views of many, like Neubauer, who believe that Japanese companies do not trust the foreign staff and keep it out of decision-making positions.

LOCAL STAFF IN DECISION-MAKING

In Japan or abroad, Japanese decision-making is a group activity. Unilateral decisions by directors or senior managers occur, but they are uncommon. Most decisions flow from an extended process of discussion involving many people. In part, this is a device to ensure that decisions will be supported throughout the company, in part a device to minimize error, by having people cross-check one another's ideas.

A model of a typical Japanese decision-making process is

shown in Figure 1. Beginning at the bottom of the page, the first four stages involve people getting together as a team, collecting information, and making a first draft of the idea proposal. This proposal and its implications are then discussed with a variety of people within the company, who have interests in the area or who could be affected by its implementation. These discussions are called nemawashi, originally a horticultural term meaning the work of binding the roots of a tree to prepare it for removal and transplantation elsewhere. From the nemawashi groundwork, a proposal (ringisho) will be prepared and circulated, and people will write comments in the margin. This nemawashi-ringisho process may be repeated a number of times until consensus seems

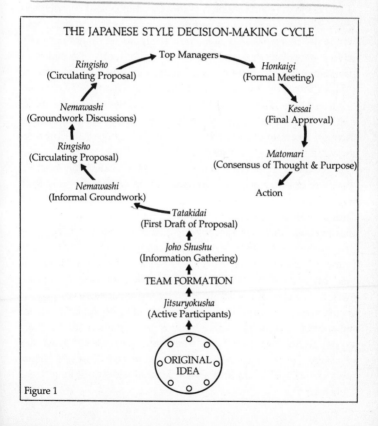

THE JAPANESE STYLE DECISION-MAKING CYCLE

Ringisho
(Circulating Proposal)

Top Managers

Honkaigi
(Formal Meeting)

Nemawashi
(Groundwork Discussions)

Kessai
(Final Approval)

Ringisho
(Circulating Proposal)

Matomari
(Consensus of Thought & Purpose)

Nemawashi
(Informal Groundwork)

Action

Tatakidai
(First Draft of Proposal)

Joho Shushu
(Information Gathering)

TEAM FORMATION

Jitsuryokusha
(Active Participants)

ORIGINAL
IDEA

Figure 1

certain, or the proposal is scuttled. From this point on, top managers (the executive committee or the board of directors) make the final decisions.

What we can see is that the heart of the predecision process—nemawashi and ringisho—is extensive, open communication between many parties. The Japanese are accustomed to its open-ended and iterative nature, and to the subtleties of communication (in their own language) that are involved. But, while Japanese know this, non-Japanese are not accustomed to such methods of communication. I believe this is a major reason expatriates tend to monopolize decision-making abroad and exclude locals from the process. Martin Carothers, senior VP for Nitto Industries in the US, told me the nemawashi system was "clumsy and complex—it gives mediocre, uncreative people too much power to delay and obfuscate." A British manager says, "the Japanese do not normally have a participatory style. . . . Creativity in terms of reaction to problem-solving is not one of a Japanese person's strong points" (Jones 1991, 70). Michael Pritchard, of the Bank of Tokyo in London, says: " the Japanese have an insatiable appetite for information and so pick up every trivial little detail . . . (They) operate through a system of . . . attrition. . . . There's none of the gut feeling which is behind decisions in US banks" (ibid., 84).

A particularly tedious example of extended decision-making, reported in every country surveyed, is agreement on new staff regulations. In every case, it took three to five years for Tokyo and local expatriate managers to agree to the content. It would seem that Japanese managers are reluctant to accept the more legalistic and explicit statements of company obligations to staff that are found in the West. In Japan, there is an unspoken but widespread view that the company and its needs and demands are more powerful than those of society or the law. To Japanese managers, it would seem impudent, arrogant, and insulting to appeal to external criteria or principles or authorities in settling a matter of individual rights and privileges. The employees should trust the company's goodwill and paternalism to receive "just" or "equitable" conditions, over and above those already traditionally established.

Meetings and decision-making are intimately connected. Japanese subsidiaries with expatriates in charge usually have weekly meetings of expatriates only, conducted therefore in Japanese. In some, but by no means all, subsidiaries, there are also regular meetings including local managers, which are occasions for exchanging views, and, many locals feel, giving the expatriates solid opportunities to practice their English. The former meetings are much concerned with decision-making, the latter not.

Board meetings regularly take place in some manufacturing subsidiaries, where most board members are at the same time working executives. Mitsubishi Electric in the UK has monthly board meetings, which report to the head of international operations in Tokyo on strategy matters, while a local executive committee deals with day-to-day operational decisions (Jones 1991, 130). On the other hand, and this seems the case especially in the USA, local managers with overall marketing/sales or operations responsibilities have individual shadow managers to report to, or an expatriate chief executive officer. There are also responsibilities to others in Japan. Rehfeld (1990) recounts: "I reported directly to the president of Toshiba America, who approved the business plan and evaluated the fiscal period business performance. But I also had a dotted line—a very thick, black dotted line—to the head of the international sales and marketing group in Tokyo. He was interested in long-term business development" (p. 174).

Smaller, nonmanufacturing businesses run by expatriates often have no custom of regular board meetings. Everything is handled by the ongoing weekly and other meetings among expatriates.

The upshot of these different customs of decision-making is to leave most local managers, below the most senior level, feeling out in the cold, without leverage upon decisions made in private, behind-the-scenes cabals of expatriates. In seeking to get decisions made on specific recommendations or projects, many local managers try to push Tokyo, but are bewildered by being unable to find out who specifically has authority to make a given decision. In extreme cases, Tokyo decisions can take as long as six months to obtain.

Leonard Bright, general manager of Japan Courier Overseas

service office in the UK, says: "I admire the thoroughness with which they plan and that they use to solve problems, but like many people, I'm frustrated by the slowness and tardiness of action. This particular organization always seems to be playing catch-up. It should be no. 1 but isn't. When our major competitors do something new, eventually two years later we do it. I'm frustrated many times by the lack of answers, therefore no decision; and when that decision affects non-Japanese clients here, it is very difficult to explain to them.

"I'm frustrated by the behavior of other JWC offices in their attitude that Japan is the center of the world. It is annoying when my clients request the LA office to send documents to London—when they ring our office in LA, they are answered in Japanese. In our industry, one of the major geographic areas is North America. Every other competitor sends stuff directly from LA to London, but not JWC. We have to send it via Japan. It's pretty hard to explain."

Bright attributes the delays in new product launches and service innovations to difficulties in decision-making at Tokyo head office. There is also a viewpoint, which I accept, that Japanese head offices, tend to look down on the overseas branches, offices or subsidiaries. Since the most cerebral and challenging activities of most businesses remain in Japan—global financial and product strategy, production planning, product development, and so on—the overseas office is often no more sophisticated than a regional sales office would be in Japan.

DECISION-MAKING AND JAPANESE ENCLAVES ABROAD

The reluctance to give foreign managers real power is often due to the overwhelming presence of Japanese assignees in the overseas subsidiary. Surveys in Europe, the USA, and the Asia-Pacific region (e.g., Nikkei Kigyo 1989, News From MITI 1990, March 1980) have shown that close to 70 percent of middle/senior managers in Japanese firms abroad are Japanese, a marked contrast to American and European multinationals abroad, where only 10 percent of the same group come from the home country. As for the CEO's of overseas subsidiaries, virtually 100 percent are home country (i.e., Japanese) nationals in the Japanese case, contrasted to 75 percent being home country nationals with European subsidiaries, and 50 percent with US subsidiaries abroad.

These differences have many consequences. Decision-making abroad tends to be firmly in Japanese hands, and decision- making meetings are held largely among Japanese only, and in the Japanese language. This is an ongoing source of resentment and frustration among local managers. When the overseas firm has more than three or four Japanese expatriates, and many have twenty or thirty or more, the expatriate group becomes a self-sufficient community in its own right; members no longer need to depend upon local people for socializing, or even for local information, and they do not. Consequently, the Japanese assignees tend to become distant, unsociable figures, their native tendencies to be shy and avoid foreigners are reinforced, and their usually limited skills in conversational English remain limited through lack of everyday practice, making the job of handing over authority to local managers even more difficult. A truly vicious circle.

In a recent survey of Japanese executives assigned to British subsidiaries, Jones (1990) found that 9 percent of all employees were Japanese, while in companies with 200 employees or less (which are more likely to be nonmanufacturing), the percentage was 15 percent, suggesting a dominant presence of Japanese among middle and senior managers. In one case—quite likely a car manufacturer—150 out of 2,000 were Japanese. Nine Japanese companies in this sample each had 200 to 500 employees (a size suggesting they are in a high growth phase), and there were a total of 356 expatriates in these 9 companies, or almost 40 per company. These are very large company populations of expatriates. One might take more kindly to such a large representation if the expatriates were abroad to train local people, which seems certainly the case with manufacturing businesses where non-Japanese have much to learn. In nonmanufacturing, however, especially banks and trading companies, I have found less evidence that expatriates are training people, or even that the Japanese abroad have any special competence to train locals in these softer areas.

This distinction is related to a matter of current concern in the USA: that Japanese companies there are discriminating against American managers in favor of less experienced, less qualified Japanese expatriates. One newspaper reports:

"Some mighty names in Japanese industry—Matsushita, Sumitomo, NEC Electronics—settled lawsuits charging discrimination against American managers just last year (1990). Beyond specific complaints of discrimination, critics say Japanese companies in the United States are top-heavy with Japanese managers. . . . The proportions . . . far exceed [those] of Europeans in the top ranks of European companies in America, or of Americans in American companies abroad. . . . In a lawsuit against a Ricoh Corp. plant in San Jose . . . Chet Mackenzie . . . says he was dismissed solely because he was American. [He] asserts that after he paved the way for the company to reach American customers with a new product . . . his functions were assigned to a Japanese . . . the federal Equal Employment Opportunity Commission found that [he] had 'reasonable cause' to sue."

(*International Herald Tribune*, June 4, 1991, p. 1)

In the context of the question of what status the local employee has in the Japanese company abroad, there is justification for concern here. Treatment of local managers as second-class, "disposable" citizens is very much contrary to the spirit of the company-employee relationship in major companies in Japan. The only explanation of this discrepancy I can conjure up is, as I have said before, that non-Japanese employees simply have temporary status to Japanese, on the implicit basis of employment conventions in Japan—as contract workers, who can be dismissed, even in Japan, without fuss. I do not mean to say that all Japanese companies have such a calculated or predatory attitude to local staff, for most of them are honorable and high-minded in their views of their own humanity and aspirations. But in the case of problems with some Japanese expatriates, three problems in particular—their consciousness of their Japaneseness, and their consequent difference from and superiority to non-Japanese; their fragile and poorly developed human contacts with and sympathies for local people; their diminished human sensitivities, blunted by the much higher priority given to the company's success—help to distort and weaken universalist sentiments or goodwill, and restrict the access of local managers to positions of decision-making authority.

THE LIMITS OF DECISION-MAKING POWER

The presence of shadow managers, discussed in the last chapter, indicates how limited the decision-making power of many local managers is. The case of Denis Pawley is instructive. He joined Mazda USA in 1985 as director of manufacturing at Flat Rock, Michigan, and was the top-ranking American manager. At that time he believed that within three to four years American managers would be able to take over. "Every American here expects that," he told the *Detroit News*. "By then, we will have illustrated our patience to learn the system, and they damn well better let us implement it. That's the reason they came here." But in three years Pawley had resigned. "It had finally become obvious to him," reported J.J. and Suzy Fucini (1990), "that he would never be given real authority at Flat Rock. . . . He had become frustrated with the constraints that the company's Japanese management had placed upon him."

Pawley had, erroneously, convinced himself that it was appropriate to expect to become the top man in the USA company. This can never have been the intention of Mazda, even if they had promised to give him the title of president some time in the future. In the Japanese auto industry abroad, Japanese are firmly in control. It is an essential part of their global strategies for quality control and product development. The fact that a non-Japanese is called president is merely, with few exceptions, a screen hiding the fact that they still report on a daily basis to a Japanese shadow manager.

When the board of Nissan Japan decided to close its Australian manufacturing operation in February 1992, the decision was conveyed by a telephone call from the chairman in Japan to the Australian managing director of the local company, who then made the decision public at a press conference in Melbourne. There were no Japanese visible at that conference. (The previous managing director of Nissan Australia, curiously enough, had re-signed just months before the decision to close down was made.) Experiences like this make Japanese hesitant not only to hand over too much authority, but, as one would suspect in the Nissan Australia case, any information about forward strategic thinking. Ironically, this is now becoming a problem in an unexpected and embarrassing way: it is Japanese expatriates, assigned from head office, who are starting to resign and take strategic information of this kind to the western competitors of Japanese companies. IBM, Burroughs, Rockwell International, a number of English and American banks and security companies, are just some examples.

FINAL COMMENTS

More than anything else, the failure of non-Japanese employees to achieve senior decision-making responsibility in Japanese sub-sidiaries is due to the vicious circle of: the Japanese belief that they will only stay a few years —> Japanese restrictions on training and promotion, of foreigners —> foreign employee dissatisfaction with the lack of training, promotion, and authority —> foreigner's res-ignation from the subsidiary, so fulfilling the Japanese "prophecy."

The Japanese manager's retort to this would undoubtedly be that Japanese employees in Japan show a much greater company loyalty and lower job turnover than do foreigners. I challenge that. The Japanese manager's view is based on data for regular em-ployees in major companies in Japan. The situation abroad is different, for two reasons. One, local employees do not feel them-selves regular employees and are treated more like non-regular employees are in Japan. Two, Japanese overseas subsidiaries are generally not "major" companies abroad. They tend to be small or medium in size, and to be so perceived. A head office in Tokyo might employ 5,000 people, while its subsidiary in New York (as an example) might have no more than 200, a size of operation which would not inspire the same respect and attachment that one does find in Japan.

The comparison with Japanese employees to the disadvantage of local employees is not, then, a fair or valid one. If the compari-son were made with the turnover of staff in small or medium-sized companies in Japan, I have no doubt at all that it would hardly differ, since labor turnover rates in that segment of the Japanese world have long been comparable to turnover rates in Western countries.

How the Japanese face up to the problem of staff turnover, especially at senior executive level, depends upon which point in the vicious circle I have described above they choose to concentrate on. To me, the obvious answer is that they must train and promote foreigners as though their lives depended on it. Naturally, they have the challenge of recruiting the "right" people in the first place. Then they have the challenge of giving them authority and a real sense of involvement in the company: not the "second-class" perception that is all too common at the moment.

There are risks in this for the Japanese. Some of the people they invest in will leave. Japanese pride will be hurt and a sense of being a victim of "disloyal" foreigners will be typical enough. The Japanese must then choose more carefully, bind them by personal affections and favors and support to the company, so making it more difficult for the foreign employee to contemplate leaving the company. This means bridging interpersonal barriers and creating friendlier relationships between Japanese and Westerners.

In recruiting foreigners abroad, the Japanese may need to create a system similar to Japan of regular and nonregular employees. This can be done by promoting existing foreign employees up to regular status, on a level equivalent in every way to the Japanese. There are already precedents for doing this in Japanese companies: there are younger shokutaku employees in Japan who do become regular employees in many companies, for instance. But it needs to be done systematically and to be driven by an explicit policy that legitimizes the ascension of foreigners.

As for the foreign employee and manager, some know perfectly well from the start that they could spend the remainder of their working life in a Japanese company, while others are reasonably certain it will only be for a few years. A more informed and thorough understanding of how the Japanese subsidiary works—its relations to head office, the roles played by expatriates, and the likely scope for and ceiling to promotion and professional development—

are important for the foreign employee. At the same time, if you choose to be patient, you are likely to find that your opportunities in a Japanese subsidiary are going to grow greatly, and beyond current expectations or imagining, in the next decade or so.

9

DIVISION AND POLARIZATION IN THE MULTINATIONAL JAPANESE COMPANY

The overriding question of this second part of the book has been whether foreigners fit into Japanese companies, in Japan and overseas. The answer, simply put, has been, "Not easily." Having two cultures in the one organization makes for frequent problems, and in some cases human and working relationships are so seriously affected that the company becomes chronically divided and polarized into two "warring" camps. A little later, we will look at some cases of such polarization. Before that, a review of the main problems adversely affecting relations between the two sides will make clearer what we have detected in the past five chapters by summarizing each chapter as a question.

1. Are Human Relations Good?

Human relations between foreign employees and their Japanese bosses and colleagues tend to be satisfactory in Japan, where foreigners who have regular employee status enjoy the same or better employment conditions and the same paternalism as do the Japanese. Abroad, there is less friendliness, far less socializing with the Japanese, and a lot more coolness and psychological distance, especially when there are large numbers of expatriate Japanese in the one company.

2. Is Communication Effective?

As long as the conversational English of Japanese expatriates remains as limited and unidiomatic as it is, face-to-face communication with local employees and managers will remain a source of cross-cultural misunderstandings, miscommunication, confusion, hostility, etc. But the communication we talk about here is not just linguistic: culture is also involved. Expatriate Japanese, for instance, do not learn enough about the local culture and fail to speak English with the smooth idiomatic (i.e., cultural) quality of the host country. Rather, expatriates tend to speak a Japanized English along with what I'll call "body Japanese." That is, the non-verbal, paralinguistic, and culturally idiosyncratic aspects of their conversational English remain Japanese, and although most expatriates may not be able to put their finger on exactly what their problems are, the Japanese do, by their stiff, un-English "body Japanese," communicate an alienness to locals that is confusing and off-putting.

In addition, there are certain practices of some Japanese that seriously impede interpersonal communication with Westerners, namely, the use of avoidance and denial, the feigned or real indifference projected by their poker-facedness, ambiguity in response, and the use of a blunt form of speech and order-giving that Westerners are unaccustomed to. Communication is also affected by expatriates' suspicion of the motives or real intentions of local staff. In short then, communication is frequently ineffective, and this contributes to unsatisfactory human relations.

3. Is the Employment and Status of Foreigners Satisfactory?

The greatest difficulty in this area is the extensive discrimination, on racial and sexual grounds, practiced by the Japanese in recruiting abroad.

4. Are the Work Conditions and the Administrative Controls upon Foreigners Equitable and Appropriate?

The most serious concerns for foreign employees abroad are,

one: their second-class status compared to regular employees in Japan, and two: their own lack of understanding of (and probably interest in) Japanese business culture. These two factors contribute directly to worsening their chances of becoming involved in company decision-making.

5. Are Foreign Employees Equitably Involved in Company Management?

The continuing second-class status of foreign employees abroad is sustained by a Japanese fear that the local staff will only stay with the company for a few years, and that therefore there should be little investment in their training, no openness with them about strategic company information, and little involvement in important management meetings or decision-making. Such situations constitute vicious cycles inviting the self-fulfilment of the prophecy that the foreigners will leave. This kind of situation is most likely when there are large numbers of expatriates in the overseas subsidiary.

THRESHOLDS FOR POLARIZATION

It is one thing for a company to be performing suboptimally, muddling along with a mediocre but not horrendous performance, with the staff doing their jobs without overt antagonism (though not exactly joyously either), and leaving the expression of their private opinions to after-hours meetings with their peers. It is quite another thing for the company to be riven daily by angry encounters and meetings, by deliberate resistance to cooperative activities, and by explicit avoidance of one culture by most members of the other culture. What has to occur to turn a nonhostile organizational environment into an unhappily polarized den of mutual antipathy? Are there any special conditions or thresholds that lead a multicultural company to become dysfunctional? I suggest that there are at least four.

1. Threats to Established Power and Position

Threats to established power and position can arise when one company merges with another, or when a new business department

develops within an organization and requires treatment or resources that are not available to other departments, or when new
managers are brought into the company and become senior to existing staff members.

2. Extreme Psychological Distance between Cultures

At various points throughout the book, I have stated that many
Japanese expatriates distance themselves from their local employees and the host culture. The weight of evidence supporting this—
in particular extensive unsociable behavior in many countries—is
considerable, and we also have the words of the expatriates themselves. Hori (1982) undertook a survey amongst Japanese expatriate managers in Sydney, Australia in 1982, and his findings
support this view. For instance, when asked, "If anti-Japanese sentiments occur in Australia, which of these reasons do you think
would be most responsible?" just about half of the Japanese expatriate respondents chose the response, "A lack of international
consciousness by the Japanese." Finding that nearly half of the
managers showed no interest in Australia, he explained the psychology of his fellows (and himself) thus:

"We are somewhat insecure here because we saw ourselves as
belonging to a different, and not very pleasant, race, in the eyes of
Australians. The more insecurity we develop, the more sensitive
and cautious we become in our thinking about what Australians
are really thinking of us." (p. 83)

Obviously, this sensitivity to what Australians were really
thinking must have occurred most frequently in the office, since
expatriates have few other opportunities to meet the local people.

Hori also draws these conclusions about the problems of
Australians working in Japanese subsidiaries:

—They excluded local staff from decision-making, or simply ignored them;

—Failed to delegate;

—Didn't spend enough time attending to the local organization;

—Failed to appreciate loyalty from local staff, and treated them as
second class citizens.

If such problems occur together, especially when the number

of expatriates is large, we can expect extreme psychological distance to arise between the cultures, and the threshold is reached at which severe, explicit polarization erupts. One problem in particular with large numbers of expatriates, where relatively few locals occupy important management posts, is their likelihood to resist change jointly and be supportive of the status quo (favoring them).

3. Accumulated Dissatisfaction

When the number of expatriates is not large (say no more than three or four), I would anticipate that the accumulation of the various kinds of dissatisfaction (reported by Hori above) over time would bring the organization to a threshold for polarization to occur. However, in such a case one would expect a great proportion of managers to be local employees, with more treatment as "equals," and therefore a speedier resolution of problems could be achieved than in the expatriate-heavy subsidiary.

4. Exclusion from Involvement and/or Power

However well treated local employees might be, there is always the probability that they will develop, as Hori says, and as we have seen throughout the book, the sense of being in fact second-class members of the Japanese organization. Seven factors in particular can contribute to this: (1) a clear ceiling on promotion, as Pawley of Mazda USA found; (2) the absence or near absence of local employees among the company's middle and senior management—this was long the case of Nancy Haughton's *Yomi-Asa Daily News*, for instance; (3) the experience of local employees who are assistants to successive senior expatriates over time whom they must train for the local post, but who are never given more senior opportunities or the chance themselves to do the job of the senior expatriate; (4) the failure to disclose information, both strategic and operational, to foreigners; (5) a somewhat common correlate of the failure of expatriates to share information is their failure to show teamwork skills when working with local or foreign staff, in spite of the Japanese reputation as good team workers. This is connected to the frequent turnover of expatriate managers—it takes time for trust and teamwork to develop between locals and expatriates; (6) the sense of exclusion is intensified by the confusion and frustration that local managers feel about who has the power to make decisions or get things done at the Japanese head office, and who reports to whom; and finally, (7) the Japanese expatriates, generally speaking, continue to rely more on interpreters and other intermediaries, or on their own poor English, in communicating with local staff, rather than working to improve their English language skills. This implies to local staff that Japanese is the language of the "ruling-class."

EXCLUSION FROM INVOLVEMENT/POWER: ONE EXAMPLE

Independent confirmation of the seven factors cited comes from the research of Pucik, Hanada & Fifield (1989), undertaken among US subsidiaries of Japanese companies. Even more striking, however, is the content of a confidential report to one of Japan's largest multinationals about the situation in its Asia-Pacific offices. The report comes from a Western management consultant hired by Tokyo head office to assess training needs and requirements among local staff. The consultant spent three months visiting each office to interview all management staff. While noting that most local staff liked working at the company, the range of dissatisfaction was considerable in every subsidiary. Here is a sample of comments from five Asian offices:

—There is a lack of equal opportunity for local managers compared with Japanese managers, due to their disadvantage in making decisions and in doing business with the head office.

—Senior local managers are not shown respect by junior Japanese managers and can be overruled by them.

—Senior local staff are unsure of when it is appropriate for them to speak with the general manager, given their relationship with Japanese supervisors.

—Japanese managers are seen as more concerned with their own comfort, rank, and getting credit from head office than with issues concerning the local staff and managers.

—Japanese representatives hide relevant information from the locals and, once they have been in the country for a few months, omit them from all decision-making.

—Local staff have inadequate basic company and technical product and process knowledge,needed to get respect from customers and to sell effectively.

—Too much important business data is in Japanese.

—Head office is not giving adequate and timely responses to inquiries.

—Japanese managers are too busy to act as mentors to local staff.

This report highlights the inferior status and limited power and involvement of local staff. The "second-class" status of the locals is made clear by lack of respect shown by junior Japanese to senior local employees. Moreover, the expatriates are evidently not spending nearly enough time and effort in training local employees or in motivating them to do the job, a point also made by Hori about Japanese expatriates in Australia. Nonetheless, the head office is concerned currently only with the training of local employees, not that of expatriate managers, and the reason clearly is that head office has no confidence that expatriate Japanese have the capacity, time, or motivation to train local staff. Even if training is undertaken, however, and is at all successful, one probable undesired side-effect will be to widen the gaps between the expatriates (who will not have experience of the training) and the local employees (who will).

The sparks of division and polarization exist in these Japanese subsidiaries, but they are unlikely to flare up as long as the local employees are powerless or, to put it another way, as long as they are easily disposable and replaceable. One can expect that dissatisfactions, covert hostilities, resentments, and even attempts to undermine or thwart the activities of disliked expatriates or the company generally will accumulate as only the more mediocre and overtly timid staff end up remaining over time. However, as long as the locals are mediocre and timid, we would be unlikely to see the appearance of flagrant polarization; perhaps we could call such situations of covert resentment no more than "smouldering" division.

FOREIGN STAFF WITH POWER IN A JAPANESE COMPANY

Polarization occurred in the Novatech organization in Japan, as reported in chapter 4, between Shinagawa, the president, and most of the non-Japanese staff involved in translation and writing. It was their large numbers (varying from 15 to 30 depending on work flow) and their relative powerfulness (they were difficult to recruit or replace, and their work output made up a sizeable part of the company's turnover) that fuelled the explicit polarization between (some of) them and the president.

POLARIZATION

Other Japanese companies in Japan where similar polarization of Japanese and foreigners into opposed and hostile groups occurred, that were also reported to me, included: a securities company, where large numbers of foreigners were employed as security analysts, bond traders, etc.; a major advertising agency where account groups tended to be foreigner only or Japanese only; a market research company serving predominantly foreign clients that had large numbers of foreigners on its staff; and the legal departments of trading companies employing many foreign lawyers offering legal services to business departments.

Polarization is not a uniquely Japanese problem. Foreign firms in Japan also experience it. It is well recognized in the expatriate "old hand" community in Japan that many of the severe personnel problems experienced during the 1980s by firms such as Procter and Gamble, IBM Asia/Pacific headquarters in Tokyo, Coca Cola, Pepsico, etc., were due to the large numbers of expatriates assigned to their Japan subsidiaries. Procter and Gamble had 50 or more expatriates at one stage, which coincided with widespread dissatisfaction among its Japanese staff members about their lack of promotion opportunities or of involvement in decision-making. When a large number of expatriates are together in an overseas subsidiary, one must conclude, they will tend to form their own social community and so minimize, and even eliminate, socializing with local staff or people.

Polarization of the bicultural organization seems to be more common overseas than in the home country. Just as American firms in Japan have suffered from it, so do Japanese companies abroad. Cliff Stratton, the CEO of Hitachi Computers in Australia, is uniquely placed to comment on this.

"I have been associated with Japan virtually all my working life—first with Fujitsu Australia as regional sales manager, then with Prime Computers Japan as president, and in my present position as head of a Japanese subsidiary overseas. From my days with Fujitsu, I learned how destabilizing a large number of expatriates can be. At Fujitsu Australia in the seventies, the more Japanese expatriates we received from Japan, and the more intense the human relations problems became, the more the company was polarized. When I took over at Prime Computers Japan, there were already a number of expatriates on the staff. From the beginning they demanded a special relationship with me—expatriate-only socializing, lunches regularly together. I understood their motivation—they felt lonely and insecure in Japan and could not communicate well with their Japanese colleagues, but I also knew it was the wrong decision, so I refused their requests. When Prime head office suggested that I take on more expatriate staff, I also refused that, remembering what had happened to Fujitsu Australia. I wanted the absolute minimum number of expatriates. Today, running the Hitachi Computers subsidiary in Australia, my policy is 'no expatriates'—and we are the better, in human terms, for it."

EXPATRIATE NUMBERS AND POLARIZATION

Polarization of the kind I am discussing seems only to begin when the number of expatriates exceeds three or four. What conditions have to exist, from the Japanese viewpoint, in order for their overseas subsidiaries to have more than this number of expatriates on staff? The sheer size of the subsidiary is obviously one factor. Manufacturing subsidiaries—especially in the automobile industry—require large numbers of expatriates, who are involved in employee training, production planning, and finance. So too do subsidiaries marketing a diversity of sophisticated or hi-tech products, such as home electronics or office automation products; for instance, product specialists and after-sales service specialists from Japan will probably be needed for each product category. Japanese general trading companies have traditionally had large numbers of expatriates assigned to their offices in countries that have significant trading with Japan. These expatriates are mostly traders, usually product or business specialists—for example, in metals, grains and commodities, petroleum, gas and coal, consumer goods, investment, etc.—and also have an intimate knowledge of customers back in Japan. For similar reasons Japanese banks, though much more recent entrants into foreign countries, often have large numbers of expatriates in order to give the expected level of service to their Japanese clients abroad.

In contrast to these types of companies, there are others that have very small numbers of Japanese expatriates. These include companies in the service and transportation industries—shipping companies like NYK, airlines like JAL or ANA, courier services like OCS, specialty banks such as the Long-Term Credit Bank, and the thousands of joint ventures overseas which are managed by locals, and usually have no more than one or two Japanese assignees.

In researching this book, I found few complaints about cross-cultural communication or human relations problems in companies of this latter type—that is, with only one or two expatriate Japanese—and no cases of polarization: understandably because there were too few Japanese to form a distinct social group. Whenever there were two Japanese, usually one was senior and the other 10 to 15 years his junior, so they did not have much in common in the first place and were forced to socialize with others, the senior usually with his (Japanese) clients, the junior either with other young Japanese in the area or with virtually no one at all. Socializing regularly with the local people is very rare among expatriates.

The few cross-cultural problems reported by people in these companies included the following: a young expatriate repeatedly and unpleasantly making demands on his local delivery people for the urgent delivery of a product to a Japanese client, without explaining why; or, a variant on this, after being told by his local staff that, unavoidably, a certain delivery could not be made on time, refusing to tell this to the Japanese client and continuing to harass the local staff to make the delivery on time; spending "too much" time playing golf with clients or other Japanese and not enough time in the office (this from the viewpoint of the local staff); making decisions without consulting local managers; failing to support reasonable requests to head office by the local managers; senior Japanese insisting that every decision, however small, be referred to them.

FLAGRANT POLARIZATION: TWO CASES

What happens when companies do polarize flagrantly? Here are two examples, both Japanese subsidiaries abroad. One is the US subsidiary of a major Japanese bank (which I will call "K" Bank), the US head office of which has fifty expatriate managers and fifty local managers in its total staff of one thousand. This bank had originally been US-owned and was acquired by the Japanese bank in 1980. From then until 1988 it had been chronically polarized, with local managers and expatriate managers showing undisguised hostility whenever they were in meetings together, and otherwise keeping strictly to themselves. Virtually everyone in the managerial corps on each side had taken sides, save for the American personnel director and his senior assistant, and three of the most senior Japanese. Meetings involving expatriate and local managers, I was told, had usually become hostile very quickly, each side (but especially the Americans) quick to blame the other for whatever problems emerged at the meetings.

The problems were not unlike those found in Western (or Japanese for that matter) companies which had been merged or acquired, putting people from different corporate backgrounds and differing ways of working in direct conflict with one another. But the competition between each side, each trying to have its ways of doing business prevail, had led quickly to chronic antagonism and polarization within which common sense and sober judgment and even a sense of fairness went out the window. The Americans felt deeply threatened by the Japanese and justified their stand by arguing that it was an American bank, doing business in and with Americans, and therefore that American ideas should prevail. Attempts by senior Japanese to confer privately with selected Americans in the hope of getting their support for Japanese innovations in ways of working failed and the Americans had a long list of complaints about Japanese working practices: the dependence upon head office in Tokyo for a range of decisions; the attempt to introduce monthly sales quotas for client deposits for branch managers along the lines used in Japan; the seemingly covert meetings held separately by the Japanese to which no Americans were invited and which were held in the Japanese language; straightforward problems of communication caused by the imperfect and not always easy-to-understand English of the Japanese—all these and many more issues merely served to sustain the divisiveness within the organization.

The bank tried many ways to improve relationships between the two sides, such as social clubs, leisure trips away, entertainments involving families, and weekend workshops on cross-cultural problems, but nothing worked. The cross-cultural workshop in particular was a disaster. The personnel director fondly hoped that making the topic "cross-cultural problems" would encourage both Americans and Japanese to talk frankly to each other. Held in a fashionable resort town, it turned out that one or the other group only went to a lecture or activity when the other group was not present. If both Americans and Japanese were present, they polarized completely, sitting as groups in extreme parts of the conference hall. The bank finally recognized in 1986 that it did not know how to reconcile the two parties and proceeded to reorganize its operations. All save a few senior expatriates were shifted into a separate organization, where they were responsible for Japanese clients only, leaving the American managers to manage the core local business. It finally resolved the seven years of difficulty, at a very considerable human and financial cost.

As discussed earlier in the case of the Asia-Pacific subsidiaries of a Japanese firm, some cross-cultural polarization can linger on without becoming as chronic as the "K" Bank case; or, to put it another way, there are overseas subsidiaries where large numbers of expatriates are present, but the animosity is dormant or suppressed, for various reasons. Clues about why this might be can be found in the next case. General trading company offices overseas seem to be rather typical examples of "smouldering" polarization. Their characteristics make them different from, for instance, the bank head office we have just looked at. These characteristics include: large numbers of expatriates in managerial positions, few local employees in managerial positions, and most local employees undertaking routine clerical, office, or administrative work. In other words, almost all the power of the subsidiaries is in the hands of the expatriates, and individual local employees, feeling far more powerless than would local managerial staff, do not enter into overt, continuous conflict with expatriates.

I spoke with two Americans about cross cultural human relations in one trading company subsidiary in the USA. One was the administration manager, Marcus Frew, who was one of only two local managers in an office with 50 Japanese expatriate managers, the total staff being 300. The other was Roger Whitmore, a former member of the company's general affairs section, where he spent as much time with expatriates as he did with locals. Whitmore is a 30-year-old bilingual white American who had spent many years in Japan. First let us hear what Frew had to say:

"Out of 50 expatriates, only two have the ability to relate to their staff and bring out the best in them. The rest are incompetent, and behave arrogantly towards the local staff. Female staff are often passively bullied. That is, they are ignored, greetings are neither made nor returned, the simple courtesies of everyday life are not extended. I report to one of the Japanese directors, and his attitude is that I know nothing and cannot be trusted to make the smallest of decisions by myself."

Whitmore agrees with the overall assessment of the company as polarized. He sees it as chronic and long-standing, although there is little open hostility. As mentioned above, the local staff are, he agrees, in too inferior and subordinate a position.

"They take their 'revenge' on the Japanese managers by backbiting comments, go-slow work tactics, and working strictly to rule," says Whitmore. "The Japanese complain about the 'stupidity' of the local staff, but in many ways they bring it on themselves. Some at least of the local staff make things difficult for their Japanese managers just to 'get their own back' for their rude or discourteous behavior."

Frew told me bitterly that, in his view, there is an obvious "expatriate syndrome," which "operates on the basis of five principles":

"One, don't tell me about the future—I won't be here. Two, don't expect any decisions, I'll be leaving soon. Three, no long-term thinking. Four, never train a successor, just throw him in the way I was. Five, never give the local staff any responsibility (with staff like this you can't expect anything anyway!). It suits the expats to downgrade the local staff, because they can then be used as scapegoats when anything goes wrong."

While I accept that there is substance to Frew's comments on the human situation in his company, we also have to recognize that this kind of thinking is akin to "slave mentality," the bruised and resentful thoughts of thoroughly intimidated, powerless people. (The behavior of the writers and translators at the Japanese company Novatech comes to mind here as well, as does Klineberg at the construction company.) It is intriguing to recall also that Gage had described many of the writers and translators as maladjusted, riffraff, etc., while, as we see in the next paragraph, Whitmore spoke in a somewhat similar vein about the caliber of the local staff in the trading company.

According to Whitmore and other informants who are familiar with Japanese trading companies abroad, there is a widespread view in the company—amongst both local and expatriate staff—that the staff they retain long-term are mediocre, the superior individuals having long since left the company because of insufficient salaries, poor quality of work, and lack of promotion opportunities. Whitmore gave similar reasons for his resignation from the company after just ten months. I have reasons to believe that other trading company offices overseas suffer from similar problems. One is that the only challenging work in a trading company is that of the traders, most of whom are Japanese; another is that personnel consultants in various countries also hold similar views, and some claim that the job specifications for personnel for Japanese trading companies abroad are deliberately designed to attract mediocre staff.

If there is anything like a slave mentality among the long-term, nonmanagerial local employees of Japanese trading companies abroad, it is probably exacerbated by some of the practices and behaviors that were reported to me as offensive to local staff. These included: directory boards that list Japanese and local staff separately, with the Japanese always on top; local staff never permitted to be in the office on their own, without the presence of a Japanese expatriate, who stays until every local employee has left for the day; refusal of heavy-smoking expatriates to cooperate in the introduction of smoke-free offices; having policies of promoting the study of Japanese language and culture but violating these in practice. As an example of this last point, one senior local manager was given Japanese language lessons regularly during the lunch hour by a Japanese secretary. After just two weeks, his expatriate manager told him that the classes could not continue as the secretary "was not paying rent for the space she was using to give the language lesson." In another case, in a trading company's US subsidiary, many of the local staff could competently speak, read, and write Japanese, with some of them even writing internal office memos in Japanese. Without warning or consultation, local staff were told that henceforth they were neither to speak nor write Japanese in the office. Everything had to be in English. The American who told me this story (a former student of mine in Japan) was subsequently reprimanded because he was caught making a memo for himself partly in Japanese!

I hope that cases like this are exceptional, although I can understand (if not sympathize with) some of the Japanese motivations concerning the learning and use of Japanese. Their viewpoint would be that, while overseas, they should use every opportunity they can in their busy work lives to practice and improve their English. But the behavior in these cases does appear mean-spirited, and can do the cause of Japanese-Western relationships little good, and either lose the Japanese subsidiary more staff (by resignation), or aggravate the cross-cultural polarization of the office.

In summing up the problems of polarization of human relations between Japanese and non-Japanese when they work in a Japanese organization, the complexity of the situation and the variety of the problems should now be clearer. In a foreign country, the greater the number of expatriates, the more problems arise in human relations; but the less power the local employees have, the less overt the problems will be. In Japan, the key variable seems to be the significance to the company of the work the foreigner does, and his or her replaceability.

COUNTERSTRATEGIES TO POLARIZATION AND DIVISION: TWO APPROACHES

1. Clever Individuals

In very small organizations and at exceptional times, polarization and division between Japanese and non-Japanese might be countered by the activities of what I will call the "cross-culturally clever" person. There seem to be a number of types. One is the individual foreigner within the Japanese company who works cleverly to either adapt to, or bring about change in, the organization. I have reported on at least four people in this category. There was Alfredo Villarante, who has worked skillfully to solve the diverse problems or overcome the many barriers that have faced him in his commitment to a lifelong managerial career in a major Japanese computer company. Next was Nancy Haughton, the journalist/editor with *Yomi-Asa Daily News*, who persevered in a difficult organizational environment until a new and superior Japanese general manager was able to draw on her skills and experience to redesign and greatly improve the work environment and employment conditions of foreigners at the newspaper. The third example was Robert Klineberg, catering manager for foreign clients at a major Tokyo hotel, who was able, like Villarante but with more positive dynamism, to create a new business within the hotel by his clever and culturally appropriate methods of eliciting cooperation. He showed cleverness in the way he got around "no" or "impossible" answers to his requests. That he was unable eventually to develop his new business department further was due to collisions with the rigid traditionalism of the hotel organization rather than to his own limitations. Finally, there was the somewhat more limited cleverness of Robert Gage at Novatech, who seemed for a time to be managing effectively the pre-existing hostile relationships between the Japanese president and the foreign writing and translating staff, but who eventually felt unable to handle the entrenched value systems of both sides.

Looking at these four cases, it is possible to identify some characteristics in common. They were all sensitive communicators, good at their jobs, interested in Japan, and had strong perseverance (the fact that Klineberg and Gage did not stay long term has, I believe, more to do with their judgment of the organization as inflexible, tradition-bound, and culturally rigid). Their strategies always seemed to be flexible; they adapted to what seemed unchangeable or inevitable but delicately worked to change what seemed changeable. Villarante and Haughton both speak and write fluent Japanese, Klineberg is reasonably competent in spoken Japanese, while Gage's Japanese was not much better than elementary. However, since language or communication problems did not appear in the cases of Klineberg or Gage, language competence was not an issue. Overseas, I met a number of local managers who demonstrated the same skills' profile. Dunwoodie of JAL in Sydney, Australia; Leonard Bright of Japan Couriers Overseas in London, England; Michael Schulhof of Sony America, fit well into Japanese companies abroad, accepting the inevitable, working delicately to change the changeable, always maintaining good relations with the Japanese. Such examples give new, more concrete meaning to the expression "cultural adjustment."

These people show that problem-solving is a critical element in effective ongoing cross-cultural adjustment. It requires the capacity to deal with the Japanese as individual human beings, not just as stereotypes. A person able to do this, as I have shown elsewhere, is a genuinely international type of human being:

"[One] who watches and listens carefully to others; deals with situations pragmatically, does not think that he has special skills [such as patience, flexibility, empathy (people who think of themselves in this way are usually not culturally sensitive or international)]; is highly aware of himself, his feelings, thoughts, and especially stereotypes about people from other cultures; checks [and monitors] his own tendency to stereotype foreigners against his observations of the foreigners he is dealing with" (March, 1988, 170).

People lacking in these skills can often end up merely confirming their own stereotypes about the foreigners they are encountering, and so can enter into a cold, distant relationship if both are constrained to the same workplace. This other type of individual, not having the personal flexibility and problem-solving skills of people like Klineberg and others, may have much in common with those foreigners in Japan whom Patrick, Gage, and others have criticized for their disagreeable or "not nice" personalities (and their coldness and disinterest in Japan and the Japanese).

At the same time, however, the Japanese are not the easiest people for non-Japanese to communicate with:

"Many people, including the Japanese themselves, have spoken critically of the Japanese as communicators. In my first days in Japan, I was most impressed by the sociability of the Japanese, especially their skills in making visitors feel welcome by solicitous inquiries about their views and situation. Like many Westerners, however, I came to find a good deal of coldness and distance after the initial period. This was puzzling to me, and I have only recently come to make sense of my experiences. The Japanese people are generally good at interpersonal communication that deals with information exchange, and the exchange of news, views, opinions, gossip, and experiences in a friendly, relaxed way. They are, moreover, polite and well-mannered, and it is important to remember that 'manners' are themselves a form of communication. On a scale of human communication that culminates in true intimacy and openness, however, communications that are concerned only with manners or information exchange are of a somewhat limited nature. To achieve genuinely open and intimate human relationships, more is needed—friendliness, interest in the other party, perceptive insight into his or her heart and mind (for often an individual is unable to clearly express what is in his or her mind, and it may take an outsider's insight to achieve that), and thus true understanding. Regrettably, many Japanese have serious limitations in their ability to achieve such an understanding with people they are not familiar with, that is, strangers or foreigners. Too often, they project themselves as cold, unfriendly, disinterested, and seem to lack the skills necessary to understand others in a human way" (March 1988, 155–156).

These limitations, we can forecast, will often become more acute for those Japanese managers abroad who also have imperfect English language skills, and thus they will contribute to on-the-job problems in the overseas subsidiary.

REUNITING THE HOUSE: THE ROLE OF CULTURAL BRIDGERS IN JAPANESE COMPANIES OVERSEAS

Largely by accident, it would seem, some Japanese companies abroad have found ways to defuse intercultural conflicts within the company. Alfredo Villarante of Hitoba America explains how he has acted as a middleman, helping to resolve problems between American and Japanese managers. Remember that Villarante is actually on the staff of Hitoba Japan and only on extended assignment to the US company. Here is what he has to say:

March: "What sort of role do you play in the company here?"

V: "My position is actually very difficult. I'm in between the Japanese head office and the local employees. In Japan, head office people complain that the locals are not doing the market-entry preparation correctly or are entering the market too late, while the local people for their part say the product is not suitable, or the product is late. I have to be the lawyer in between.

"The other difficulty comes from the Americans. They know I'm not Japanese and they know the real power is with the Japanese. There are competitive guys here who want to deal directly with a Japanese. If I were Japanese they would accept me. But they say, he's a Filipino, so why the hell do we have to go through him? Let's go straight to the Japanese, let's go straight to Japan. That's a very delicate thing for me to manage. On the other hand, the Japanese office sees me as their representative here. They see me in a way as indirectly or directly responsible for what happens in the area that I look after. Sometimes when I say to some of the local guys, you can't do this, this is not the way it has to be done, they look coldly at me, saying, 'You're not a real representative, let's phone Japan.'"

March: "What happens when they phone Japan?"

V: "The Japanese back me up 99 percent of the time."

March: "Do the Americans feel some resentment against you?"

V: "Yes."

March: "Do they feel that because that happened, you must be blocking them? That confirms their original fear?"

V: "Yes. They feel that because I am here I must accept the local view, whatever that is. They feel their view is the official view of the local company, and I should not have a view. On the other hand, I do have my own views, which sometimes don't match theirs. When they know that my view differs from theirs, they get very upset."

March: "Is part of the problem that because you're not Japanese they don't completely trust what you say?"

V: "Not really because I'm not Japanese. The thing about a liaison officer is you are not in the direct line. My position is mainly based on my technical skills and my ability to influence people. I think I've been quite successful in that. Maybe more successful than a Japanese would be."

March: "How would you map out Hitoba America as a social entity? Let's look at the Americans first of all. There are probably Americans who, for example, want to use you and relate to you and see you as a very important and powerful person. Then there may be another group which resents your role and wants to go direct to Japan."

V: "In the initial stages, they don't know about Japan at all. So I'm their savior. They need something from Japan, or Japan gives them a negative answer, so they come to me and say, Alfredo, can you please talk to them again and solve this problem? That's great. I'm their hero and the great helper.

"The second stage is when they start going to Japan and get to know the people there directly. They say, I know the guys, I shook hands with them, so I'll just phone and sort out everything. Up to a certain level that's fine, but after a while they find out that it doesn't work in a lot of instances because of the distance, because of the language, and because in a way the Japanese trust my views more than theirs. They know I understand both sides. So the Americans get into a position where they can't solve problems, or their confrontation doesn't work, so they start coming back to me."

Villarante, it can hardly be doubted, contributes to the good organizational health of Hitoba America by soaking up American resentments that would otherwise stick on the Japanese. His qualifications are impressive. He is perceived to be neither Japanese nor American. He is fluent in both languages. He is a member of both organizations but has credibility in and leverage with the head office that no American could ever achieve. Neither side can stereotype him as a member of the other group—he acts as a member of both, not taking sides, and he is not a decision-maker on either side. Altogether, he represents as good a solution as one could devise.

Hayashi has reported a different kind of "solution" to the potential problem of cross-cultural misunderstanding in his case study of Alpha Electronics America Inc., a Japanese subsidiary manufacturing TV receivers. Alpha America has a Japanese president, Takashi Mino, responsible for strategy and long-run decisions, and an American vice president, William Nelson, in charge of daily operations. These two have worked closely together for six years.

"Mino is able to explain head office's requirements to Nelson in English to a reasonable extent . . . [while] Nelson is able to ask the right questions to elicit and clarify points that Mino is not able to explain clearly. . . . When a strategy is finally decided on, Nelson issues operating instructions to the American work force entirely in US terms. . . . Thus, between them, working as 'cultural interrelators,' they internalize head office input and transform it functionally and culturally into American output" (Hayashi 1989, 49–50).

Mino and Nelson see themselves as transforming demands from the head office. Some they reject, most they revise and modify before issuing them as instructions to their local staff. On the basis of their past performance, Mino and Nelson have been given a high degree of trust and autonomy by their head office, and Mino has been able to avoid appearing to be merely a "guard dog" for head office interests.

"The only way I can prove to my American managers that I am not a guard dog is to 'bite' head office executives when they visit. I have to be seen supporting local feelings and arguing for local interests and perspectives. It is a bit of a balancing act, because if I do it too often, they may decide I've gone native—and recall me. Fortunately, and this is critical to my success, I have close relationships with some very senior managers back home."

Mino shows a high order of adaptive intelligence in the way he manages, simultaneously, relationships with his subordinates and head office. The metaphor of the biting dog is instructive (though it shouldn't be taken too literally—this after all is a highly savvy Japanese manager). It not only signals his local affiliation but it also suggests that he plays the role of educator, in informing head office executives about the US market.

In another Japanese subsidiary in the USA, Theta Machinery Company, a new Japanese president decided to increase the degree of Japanese-style management by introducing bright young Japanese from the head office with roving commissions as cultural facilitators and problem-solvers. Their role, in particular, was to work on problems emerging from the greater in-company emphasis on Japanese-style management. As so often happens, they were not given specific briefs but had to create their own.

One of these young men was Yoji Sakuma. Sakuma soon discovered that the biggest problem by far was to get the trust of American managers. This led him to start representing the Americans in their negotiations with the Japanese management. Although at first he seemed to be only an interpreter, the Americans soon realized that he was also a valuable negotiation resource for their dealings with dour and obstinate Japanese senior directors. Eventually, he became a leading spokesman for the American side, while ruffling the feathers of the Japanese. In turn, the senior Japanese became deeply suspicious of Sakuma's loyalties. As he is reported to have said:

"I sometimes felt it was the Japanese side that needed the assistance of cultural facilitators, not the American. The Japanese, for instance, would feel offended and a little disgraced to be put in the position of accepting or rejecting proposals from junior American managers. This would not worry many American top managers—but, being Japanese, they had the sense of somehow dishonoring themselves, so I had to step in and adjust the relationships, smooth the egos of the senior Japanese. And it had to be done with the utmost delicacy" (Hayashi 1989, 55–56).

Sakuma plays the role of what Hayashi calls a cultural spanner, but unlike Villarante, Sakuma is hobbled by not being fully integrated into the overseas organization. It is only clever managers like Villarante, bicultural and bilingual though not Japanese, who are going to make overseas subsidiaries work more effectively as human and productive organizations.

2. Policies and Practices

A focus on the use of culturally clever individuals seems to be of only limited value as an antidote to any of the dysfunctional organization states—from accumulated discontent to flagrant polarization. Cultural spanners look at specific here-and-now problems but not at the overall organization. Hayashi, it is true, does also talk about the value of a "third culture pair," of, for instance, a pair à la Mino and Nelson above, whose synergistic cultural sensitivity permits them, as a team, to solve problems as they arise.

Beyond the culturally clever or culture-spanning individual or partners, what is also needed is a broad policy orientation within the overseas subsidiary aimed at minimizing the multiple causes of polarization. A few overseas subsidiaries have developed practices and policies that go some way toward this, including:

a. More predeparture training for expatriates, to prepare them for the overseas tasks. (But a number of companies are becoming sceptical of this type of training.)

b. Pairing expatriate with local managers to speed up development of mutual trust and local manager skills.

c. Employment of specialist interpreters to assist communication between expatriates and locals.

d. Organizing more business and social interaction between the two groups, including organized social and sports outings and picnics; meetings where the opinions of local employees are treated as important and carefully listened to; regular executive staff meetings in English; entertaining of local staff and their spouses at home (by expatriates); joint meetings to discuss management principles and methods, globalization and localization, etc; at twice-monthly recreational club meetings, operating a special "communication time" period outside of working hours; formal and informal meetings/classes, etc., to help improve the expatriates' English language skills; meetings at different levels, with the president, divisional managers, and others.

Unfortunately, these policies and practices do not go far enough in creating an informed and productive policy orientation for the more effective functioning of a multicultural organization. The big problems not yet resolved are these:

a. Failure to improve the caliber of local employees by better recruiting and job enrichment, in order to retain the most able. Very few companies have as yet faced up to this problem; the solution, whatever it is, is still on the drawing board for virtually every Japanese company.

b. Failure to reduce the number of expatriate Japanese. Those overseas subsidiaries with large numbers of expatriates are aware that overseas subsidiaries cannot continue to afford, financially, to support expatriates. Until they are able to develop better-quality local staff, however, and so to replace the expatriates (at least in part), it is just not feasible to reduce expatriate numbers: investments abroad by the Japanese are large, Japanese clients depend in various ways on overseas subsidiaries and require expatriates to be on hand when they make visits abroad, and there is a fear that company honor would be somewhat damaged if expatriate staff were severely reduced.

FINAL COMMENTS

In the final analysis, any company has the power to make "surgical" changes to its organization whenever it suffers from any of the dysfunctions and polarizations we have looked at in this chapter. "Troublemakers" can be transferred to outlying departments or branches, and other corrective tactics can be attempted. For instance, expatriates can be reassigned to an expatriates-only subsidiary rather than to the company's operating subsidiary, which can then be (seen to be) managed largely by local staff. Again, high-caliber local managers can be given a status equivalent in every way to that of expatriates—if the Japanese company so wishes. In extremely dysfunctional situations, professionals specializing in the enhancement of organizations might be invited to use dialogue and negotiation techniques between the polarized Japanese and non-Japanese sides to restore some sanity and everyday goodwill to the organization.

CHAPTER
10
THE JAPANESE MANAGER ABROAD

It is important to understand that the Japanese working abroad are not overseas because they volunteered. They are selected for postings, usually by their general manager or a responsible vice president, very occasionally by the personnel department. Few have much influence on the decision and virtually all feel obliged to accept the request from their superior. The reasons why they personally are selected fall into three categories: one, they have the experience and skills that the job overseas requires; two, they have had previous experience abroad; or three, they have special skills that would be useful abroad, such as language competence or cultural adaptability. Today the connection between overseas appointments and career advancement is growing increasingly important for the Japanese. Nakamura, in a 1989 paper, reports the relationship between appointments overseas and career advancement within a large Japanese automotive parts maker. Based on evaluations of the suitability of white-collar employees for overseas appointments, a "stock" of 700 potentially suitable young staff members (who had joined the company since 1977) was developed, from whichoverseas appointments would be made. The criteria used included: product knowledge, knowledge of trade practice, basic financial skills, price estimation ability, persuasiveness, negotiation ability, sales "mind," and English language skills. Personality and individual temperament of individuals were not apparently considered.

In setting up this system, the company philosophy was that employees without overseas experience would suffer in their promotion prospects at home—this no doubt motivated in part by the reluctance of many young men to volunteer for foreign appointments—and overseas experience is now officially regarded as just another variant of on-the-job training. Nonetheless, Nakamura reports, few employees want to go overseas. In the accounts department (a major source of overseas appointees), this was particularly noticeable, even though something like one in every three members of the accounts department was in an overseas post at her time of writing. With this lack of enthusiasm for overseas postings, plus the fatalistic acceptance if one is appointed, it can be no surprise that Japanese abroad perform poorly as people managers and show little interest in adjusting to the local culture.

PREDEPARTURE TRAINING

According to a study of the Japan Overseas Enterprises Association (JOEA), predeparture training for overseas appointees is deficient in at least three areas: education in labor management overseas, including labor-management relations in the host country; skills training to solve problems that arise in a cross-cultural environment; and interpersonal skills. In 1986, I studied predeparture training in 40 major Tokyo companies, and found that half were active in providing training for their managers being posted overseas. Of the remaining 19, one, Honda Giken, was to start that year, and a further three (Kirin Brewery, Kajima Constructions, and Tokyo Denryoku) currently had it under consideration, but the remainder either had no interest or said they relied entirely on on-the-job training or on outside programs. Sumitomo Trading Company was one of the most sophisticated companies as far as international predeparture training was concerned, with heavy investment in overseas university courses in management and technical subjects. In addition to these external, overseas courses, trainees undertake internal courses, run by the personnel department, which include: area studies, manners and etiquette, how to train and manage local staff, how to negotiate skillfully. A basic textbook, *The International Manager's Handbook*, has been produced by Sumitomo and is a key resource in the training. Very few Japanese companies have programs as comprehensive as Sumitomo's, however.

WORK CONDITIONS OVERSEAS

The JOEA survey also provides the best information about the work conditions of Japanese managers overseas. Based on replies from 324 respondents currently overseas at the time of the survey, it is comprehensive and enlightening. Most of the respondents (98 percent) were married, although 18 percent of these men had left their families back home, in almost every case because of the schooling needs or stage of children. For half, it was their first trip abroad. I will list the key findings, then discuss their implications.

Hours worked beyond the usual:

Seventy-three percent of the managers worked at least 10 hours a week more than normal business hours, the major reason by far being the need to entertain and show Japanese visitors around.

How leisure time is spent:

Given three choices from a list, 78 percent said they spend their days off at home, 73 percent said they adjust their program to fit in with family activities, 18 percent said they spend time with non-Japanese friends, and 30 percent said they spend time learning about the local culture, history, music, etc. However, 43 percent said they play golf with other Japanese, 15 percent said they play tennis with other Japanese, while 5 percent said they play mahjong or sing karaoke.

Satisfaction with the local environment:

While there is general satisfaction with local food, medical services, housing, and climate, there are also a number of dissatisfactions. These include: the cultural environment (52 percent dissatisfied), human relations in the workplace (16 percent), work conditions (32 percent), public safety (44 percent), relationships with the local people (37 percent), "ease and convenience of everyday life" (43 percent).

Complaints, Difficulties, Hardship, Stress:

Two out of three managers say they have complained about troubles in their posting. Those who have not complained said that the reasons for not complaining were: they communicate their complaints through others; or, they are being misunderstood, so they are patient and keep quiet; or, complaining works against you, so grin and bear it.

Only 8 percent said they were satisfied with the post, 53 percent said it was just all right, and 39 percent said they were dissatisfied. Virtually everyone felt his salary abroad was inadequate, and 80 percent expressed a sense of hardship in their lives. Their recommendations to alleviate this included: making clear what the period of posting is; improving salaries and housing abroad; improving "hardship" allowances; giving greater emphasis to the individual's wishes as far as postings on return from abroad are concerned; getting support and understanding from head office about hardships abroad.

Other negative points about the foreign posting were: becoming distant from what is going on at head office; the problem of the children's education; falling behind the rapid progress in Japan; uncertainty as to what posting they will receive on their return to Japan; missing out on financial opportunities (in Japan); and, from the danger that one can get the reputation of being a suitable man for overseas postings generally arises the fear that they might leave one there forever!

Many Japanese have unpleasant or threatening experiences abroad. One in five of these Japanese had been robbed or suffered some damage while their house was unoccupied, one in seven had been affected by guerilla activities, or terrorists, or revolution; 12 percent had been investigated by troops or police; one-third expressed uneasiness about their public safety and about their health; and smaller numbers had been deceived by confidence tricksters or been threatened with violence.

HOW THEY VIEW THEIR POSTING

They see the beneficial aspects of their overseas posting as: broadening their perspectives; enabling them to acquire an international outlook; permitting them to travel frequently to new places; allowing them to make contact with different cultures; enabling them to have memorable times with their families; and improving their linguistic abilities.

Asked what their reaction was to the notice of the posting, 54 percent said that as they were "salarymen" (staff employees) it was not possible to avoid the posting; 28 percent said they were able to reject the posting; and 13 percent said they were able to state to what country they would like to be posted.

Generally speaking, Japanese business people abroad find much to complain about in the overseas work experience: inadequate salaries, threats to personal safety, shortcomings in local culture, as well as feeling penalized by missing out on opportunities back in Japan. This complex of complaints, concerns, and dissatisfactions provides a new dimension to our understanding of the state of mind of Japanese expatriates. These problems add to the stresses inherent in the foreign posting itself.

SOME SPECIFIC FACETS OF THE JAPANESE MANAGER'S LIFE ABROAD

The typical Japanese expatriate manager is, in some key respects, not well equipped for his first post overseas. The problem lies in the kind of education he has received, an education which sets up certain erroneous expectations and assumptions about human behavior. One Japanese colleague puts it this way:

"Japan's education system has to be changed. It makes everything look as nice as pie, everything sweet and clean . . . wherever you go, you're treated kindly, life is nice—it's an idiotic thing. The fact is, this world is full of pirates and brigands. Once you leave Japan, you have to face them and cut them down, one after the other. That is how we ought to think. It's really too much how school teachers do this. There are lots of teachers in America who had experience first in the practical world, but Japanese teachers go straight from university into teaching, and make it their life's work. Crazy!"

The focus of Japanese education is on factual retention. Issues are not discussed. The focus of the schoolroom is on the children being good boys and girls, behaving properly, pleasing teacher, being on good terms with one another, and certainly not fighting. There is some, very limited, "moral" education in Japanese schools, but being predominantly concerned with respect for the aged, it is considered as largely irrelevant to living one's life by the young Japanese I have discussed it with. This mindset of nonaggressive, proper behavior is not useful for entering other worlds where people do behave aggressively toward each other, where people are challenged and are expected to respond to challenge, and where avoidance tactics (much used by the Japanese) provoke explicit annoyance.

In dealing with their subordinate staff overseas, inexperienced Japanese managers face the problem of staff behaving in ways unthinkable in Japan, such as asking questions if something is unclear; speaking up or being critical of others' proposals; showing animosity toward behavior that might be acceptable (or not provoke response) in Japan. Such behavior could make a very long list. Simple examples might be: having a cluttered desk (no problem for many Japanese, but not acceptable in many efficiency-oriented countries); not using greetings to others when arriving or departing; sleeping at one's desk or on one's couch; and the many other examples given in Chapter 5.

We have already seen that many of these problems stem from the limitations of English language ability among Japanese. That this is not a recent problem is clear from the preface to a book written in 1930 about the problems that Japanese were having in adjusting to life in Seattle, Washington state. The author/researcher S. Frank Miyamoto had this to say:

"The very lack of proficiency indicated by the Japanese in their use of English, despite the fact that they attempted to study it, is the result of their effort to gain a knowledge of the language from books rather than by daily practice in conversation.

"To practice the language before others and to make errors during this training does too much violence to the Japanese feelings of reserve and 'front,' and thus the very desire for status which gives them interest in studying the language becomes, at the same time, a hindrance to the natural progress of the learning process."

Miyamoto brings out how the excessive Japanese concern to preserve "face" becomes a positive hindrance to effective communication with English speakers. Nothing has changed in this respect since 1930. The foreign employee is often puzzled by conversations abbreviated or prematurely terminated by Japanese expatriates desperate to maintain their face and avoid errors in English.

In a recent movie about the life of Japanese salarymen (men like expatriate managers), called *Bakayaro!*, one scene depicts a businessman just assigned to Chicago. His boss forces him to attend an intensive English course, but he is mocked by the other expatriates for his appalling English. Finally, fed up with the infatuation of these other Japanese with the English language, he yells in Japanese, "You can take your English and shove it!" The director well knew that this scene would engender a strong sympathetic reaction in Japanese audiences.

A different problem comes up as a result of the absence of Japanese customary manners in the overseas country. Some younger men feel they can behave in ways that would be improper at home, such as cutting one's nails or combing one's hair in public, without realizing that they may be contrary to local good manners as well. The boyish rowdiness of Japanese male groups, their undressing down to underwear, barefootedness, etc., on the other hand, while accepted at home, is usually offensive abroad, but group behavior tends to dull the sensitivity of individual Japanese to the obvious displeasure of local people.

A Japanese senior manager friend gave me his view on the expatriate problems:

"The problem is connected very much to the shyness of the Japanese—and I think that it's increasing. You see this often at parties. Before you know it, the Japanese have formed themselves into one group, while the other guests are talking elsewhere. When I see things like that, I have to conclude that it is not a linguistic gap. There is no bridge between us and them. If you think about this anthropologically, the Japanese are just too quick to make a community. . . . If you Westerners have something interesting or amusing to say, you can just hop into a group. But you don't see that much with the Japanese. They hesitate, flinch, on the outskirts. I think we are an awkward, introverted race."

We have already seen how widespread the problems of shyness with strangers and the gaijin complex are with the Japanese, so it is no surprise to find them so socially encumbered when abroad.

HONDA IN MARYSVILLE

A good example of Japanese thinking about how to adapt abroad comes from Honda expatriates in their early days of setting up the Marysville plant in the USA.

"Japanese first appeared here in Marysville a few months before the Honda plant opened," my informant told me. "They wanted to avoid any appearance of a Japanese occupation, so they set up rules—no shouting out in the factory or on the street; no groups of Japanese only playing golf; no groups of roistering Japanese in local restaurants.

"The Japanese in Marysville put more emphasis on communal living Japanese-style and reinforcing their common links with one another, than on adjusting to the new environment. Wouldn't it be nice to be back home? they would say to each other when relaxing. Having farewell parties (*sobetsukai*) and singing karaoke together seemed to be the things they talked most about, or had written about. Concerns about children's education were also prominent, even though there were Japanese families that sent their children to local schools. The education system back home doesn't help. One Japanese vice president of Honda made a special trip back home to see if his daughter could go back to Japan and attend school for just three months. The school said that it was impossible for anyone not having a resident's registration (*jumin toroku*).

"However, there are many pleasures to enjoy in the US that they did not anticipate, since they had believed prior to coming that if they didn't live in New York or Los Angeles, it would be the boondocks. Now they have discovered that they can drive 30 minutes into Columbus and see a Broadway show. They can skate and ski in winter, watch pro basketball on TV, drive to Florida or New England, play golf at the local country club, go to the motor-bike club nearby for the kids, or watch hot-air balloon races in the local town."

The rules—no shouting, etc.—are intelligent and sensible. As we saw in the Mazda case, there are many parts of the US where behaving in an ostensibly Japanese way invites aggressive remarks and possibly worse. The discovery of the variety of activities available nearby is a nice plus for the Japanese—in their own country outings are more demanding and less exotic. As for the remarks on the Japanese communal living and life-style, it is hard to miss a rather pathetic tone. These Japanese seem convinced that they must fall back on themselves, persist in their Japan-side customs, sentimentalize the life back home. There is no hint, unfortunately, of any attempt to integrate or adjust to the local culture, to make local friends, or to try out new behaviors.

TIME MANAGEMENT

One of the commonest complaints that the Japanese themselves make about expatriate Japanese concerns is their failure to be more oriented to the local culture and so to spend more time with local people. As we saw earlier, most expatriate Japanese spend their weekend free time playing golf or tennis with other Japanese—socializing with locals is minor, a point repeatedly verified by oral comments and observation. One senior Japanese manager puts it thus:

"Most of the middle-aged, highly qualified Japanese people stationed in foreign countries working for Japanese companies go to the office every day, even on Saturdays, and watch the telexes come in from head office and decide what kind of response they should send back immediately. But they do not pay attention to what they could contribute to the society in which they are living at the time" (Makio Matsusaka, *Japan Economic Journal*, Aug. 2, 1986).

Shioya Ko, publisher of *Business Tokyo* magazine, sees the failure of Japanese expatriates in the USA to integrate more with American society as one important cause of Japan-bashing in that country. He observes:

"Japanese who go to the US on assignment must make a determined effort to fit into their communities, joining service clubs, taking part in parent-teacher activities, contributing to local charities. For what purpose? To demonstrate that they don't have horns and tails, that they are not money-hungry raiders, that they are good citizens interested in the welfare of their temporary home communities" (Hotel Okura *News*, June 1990, 3).

Unfortunately, in spite of all the good advice the Japanese give one another, the will to relate to the local community is not developed in some Japanese people. Professor Ikuo Seki surveyed 39 American families who were hosts to Japanese students during the 1989 summer. There were problems in a number of homes including the students' poor English skills and failure to try to learn; superior "I am a Japanese" attitudes; and many complaints that they were insensitive, uncooperative, and uncaring. The complaints were about simple matters, but telling for the host families. A Japanese would change channels on TV without asking any of those also watching. At weekends, when everyone was cleaning house or shovelling snow, the students did nothing. As they were paying a fee for staying, they "expected to be waited on hand and foot" (Reported in Japan *Free Press* 34, 1990, 1–2).

CAN THEY GO BACK HOME AGAIN?

The good side to this grim picture is that the Japanese are becoming aware that there are problems. The fact that the results of Professor Seki's small survey were published in a national daily newspaper indicates how significant the findings were. Moreover, overseas experience can be so positive and even exhilarating for some expatriate Japanese and their families that the experience leaves them irretrievably changed. In a few cases, they resign from their blue-chip Japanese company to stay in the host country (particularly the USA, Australia, or Canada); in most cases they treasure the foreign connection in manifest ways for the rest of their lives. This reminds me of a pathetic story about a Japanese expatriate who had been a senior manager in a Japanese subsidiary in Australia. He fell in love with the country but could not find the courage to quit his company and stay in Australia. However, back in Tokyo he reserved one drawer in his tiny desk exclusively for an aerial photograph of Sydney Harbor. On days when he was feeling especially blue, he confided to Australian staffers visiting Tokyo, he would open the drawer and gaze upon the beauty of the harbor and the blue skies—and dream of returning one day. More usual are the stories of Japanese wives who experienced a new surge of freedom and individuality, like Noriko Kashima, wife of a trading company manager. In the US, she wore her hair styled in a Cleopatra look and played tennis and bridge regularly. "In America, I was alive," she said. "But as soon as I arrived back in Tokyo, I started to die. I have no friends nearby, and none of my friends can understand or share that magical life I led."

After leading the good life abroad, can they ever go home again? Most can and do, because they remained secured in their Japanese community abroad, making readjustment easy and painless. Their choice is understandable and prudent. Japan is a homogeneous country, and its people at home are intolerant of deviation from the norms of good conduct. As long as Japanese culture remains like this (and I have no cause to believe that it will change in any significant way), we can expect most Japanese abroad to continue to mix with their own kind. However, it is these same people who are likely to create problems abroad, failing to settle into their local communities, preserving a Japanese ethnic exclusiveness, and, because Japan and the Japanese are regarded so ambivalently by so many other peoples, helping to provoke those attacks we call Japan-bashing.

THE PRICE OF THE CULTURAL CROSSOVER

There is a price to be paid for the Japanese effort to survive abroad by living within a Japanese enclave. Life is not always easy in the enclave. People who would ordinarily find little in common may be thrown upon one another's resources. People may differ in age and seniority, and, being Japanese, that means the families must observe the niceties of protocol towards the husband's senior's family as well. Rivalries between companies, usually intense in Japan, mean that relationships between members of different companies could simmer unpleasantly just below the surface. Isolated and usually lonely resentments (as illogical as they may be) easily emerge against sundry other targets—head office, other Japanese, the local community, the neighbors, school teachers, one's children's playmates, etc. The projection of anger onto any of these, especially Japanese, results in scapegoating, and hostility feeds on itself to make people feel even more distant from others, and more lonely.

One of Japan's leading specialists on problems of Japanese living abroad is psychiatrist Hiroshi Inamura. Inamura (1987) puts suicide at the head of the list. Whether it is in a developing or advanced country, there are suicides each year among Japanese abroad. These include single suicides by the expatriate or by his wife, and family suicides (*muri shinju* in Japanese) in which the couple or the entire family commits suicide, except that the children are usually murdered first. Inamura gives the following examples:

"A 40-year-old housewife. She went to the US with her husband, a trading company employee. The husband was late every night, being extremely busy, and the wife became desperately lonely. Although she eventually consulted an American doctor, she simply walked out one morning, leaving her husband and two children, and committed suicide. She had always been an introverted and socially isolated person, shut up in her own house.

"A 20-year-old male company technician. He was sent to assist in the construction of a dam in Indonesia. He was isolated in the country with only locals employed by sub-contractors. Suddenly, without warning, four months into his contract, he committed suicide, leaving a note complaining of the heat, the bad food, problems in interpersonal relations, and so on.

"A 30-year-old bank employee. He was sent on his own without out his wife or children to live in a city in a foreign country. He worked hard and was good at his job, but his evenings were very lonely, and he had a lot of time on his hands. He became involved with a cabaret hostess and at first thought he could have a light relationship until his wife arrived from Japan. But he became deeply involved with the hostess, and when his wife arrived he was unable to break off. Finally, when he did, the hostess committed suicide."

Suicide is commonly recognized in Japan as a problem for Japanese abroad but is not usually discussed, so it is hard to assess its frequency. In 1986, a Japanese friend told me the story of two Japanese expatriates in New Jersey, one the successor of the other, both of whom committed suicide within 19 months of each other. When I tell the story to Japanese friends, even today, no one is surprised. They nod sagely and opine, yes, it can happen. Unfortunately, many companies seem to have no idea that some people are better suited to living and working abroad than others.

WHY JAPANESE FAIL TO ADAPT OVERSEAS

1. Familiarity Based on Homogeneity

The Japanese people have one language and a religious background that is close to homogeneous, which enable them to become easily acquainted and familiar with one another, at home, in the neighborhood, at work, anywhere in Japan. They become "well tuned" (*tsuka*) to one another. In this kind of country, with few problems and everyone well adapted, nothing seems strange. When they go to other countries, they find contradictions. No other country has the homogeneity of Japan, and it confuses them. In Japan, they are accustomed to communicating by nuances, indirect expressions, in a decorative way, meaning you as the listener must think carefully about what the other person is really saying. It is like a password or secret sign language, and if you get it wrong it could be totally wrong. In other countries, people emphasize clear communication with unambiguous expressions, whereas the Japanese often leave word and sentence endings indeterminate.

2. Abundant Goods and Convenience

Everything is abundant and convenient in Japan. In other

countries, products and services are, in comparison, not as easy to come by. It is perhaps not surprising that the Japanese in developing countries often feel a sense of desperation at the poverty of products or lack of convenience, but this tends to be so even in developed countries. The previously unimagined scarcity of certain goods and services makes life itself seem impoverished.

3. Family Unity

The Japanese feel that family unity is something that extends beyond the immediate family, into the neighborhood and the workplace, where everyone feels a family-like connection. The life-long employment system expresses the caring for people over a lifetime, while the school sports carnival, school holiday travels, and company welfare systems are means of looking after people. The concept of Japan Inc. is similar. The sense of separate identity is weak and people tend to depend on one another. No other country is like this, and the Japanese feel particularly weak when they can find no points in common with others as a basis for the development of interdependence and intimacy.

4. Abundant Information

There are few countries with the wealth of media coverage that Japan has: daily newspapers; national and regional, weekly and monthly magazines of all types; as well as a number of TV channels that go to late at night. The information environment in Japan is highly enriched and stimulating. This absence abroad can lead to something like the withdrawal symptoms of drug addicts.

5. Skills and Promptness

The Japanese have made a great point out of their people having superior skills and being able to do things with great swiftness. From afar they look impatient and irritable, but within Japan it just seems matter-of-fact. So, in developing countries the tempo seems slow, almost a curse, and they become irritated and flinch from contact with locals, imagining their clumsiness and slowness as moral defects.

6. Passion for Learning and Exam Competition

These are very intense in Japan, and impossible to avoid being affected by. This is the background to the consciousness of exchange students abroad, and the national learning orientation generally.

FINAL COMMENTS

Looked at from the Japanese viewpoint, postings abroad are pleasurable for some, but difficult for many Japanese. Overall, the tone is on the "blue" side: there is much to complain about, and free-floating anxieties about safety, relationships, money, etc., abound. Some feel a (suppressed) sense of unfairness that they have been posted abroad without any say in the matter. Many feel they are in a backwater, while life in the great ocean of Japan passes them by. Abroad, they organize themselves well to minimize external threats and loneliness, at the price of distance from the locals, not to mention their own avoidance of opportunities for new personal growth. But, generalizing, they cannot be said to be enjoying themselves, and the expatriate manager whose personal life is not working well cannot be expected to be at his best in managing local staff or relating to local people. And, in his heart, so often he doesn't want to be there!

CHAPTER
11

PROBLEMS IN
THE COMPANY—CULTURAL
MISUNDERSTANDINGS
OR HUMAN NATURE?

Entering a Japanese company, even if it is overseas and in your town, has much in common with entering Japan itself. Adapted as it may be to fit in with your home culture, it will still retain many authentically Japanese characteristics. The presence of Japanese staff in itself is influential. They bring with them workways, business practices, and values that are different from those of local companies, not to mention general differences in personal values, and interpersonal communication style. If we don't know what the cultural differences actually are, then the ideas, values, and customs that we non-Japanese and Japanese each bring into the corporate bicultural environment become our expectations about how others ought to behave. When expectations differ, confusion, misunderstandings, irritations, and conflict easily arise. Here is a set of the commonest expectations, developed from my own consulting and research, that Japanese and Western business people carry into the bicultural workplace concerning their job, as well as their Japanese bosses and colleagues.

A) WHEN WORKING IN JAPAN

ADJUSTMENT EXPECTATIONS

Japanese Expectations	Foreigner Expectations
Foreigners will only stay a few years	You will get valuable experience that will help your future career
Foreigners are forthright people who will stimulate their Japanese colleagues	As a foreigner with special skills and English abilities, you will have a special status in a Japanese company
After a few years' training, the foreigner can go back to his or her country and be a manager in our subsidiary there (this is more a reflection than a strong expectation, unless special plans are made)	If you are married to a Japanese, or if you are home from a developing country, or if you are pessimistic about finding a worthwhile job back home, you will probably stay in Japan permanently

Generally, there are few serious violations of expectations in Japan. Since foreigners have to fit first into Japanese society and usually do not stay if they feel uncomfortable there, most have culturally adjusted before joining a Japanese company, especially those who become regular employees (sei shain). In other words, cultural learning helps materially to reduce unrealistic expectations, the reverse of which is made clear in the next section.

B) WORKING FOR THE JAPANESE COMPANY ABROAD

I. LOCAL STAFF GENERALLY

Your Japanese Manager's Expectations	Your Expectations
You will need time to settle in and won't feel competent to propose new initiatives for a year or so	Your boss will want you to show quickly what you are capable of doing
Outcome: *You make major proposals quickly but your boss doesn't take them seriously, offers no feedback.*	

Your Japanese Manager's Expectations	Your Expectations
Local staff are rarely as competent or cooperative as Japanese.	If you're capable, you can become the top manager.
Local staff are not real members of the company, even if they spend their lifetime there.	The Japanese will eventually hand over decision-making.
Local staff are only there to operate the business, not to plan strategies or make managerial decisions.	
Local staff members will always have to report to a Japanese and check decisions with a Japanese, no matter how senior their position.	

Outcome:	*You learn slowly and with increasing bitterness, as a local employee, that you will receive only limited respect for your work and managerial skills, and that there was never any intention to give real managerial responsibility to locals. The longer you stay, in fact, the more you see competent local managers come, then go, as they realize how low the ceiling of opportunity is; and you see that those locals who remain are not the best talents.*

II. FEMALE LOCAL STAFF

Your Japanese Manager's Expectations	Your Expectations
No local female employee will stay long-term in the company, as each will probably marry and have children.	You're not sure how long you will stay with the company, but you could stay on even if you have children.
Female executives will be treated formally, on their merits.	You will be mildly discriminated against by chauvinistic Japanese.

Your Japanese Manager's Expectations	Your Expectations

Outcome: *As you learn what their expectations are, your vision of a long-term future with the company is diminished. However, if you are a specialist manager, you are pleasantly surprised by the absence of chauvinism in how you are treated by male Japanese.*

III. EXPECTATIONS CONCERNING THE CROSS-CULTURAL MANAGEMENT INTERFACE

Japanese Managers	Local Staff
Excellent Japanese business experience and training will be useful overseas.	The Japanese are people managers.
English may not be good enough for business discussions.	There will be no communication problems.
No special study of the country is required; it can be picked up as one goes along.	The Japanese understand almost everything; you need not make any special effort in communicating with them.
I will not feel too forlorn there, as there are many other Japanese to socialize with.	You will make good friends of some of your Japanese colleagues and bosses.

Outcome: *The usual reality overseas is that Japanese businessmen experience far more problems in managing and communicating with local employees than they had anticipated and, in their initial years overseas, fail to learn about, comprehend, or endeavor to adapt to the local differences in employment laws, work culture, and interpersonal relationships. As for the local employees, they generally find that a wide gap develops between them and their Japanese colleagues and bosses. Friendships do not occur; there is little socializing outside the office; the Japanese learn little about the local culture or current events; there are many misunderstandings in interpersonal communication; the Japanese do not learn how to manage local people in other than a rough, near-authoritarian manner; and few of them take any interest in management training for local personnel.*

ARE CROSS-CULTURAL PROBLEMS INEVITABLE ABROAD?

The Japanese are not alone in experiencing problems when managing or working abroad. Most people have some difficulties even when fitting into cultures that have strong similarities—Canadians in the USA and New Zealanders in Australia, for instance. A few people seem able to avoid problems, though the number is minuscule when we are looking at extremely contrasted cultures like Japan and the USA or other Western countries.

Why do problems arise? One major reason is that visitors to another culture typically experience threats to their personal identity and values in the alien culture. In the case of Japan, many Westerners feel (at least initially) intimidated, for instance, by the claims of cultural excellence advanced for Japan, or by the allegedly superior cultivation and skills of the Japanese people. The threat seems to be our perceived inferiority to the Japanese. Again, superior technology and management know-how have been repeatedly claimed for the Japanese, though we have reached a point generally where the personal threat has weakened and we want to learn everything we can from them. This desire seems to be coinciding with increased Japanese efforts to explain and export their management philosophy and methods to the rest of the world.

ARE JAPANESE MANAGEMENT METHODS EXPORTABLE?

We need have no doubt that Japanese manufacturing techniques have been successfully exported. But can the same be said for "soft" management know-how? If it is true, then we ought to find such know-how successfully transplanted into overseas subsidiaries. The evidence presented and discussed in Part 2, however, does not add up to much confirmation at all. To understand this, we should first look at some key facets of Japanese management know-how at home.

1. Japanese companies in Japan are hierarchical in structure. Japanese management theorists and philosophers make much of the egalitarianism of Japan's people-centered management style. The suggestion is that the Japanese company is "flat" and that

every employee has the opportunity to reach the top. This is true, however, of male, university-graduate regular employees (sei shain) only; with the further proviso that in most major companies only one or two in a hundred will ever be promoted, and less than one in a thousand will make it to a senior position. But beneath this male elite group at the top of the pecking order there are other groups as well—female staff and shokutaku staff (including foreigners, seniors staying on after retirement, specialists, loan staff) as well as factory operatives and part-timers. Therefore, the Japanese company is hierarchical in structure, and promotion opportunities are severely limited.

2. Company membership and employee sovereignty (where stable employment takes precedence over profits, etc.) are the perquisites of the elite sei shain group only. Nonmembers, in other words, have less guarantee of stable employment than do members, a fact which becomes clear in those cases where Japanese companies abroad have retrenched local managers, but retained more junior or experienced Japanese managers.

3. Japanese management style is situational. Its success depends upon the common culture of its members, which ensures harmony and cooperation within a hierarchical structure. Teamwork and consensus decision-making require continuously suppressed competitiveness and avoidance of disputes to work effectively.

4. Obedience, conformity, and cooperation are rigorously demanded in Japanese companies through "exploitation" of national shame psychology, implicit threats and coercion (especially the threat of ostracism from the group), economic threats for late attendance, social threats such as of public ridicule, chastisement, etc. These make for a highly sophisticated "good boy/good girl" style of overt behavior.

5. Recruitment into the elite regular staff group is highly discriminatory and promotes arrogance and exclusivity toward out-

siders. The Japanese themselves recognize this, having been described as "intolerable prigs" (*hana mochi naranai*) for the way they act as though they were owners of the business, especially maintaining this posture toward overseas staff (see for instance the article on "Cross-cultural Communication" in the *Japan Economic Newspaper*, Feb. 9, 1989). Usually only "pure" Japanese are eligible to be regular staff, in practice meaning Koreans and the former pariah class are excluded. Some non-Japanese, mainly Chinese and Anglo-Saxons, are being admitted in a few companies provided they speak Japanese and show good evidence of cultural adjustment. It remains to be seen whether they will be given equal opportunities for promotion.

WHAT DO JAPANESE COMPANIES ACTUALLY TRANSPLANT ABROAD OF THE JAPANESE MANAGEMENT STYLE?

It is no secret, and to the Japanese no shame, that they export abroad a company structure where policy strategy and decision-making are in the hands of Japanese expatriate managers and operations are in the hands of local managers, and where local managers and staff have good job security but very limited opportunities for promotion to senior management positions (unlike the Japanese expatriates). Expatriate managers find that the subtly coercive skills for motivating and directing staff that work well with Japanese staff do not work well with Westerners, and a further problem is that expatriates share a common organization culture defining them as superior and elitist and fostering attitudes to outsiders and local staff that tend toward arrogance and condescension. The expatriate group is ultimately exclusive and cohesive.

In practice, we find that Japanese companies abroad, when there are sufficient numbers of expatriates to constitute a distinct social group, tend to separate expatriates from locals, with latent or explicit antagonism between the two sides and a psychological distancing and separation that makes for standoffish, mutually suspicious human relations, cautious interpersonal communication, and shallow friendships.

UNDERLYING FACTORS IN CULTURAL POLARIZATION

In the previous chapter we looked at many of the concrete faces of polarization in Japanese companies. In the present context of seeking fundamental explanations of the problems in these companies, I want to single out two key variables: psychology, and power, both being the responsibility of the Japanese.

I. PSYCHOLOGICAL FACTORS UNDERLYING POLARIZATION

These include:

a) The expatriate sense of being responsible for the company and its activities as quasi-owners.

b) The view that the local employees cannot have the same sense of responsibility, since they do not have quasi-owner status.

c) A sense of unease with foreigners (which we discussed earlier as a foreigner complex), which inhibits the development of open relationships.

d) The sense that Japanese really are superior to other peoples, making for insularity, and a lack of international feeling or emotional solidarity with other people.

e) The view that non-Japanese cannot understand Japanese-style indirect communication or allusiveness, and cannot read between the lines.

f) The perception that a Japanese puts the company first always whereas locals put themselves first, so weakening a link (company membership) they might appear superficially to have in common.

II. POWER/CONTROL FACTORS BEHIND THE SEPARATION

a) Control has to be retained in Japanese hands since non-Japanese cannot be completely trusted (they have not been properly trained or socialized in Japanese ways).

b) Control is necessary to ensure consistency of quality in corporate behavior and products.

c) Control remains with the Japanese when consensual decision-making is demanded. This then gives powers of veto, post-ponement, etc. to senior Japanese.

d) The Japanese refuse to be subordinate to local managers.

The combination of a psychology that makes for human re-moteness from non-Japanese and a set of behaviors that empha-sizes how securely they maintain power and control is obviously the most important cause of the de-motivation and even intimida-tion of non-Japanese managers and employees, and of the failure of Japanese expatriates in learning how to be effective middle managers abroad.

Some extravagant claims have been made by some Japanese (e.g., Itami 1986, Hasegawa 1989) on the universality of Japanese management. Itami, for instance, says that Japanese "peoplism"—where employees have priority over stockholders—"supplements and can even be an alternative system to Western-style capitalism, and the spread of this system as Japanese firms internationalize is potentially of worldwide importance." Alas, as noble and grand as it sounds, Japanese peoplism does not transplant. If it did, we would have local managers managing the overseas subsidiaries. The well-tried Japanese philosophy that "the strength is at the grass roots, where the action is" (*genba wa tsuyoi*), in Japan means that the people on the spot in selling, in the factory, and so on (when abroad, the local staff), should be used as experts on what is happening there. But the philosophy breaks down abroad. Non-Japanese, untrained, unsocialized, and untested for endurance or loyalty to the company, cannot be trusted. This is one good reason why Japanese expatriates have to be abroad: to say what is hap-pening on the spot, in a voice that is trusted. In doing that, they also demonstrate that the company still belongs, wherever it is abroad, to them, not to the local employees, whose status is shown by the fact that virtually no Japanese report to foreign managers; by discriminatory hiring of locals whenever possible; and by local staff being given no decision-making responsibilities.

CAN ALL JAPANESE MANAGEMENT "ODDITIES" ABROAD BE EXPLAINED AWAY BY CROSS-CULTURAL DIFFICULTIES ALONE?

Earlier in this chapter and elsewhere in the book, I have pointed out how Western managers in Japan, somewhat like Japanese managers in the West, fail in many ways to be effective people managers or trainers. At face value, this would suggest that all of us, whatever our cultural background, are subject inevitably to the ills of cross-cultural maladjustment in business life and that perhaps there is not much we can do about it. If fault is to be found, it would be equally on both sides. Is this so?

According to Hayashi, who has studied US and Japanese subsidiaries in Japan and the US (1989), American managers working for Japanese subsidiaries in the United States are more frustrated than Japanese managers working for American subsidiaries in Japan.

"They were frustrated because they were not able to understand what was really going on [and did not] participate effectively in decision-making. . . . [whereas] Japanese managers in US subsidiaries in Japan clearly have accepted the American style of management as inevitable" (p 58).

Hayashi proposes to explain this difference through five "conjectures", namely, Japanese concepts and practices are complex, not logical; verbal explanation is rare among the Japanese; American practices are easily explainable; the Japanese feel that local staff are not true members of the firm; and the Japanese exercise much closer control over subsidiaries than Americans can do. These conjectures of Hayashi are entirely consistent with the findings of the present book, and help to make sense of the greater frustration he found among American managers in Japanese US subsidiaries. They demonstrate also how "locked in" the Japanese are to management practices that, as functional as they may be in Japan, tend to be dysfunctional abroad, at times even "deviant" (i.e., deviating from, say, the American norm).

If this were the whole story, then the issue would come down to the challenge of new culture learning for Westerners (remember the Japanese are much less frustrated, more at home with Western management, according to Hayashi). But it is not the whole story. In spite of the advocacy of Japanese "peoplism" or people-centered management, there is hard evidence to show that in many ways Japanese management is less people-centered than that in the West. In 1984, the Japan Productivity Center undertook a large-scale cross-national comparison of managerial behavior in Japan and the USA, based on responses from 482 businesspeople in the US and 917 in Japan.

To the surprise of many, the researchers obtained results which, as they said, "contradicted established beliefs." These were:

1. American managers show more consideration for subordinates than do Japanese.

2. American managers pay more heed to subordinates' opinions than do their Japanese counterparts.

3. American managers give more consideration to their subordinates' future in decisions on promotion/rotation.

Personally, these findings were no surprise. In my view, Japanese managers are more autocratic and coercive than Western managers: Japan is a "culture of command." Japanese culture has little place for verbal discussion between superiors and subordinates. If you are a subordinate, you behave deferentially, do what you're told, respond quickly—without demur or question—to orders. If you are a superior, it is culturally appropriate to give orders, with the expectation that a subordinate can work out how to execute the order without detailed discussion or guidance. The Japanese emphasis on recruiting candidates having flexibility and a good "attitude" stems from these social role expectations. Such candidates will do what they are told without argument or demur, it is believed.

So, when we look at the ineffective managerial behaviors of expatriate managers in Japan or in the West, we should, I believe, look at this "culture of command" in Japan. It is in very marked contrast to the Western "culture of persuasive argumentation." To put it simply, in bold strokes, Japanese expatriates tend to be nonplussed whenever their local staff are not only unfamiliar with, but hostile to, a command culture. Such local staff expect, are accustomed to, more consideration, more discussion, more friendly concern for their welfare, than the Japanese have been accustomed to—their bosses did not behave in such a way, and even if they had, they would have been branded, by Japanese conservative male cultural values, as "wimps" or "sissies" (*memeshii mono*). A "real man" doesn't, in fact, talk much at all in Japan. He is "still waters running deep," keeping his own counsel. These conventional stereotypes of "proper" behavior become the greatest barrier, in the last analysis, to Japanese managers adjusting effectively to their foreign workplaces and local staff.

CHAPTER
12
SOME WORDS OF ADVICE -
AND WARNING

A. ADVICE TO JAPAN AND THE JAPANESE

This book has put Japanese managers under the microscope, notably those overseas. There are many special problems, which they themselves recognize, though most feel powerless to do anything about them. Westerners have problems overseas, too, but they haven't drawn attention to themselves as much as the Japanese. This is ironic, when you understand how much individual Japanese, wherever they are, try to avoid attracting attention to themselves.

A modicum of the book's content was called "sensational" by some of my early readers, and there might also be suspicion that I set out to write a sensational book. The truth is only that I set out to write a fair but penetrating account of the Japanese manager in the cross-cultural setting. I did know something about this topic previously, having worked in Japanese organizations in Japan, and having acted as consultant to foreign companies in Japan and foreign and Japanese companies abroad on Japanese-foreign work and human relationships. But the more research I did, and the more I talked to Japanese and foreigners about their experiences, the bigger these cross-cultural problems seemed to appear, and the more widespread, serious, and even crippling the shortcomings of Japanese managers (notably junior and middle managers) in their dealings with foreign staff and subordinates seemed to be.

The perspective I came to adopt was this: that the difficulties of Japanese managers abroad, the troubles created by their presence, their often dysfunctional mode of managing, and the various constraints put upon foreign staff (such as restricted responsibility, limited decision-making authority, restricted freedom to deal directly with head office) are of a more general and serious character than I had imagined or that anyone has so far hinted at. What do I mean by "serious"? Let me put it this way: Sooner or later, the severe labor shortage in Japan and the huge cost of maintaining expatriates abroad are going to make it impossible for Japanese companies to keep increasing the number of people they are sending overseas. At that point, or well in advance of it, they will have to recruit senior local (non-Japanese) managers and give them real decision-making responsibility. Those senior locals will have to become genuine full members of the Japanese corporation, with the same company status as Japanese staff. This will mean, among other things, that some Japanese staff will also have to report to them, that the "Japanese-ness" of the company will start to be diluted.

For this to happen, far-reaching changes in the culture of the Japanese firm and in the values and attitudes of the core management elite ought already to be starting. We ought to be seeing already a demand that Japanese managers overseas modify their management style to fit different circumstances and different subordinates. But we are not. We ought to be hearing calls for Japanese managers to extend their touted "generalist" management abilities to cover managing abroad. But we are not. We ought to be hearing calls for a global egalitarianism of company personnel, where everyone, irrespective of race, has the same opportunity to succeed, to be a leader or a follower. We are not. We ought to be hearing company presidents telling their new staff, "don't expect to succeed in our global enterprise just because you are Japanese. It is your humanity, your flexibility as a businessperson in any culture setting, your development of management skills that transplant quickly in other cultural soils, that will make our company flourish in the 21st century." We are not.

Calls for such a shift in values, from nationalist to transnationalist, will sound anti-Japanese, unpatriotic, and disloyal to many Japanese. But such a shift is conceivable. It is conceivable that some company presidents could begin to say this; they are, after all, encouraged by the culture to think in visionary terms. They also have a sense of fashion in ideas, as you will see if you follow the content of annual presidents' speeches each April to newly recruited employees. Another reason for this being conceivable is that the Japanese people do tend to be followers. Make the concept significant enough for the welfare of the country or the enterprise and people will feel they ought to follow. Unfortunately, the very addiction of the Japanese to fashion, in this case fashionable ideas, reminds them constantly that fashions are short-lived, not to mention that the flashy rhetoric of company presidents is also seen by many Japanese as what they call *tatemae*, utterances having a pleasing and flattering ring to them, but not meant to be taken too seriously.

Better training for expatriate Japanese, to help them manage and adjust better abroad, might seem another option. It is true that a few companies, such as Nomura and Sumitomo, put their staff through formal training courses prior to departure abroad. But the overall picture is of little being learnt prior to arrival overseas. Once there, an informal learning process does begin, as they learn from their local staff and, especially, from other Japanese expatriates who themselves, given their usually sheltered lifestyle, are not exactly steeped in the local culture. My general impression today is that they learn a minimum for survival, after which the light of learning (as a businessperson) is extinguished.

I haven't always thought this way. While I was living full-time in Japan (until 1988), I let myself believe that expatriate Japanese were no better or worse in these respects than expatriates of other nationalities. When I would go overseas to do training programs on how to deal with or negotiate with the Japanese, I would always be asked: Do the Japanese try to learn about us in the way that we try to learn about them? To be frank, I always chose to defend the Japanese against the implicit charge of indifference (which was always there behind the question). In part, this was tactical. It does no good in a training course to sympathize with participants about their feelings of being treated condescendingly and unfairly, or of being victimized, for it takes the focus away from the individual participant and his new learning. But I had also believed, which I now regard as a mistake, that the Japanese abroad were no more and no less interested in the foreign country than, for instance, some of those Western expatriates who hold up the late-night bars of Tokyo. I now think I was mistaken about this as my overseas experience since then (in addition to the evidence acquired in researching this book) has convinced me that the Japanese are not only more uninterested, but will actively avoid undergoing training about the local culture or business environment, even if it is offered. Participation is always voluntary, and the motivation is, as I said earlier, simply to pick up the minimum for survival. A story by a fellow consultant tends to support this.

He began lecturing in a predeparture training program with just four Japanese present. Within thirty minutes, however, they had all disappeared. He was about to pack up when another man arrived, so he continued lecturing. This last Japanese man showed great interest in my friend's talk, which cheered him up no end. On finishing, he thanked that sole audience member warmly—only to discover that he was the next lecturer in the program!

Ultimately, I have reached a pessimistic conclusion about the likelihood of change occurring among the Japanese. In some ways, it is even impudent of me to be expecting them, not us, to change. I can understand that viewpoint. But it is the Japanese, not us, who are "invading" other societies, bringing in workways and decision-making styles that are alien to our cultures, utilizing corporate structures that put local people in subordinate roles, and who "provoke" local feelings of being treated as "second-class citizens." How should we respond to this? For one thing, a good deal of the awkwardness of Japanese managers abroad, in their handling of foreign staff, is to be attributed not to their being Japanese but to their lack of foreign experience; personal immaturity; poor empathy with non-Japanese; inadequate sense of judgment; and defensiveness and stress under unfamiliar and threatening circumstances. On the other hand, this list of shortcomings is so long that we ought to wonder about the quality of the managers back at the head office who, in the first place, sent them abroad so ill-prepared. Japanese companies seem to lack realistic policies for the training of appointees abroad. Or we might suspect that the head office had little choice of whom to send. Perhaps the head office was desperate and had to send whoever was available.

The personal characteristics of the expatriate Japanese are one factor. Another is the dual structure of the Japanese company abroad, the tight control maintained in most cases over people and projects, and the seeming inability of the Japanese corporate system to integrate, motivate, and reward senior foreign managers in a satisfying way (though Sony and a few others are striking exceptions). Something will and has to "give" here, as the supply of Japanese available for overseas posting declines. (Another not inconsiderable problem is changes in immigration policy in foreign countries, leading to a reduction in the number of visas that a Japanese company is permitted for expatriate staff. These management problems are thus also political problems.)

There is also the interesting role of Hayashi's cultural spanners, that is, people within the organization who command both languages, are "acquainted with the knowledge, values, and meanings" of both cultures, and who are legitimate members of one or both of the two cultures (Hayashi 1989, 34). The notion of cultural spanners is still a very novel one, although Hayashi has communicated his ideas well to Japanese big business through his books and lectures. There is a very good chance, unfortunately, that this concept will go the way of other "fashionable concepts" and never really be accepted as a necessary, integral function within the multinational organization. In principle, cultural bridgers need to have a full-time role as problem solvers, two-way communicators, negotiators, counsellors, and probably interpreters as well. They also need to have the ear of powerful figures within the organization to help bring about changes which they have found must be made for the well-being of everyone involved.

Another danger in the cultural spanner idea is that, in any

attempt to make the concept work effectively, the Japanese company will ignore the other opportunities to make all expatriate and local staff more cooperative and more insightful about intercultural problems. There are a lot of "needs" and "musts" here, and as sensible as it appears, I cannot see much being done on a long-term basis in Japanese companies, unless, and this is not too implausible, the Japanese president overseas is himself a bicultural person (who could have lived abroad as a child) and so has the precious insights, empathy, and communication skills necessary to see issues and problems from the viewpoint of both sides, and to take a leadership role to resolve matters.

It has to be said that business difficulties abroad (especially in the USA) ought to be managed by the Japanese business community and the government more effectively, in order to minimize problems and contain both human and political damage. I hope, for the sake of Japan, that someone in the upper echelons of Japan is listening, understands how potentially explosive the problems of Japanese companies abroad are becoming, and recognizes that the solution lies, not in more PR and lobbying activity in Washington, but in the enhancement of a genuine international sense among the Japanese. Overseas postings have to be made much more attractive than they now are, and better salaries and overseas allowances (especially for unpopular locations) will certainly help. Japanese people should want to go abroad and should compete for the opportunities to do so, not be ordered like children to do some years of often painful and unavoidable overseas duty. When finally the Japanese people really want to be more international, the problems will have begun to be resolved.

Those non-Japanese who know Japan well may react cynically to the notion of the Japanese generally becoming more international, in the sense of genuinely wanting to serve and live abroad. After all, in every country the diplomatic service has a problem in inducing its diplomatic staff to take up third world postings. And they are career diplomats! What chance, then, of success in turning around the pathetic negativity of introverted Japanese business people? Let me make some modest suggestions. One, offer more economic inducements to serve effectively abroad as a hands-on manager of local staff. Increase salaries, and offer bonuses for good performance. Two, follow a type of personnel system that makes overseas experience essential to organizational advancement, such as that described in Nakamura (1989). Three, emphasize the quality of overseas experience, not sheer time abroad. The Japanese need to avoid posting abroad those negative-thinking individuals who try to merely hang in and endure the unpleasant posting (what the Japanese call *gamanzuyoi*, meaning "long-suffering"), but who often end up as highly stressed, psychosomatically disordered candidates for suicide. Four, appoint more Japanese who have spent some of their childhood overseas and are fluent in another language. These so-called "returnees" (*kikokushijo*) are well known in Japan as being more positive-minded, optimistic, and sociable than Japanese who have never lived abroad, and can handle appointments and life abroad more effectively. Five, make appointments abroad more voluntary, i.e., minimize coercion. Six, take a leaf out of the book of European businesses and appoint managers abroad for long periods, ten years or more. Seven, drop all the nice-sounding tatemae (face-saving) statements about localizing sometime in the future—that is, replacing Japanese managers abroad by locals—and start at once to recruit successor candidates, giving them regular employee status and seniority equivalent to Japanese employees. Eight, take the difficult steps required to modify the management of subsidiaries abroad so that their future foreign managers are left in no doubt that they will become responsible decision-makers. Nine, drop once and for all either the explicit or implicit need for anyone in the organization in Japan or abroad to be Japanese in order to be promoted or to take a leadership position. In short, let Japanese-ness be diluted in the company. Ten, and finally, do battle with the pettiness and small-mindedness of those Japanese who, when abroad, treat local staff in other than a responsible, mature, respectful fashion.

If a sincere committed attempt to bring about these changes and improvements is made by Japanese companies, based on explicit policies binding upon everyone in the organization, we would expect to see a rapid breaking of the vicious cycle of Japanese suspicion that Westerners will only stay a few years, leading to restrictions on training and promotion, thus inducing short-term employment through employee dissatisfaction. This will bring about the real beginnings of an overseas localization policy for Japanese companies.

B. ADVICE TO FOREIGNERS ABOUT WORKING FOR THE JAPANESE COMPANY

If you are non-Japanese and have read this far, you may have sensed a pessimism on my part about the likelihood of any change in Japanese companies that will materially improve your prospects of climbing high into its senior managerial and decision-making echelons. If so, your sense will be more or less correct, with a few provisos: one, if, like Villarante, you join the company in Japan in your twenties, already speak the language and feel a lifelong commitment, I believe you may, with patience and perseverance, go very far indeed; two, if you are abroad, and aspire (as most do) to be head of the subsidiary there, you will have a far better chance if there is only a small number of expatriates assigned there; three, certain types of Japanese companies abroad offer good opportunities for local senior executives to enter at or close to chief executive officer level. This is especially true for joint ventures and for subsidiaries which depend on local non-Japanese clients for much of their turnover. The fourth and final proviso on my pessimism is this: your success or failure in a Japanese company depends partly on Japanese management and staff, partly on you and how you adapt and contribute to it. This book, in focussing on the "warts and all" of the Japanese, has largely left the Westerner out of the picture, but we have been able to see that, depending on personality skills and motivation, a few non-Japanese at least are entitled to feel optimistic about their position and prospects in the Japanese company.

IDENTIFYING JAPANESE COMPANIES THAT OFFER OPPORTUNITIES TO FOREIGN STAFF

If there are Japanese companies that do offer good opportunities for advancement, we should try to identify them. In a moment, I will suggest how you might go about doing this, by acquiring information about their policies, work and employment practices, and the benefits and equal opportunities (vis-a-vis Japanese employees) they offer you. First, however, let me offer a sketch of what I see as the ideal characteristics of a Japanese company for the non-Japanese to work for abroad.

1. It has only one or two expatriates, and there is little likelihood that the number will increase.

2. The industry is one that needs local people to manage it.

3. The company is in a growth industry, and can expect to be one of the local industry leaders in the next five to fifteen years.

4. The subsidiary is already operating in the black.

5. The replacement of expatriates by their successors has little effect on business performance or organizational climate.

6. The Japanese head office exercises the minimum control over your business, and you feel largely autonomous.

7. The absolute number of staff in the subsidiary is unlikely ever to exceed a few hundred (large numbers may provoke head office again to start exercising more control over your operation).

In brief, I would advise non-Japanese to seek out as employers Japanese subsidiaries that have small establishments, high growth potential, and an established, profitable position in the local market. This will minimize head office interference in decision-making, maximize local staff involvement in decision-making, and foster "healthy" human relations between local staff and Japanese.

EVALUATING JAPANESE COMPANIES AS EMPLOYERS OF NON-JAPANESE

Identifying candidates for the "ideal" Japanese employer company should not be too difficult, if you start by identifying high-growth industries in your country and then look for the Japanese members of that industry. But this technique will not work for everyone looking for a Japanese employer, such as those looking at industries they are already familiar with or who seek specialist positions that are only available in large companies. There are also important questions about the company and its work conditions that many will want to ask in company interviews, the answers to which may help frame both your decision on any offer and conditions you would want to demand. Even if you are already working for a Japanese company, the answers you obtain to these questions may help you clarify what changes you would like to see in the company, as well as giving you the means to make an overall assessment of it as a place for foreigners to work.

EVALUATION QUESTIONS ABOUT JAPANESE EMPLOYERS

A. Corporate Philosophy/Strategy

To what extent does management expect to extend Japan-side management philosophies and practices to overseas subsidiaries? What importance is attached to corporate "globalization" and "localization"?

What corporate commitment is there to the employment of non-Japanese as equal in status to Japanese?

What commitment is there to future investment and diversification in your country?

What commitment is there to equal employment opportunity (EEO)?

B. Policies in Practice

How far has localization (the replacement of expatriate managers by local employees) actually proceeded? What is the company actually doing at this moment to speed up localization? Ask for concrete examples of what is being done.

Are minorities discriminated against, even covertly? How does minorities' representation in the local population match their representation in the company labor force?

What degree of autonomy does the subsidiary have from head office, especially in respect of the functional areas you will be involved in?

What decisions are individual local (non-Japanese) managers able to make without referral?

What decisions must/need not be referred to head office?

What is the actual involvement of local managers in the subsidiary's decision-making? How much pre-decision-making discussion within the company are local managers involved in? How much is carried out exclusively by expatriates, in Japanese-language meetings?

How often have board meetings, executive committee meetings, and general staff meetings been held in the past twelve months?

C. Work and Employment Practices

What is the actual employment status of local managers as compared to expatriate managers of the same age? Is a Japanese-style seniority and promotion system used?

What are the seniority and promotion systems?

Are those local managers hired in midcareer given advanced seniority status to match them with their expatriate peers?

If you are a woman or minority member hired by the company, will your career prospects be adversely affected compared to other local employees?

What training is offered or supported by the company? Does the company send staff to Japan for training? Does the company subsidize Japanese language or other study?

Are expatriates concerned that you will only stay with the company for a few years? If so, in what ways will your treatment and acceptance be inhibited, it at all? Do you want to allay their fears on this? How might you do that?

How many expatriates are there? How many will you have to report to?

Will you receive a job description, or some indication of what is expected of you, especially in the first year or so?

What are the basic rules—formal and informal—about the workplace? What are the basic expectations held by expatriate managers of you as a local manager or staff person? Is the company involved, or has it been involved, in any EEO or similar litigation?

D. Organizational Climate and Human Relations

What are current relationships like between expatriates and local staff?

How much cross-cultural socializing has actually occurred in the past three months, including home entertaining, sports or family events, company outings, after-work socializing?

How much socializing with staff has actually been done by the two or three top expatriates?

How well do expatriates communicate with local staff? To what extent are interpreters needed to facilitate on-the-job communication?

If you speak Japanese well, will your use of it on the job be welcomed (a) by expatriates, (b) by head office?

If you don't speak Japanese, will you be able to communicate effectively with all of the expatriates you have to report to?

How are relationships between male expatriates and female local staff? Do female staff members have any sense of being discriminated against in promotion or salary increases?

How will expatriates react to any idiosyncratic work practices of yours, e.g., starting early, finishing early, orderliness in the workplace?

In offering this set of questions, I do not necessarily mean to say that you should put these questions directly to the Japanese. Many, perhaps most, of these questions if asked directly would be regarded as offensive. You need, in dealing with the Japanese, to let them do the talking, encourage them to reach the point where they feel relaxed with you and will speak frankly, for instance about the prevailing organizational climate. You will have to guess at the answers to many questions, though if you feel it will be helpful, you might ask if you can speak to other company employees, local as well as expatriate.

Finally, Japanese managers can also use these questions and their answers as a means to better understanding what they could do to employ foreigners productively and intelligently in the long term. I would welcome hearing from those who are able to find inspiration or guidance in this book, toward the solution of any of the many problems facing Japanese companies and their Japanese and foreign employees.

BIBLIOGRAPHY

Abegglen, J.C., and G. Stalk. *Kaisha: The Japanese Corporation*. New York: Basic Books, 1985. Reprint. Tokyo: Tuttle, 1990.

Adams, Roy J., R.B. Peterson, and H.F. Schwind. "Personal Value Systems of Japanese Trainees and Managers in a Changing Competitive System." *Asia Pacific Journal of Management* 5, no. 3 (1988): 169–179.

Aida, Yuji. "International Understanding: An Illusion." *Japan Times*, 26 March 1986, 16.

Alletzhauser, Al. *The House of Nomura*. London: Bloomsbury, 1990.

Armbruster, W. "Cultures Clash as Japanese Firms Set Up Shop in the US." *Journal of Commerce*, 1 March 1989: 1–4.

"Attitudes Towards Japanese Business Activity in Australia." Sydney: Malleson, Jacques & Stephen. Undated.

Beasley, W.G. *The Modern History of Japan*. 3d ed. Weidenfeld & Hudson, 1981.

Beauchamp, E.R. and A. Iriye. *Foreign Employees in 19th Century Japan*. Westview, 1987.

Benedict, Ruth. *The Chrysanthemum and the Sword*. Tokyo: Tuttle, 1972 (First edition, 1946).

Browning, E.S. "Japan Shuns Those Back from Abroad." *Asian Wall Street Journal*, 14 May 1986.

Christopher, R.C. *The Japanese Mind*. New York: Simon and Schuster, 1983.

Chrysler, M. "'Integration' Problems Plague Japanese Employees." *Daily Yomiuri*, 27 June 1990, 3.

Clark, Gregory. "The People are the Enterprise." *PHP*, Dec. 1981, 31–58.

Cole, R.E., and D.R. Deskins Jr. "Racial Factors in Site Location." *California Management Review* 31, no. 1 (Fall 1988).

Cross, Michael. "Down and Out in Tokyo." *New Scientist*, 8 September 1990, 36–39.

CSBK (Chikyu Sangyo Bunka Kenkyusho) [Global Industry Research Institute]. "*Keizai no Guroobaruka ga maneku Bunka Masatsu to Taio*" (Cross-cultural friction stemming from economic globalization, and how it is coped with), May 1991.

"Culture Shock at Home: Working for a Foreign Boss." *Business Week*, 17 December 1990, 80–84.

"Current Situation of Business Operations of Japanese Manufacturing Enterprises in Europe." JETRO, March 1990.

"Current State of Resident Japanese Companies, The." JETRO, Sydney, July 1989.

Doctor, R. et. al. "Culture as a Constraint on Productivity." *International Studies of Management and Organization* 15, Issue 3/4 (Fall/Winter 1985, 1986).

Dower, J.W., ed. *Origins of the Modern Japanese State*. New York: Pantheon Books, 1975.

Emmott, Bill. *The Sun Also Sets: The Limits of Japan's Economic Power*. New York: Random House, 1989.

Esaka, A., and K. Kimindo. "Farewell to the Corporate Warrior." *Japan Echo*, Special Issue 17 (1990): 37–41.

"Current State of Resident Japanese Companies, The." JETRO, Sydney, July 1989.

"Export of Management Style Is Delicate Matter." *Japan Economic Journal*, 4 November 1989, 21.

Fairbank, J.K., E.O. Reischauer, A.M. Craig. *East Asia: Tradition and Transformation*. Boston: Houghton Mifflin, 1973.

Fallows, James. "Containing Japan." *Atlantic Monthly*, May 1989, 40–54.

"Foreign-Capital Business Faring Well." *Journal of Japanese Trade & Industry*, no. 2, 1986.

"Foreigners are Back." *Tokyo Business Today*, May 1988, 14–20.

Fucini, J.J. & S. *Working for the Japanese*. New York: Free Press, 1990.

Fujita, F. "Encounters with an Alien Culture: Americans Employed by the Kaitakushi." In *Live Machines*. See Jones 1980.

Gaijin Scientist. Science & Technology Action Group. British Chamber of Commerce in Japan, 1990.

"Gaikokujin Chishiki Rodosha no Koyo Jittai" (The recruitment of foreign knowledge workers). *Rosei Jiho*, 6 May 1989, 47–52.

"Gaikokujin Howaito Kara: Saiyo Saizensen" (Foreign white collar workers: The hiring frontline). *Nikkei Sangyo Shimbun* (Nikkei Industrial Newspaper), 10–11 September 1991.

"Gaikokujin Koyo no Genjo to Kongo no Hoko" (Current trends and circumstances in the employment of foreigners). *Kyokai Jinryu*, 6 May 1989, 53–58.

"Gaikokujin Rodosha Mondai" (The problem of foreign workers). *Kokusai Jinryu* 3, 1990, 11–18.

Hall, J.W. *Japan from Prehistory to Modern Times*. London: Weidenfeld & Nicolson, 1970. Reprint. Tokyo: Tuttle, 1987.

Hansen, Karen. "American Women in Japan." Aoyama Gakuin University, December 1986. Typescript.

Harada, Yukio. "Zaibei Nikkei Kigyo no Jinji Kanri Shisutemu" (The personnel management systems of Japanese companies in the USA). *Zaigai Kigyo*, March 1990, 22–35.

Hasegawa, Keitaro. *The Theory of Japanese Management*. Tokyo, 1989.

Hayashi, K. "Zainichi Gaikokujin no Mita Nihon no Bijinesu o Yomu" (Understanding how foreigners resident in Japan perceive Japanese business). In *Bijinesu Senryoku Senjutsu Koza* (Studies of business strategy and tactics). Kodansha 12 (1988): 375–385.

Hayashi, K., ed. *The US-Japanese Economic Relationship: Can It Be Improved?* New York: New York University Press, 1989.

Henderson, D.F. *Foreign Enterprise in Japan: Laws and Policies*. Chapel Hill: University of North Carolina Press, 1973. Reprint. Tokyo: Tuttle, 1975.

"Here's Where Trouble Develops During Home-Stay Programs." *Japan Free Press*, no. 34, 1990, 1.

"Hito no Genchika Tachi Okure" (The localization of people is running late). *Nikkei Sangyo Shimbun*, 11 December 1991.

Holusha, J. "Japanese Faulted over Black Hiring." *New York Times*, no. 27, 1988, 28L.

"Honda to Pay $6 Million in Rights Settlement." *New York Times*, 24 March 1989, A18.

Hori, T. *The Japanese and the Australians*. Pergamon, 1982.

Huddleston, J.N. Jr. *Gaijin Kaisha: Running a Foreign Business in Japan*. Armonk, N.Y.: M.E. Sharpe, 1990.

Inamura, Hiroshi. *Nihonjin no Kaigai Futekio* (The maladjustment of Japanese overseas). NHK Books, 1987.

Inohara, Hideo. "Human Resource Development in Japanese Companies." Asian Productivity Organization. Tokyo, 1990.

Itami, Hiroyuki. "Global 'Sharing': Can Japanese 'Peoplism' Catch on Abroad?" *Look Japan*, 10 June 1986, 4–6.

Iwai, Hiroshi. *Yugamerareta Kansho Nihonjin no Taijin Kyofu* (The distorted mirror image: The interpersonal fears of the Japanese). Asahi Shuppan, 1982.

Japan Productivity Center. "Management Behavior in Japan and the USA." JPA. Tokyo, 1984.

"Japanese Companies Continue to Pursue Good Corporate Citizenship." JEI Report, 4 May 1990.

"Japanese Executives in America Often Find Themselves Engaged in a Dialogue of the Deaf with their American Colleagues." *Economist*, 24 November 1989, 71–72.

"Japanese Management/Matsushita Management." Overseas Training Center, Matsushita Electric Industrial Co. Ltd. Undated.

"Japanese Manager Meets the American Worker, The." *Business Week*, 20 August, 1984.

"Japan's Foreign Workers." *Japan Economic Journal*, 27 May 1989.

"Japan's New Cosmopolitan Workforce." *Focus Japan*, August 1990, 1.

JOEA (Nihon Kaigai Kigyo Kyokai). *Nihon Kigyo no Naka no Gaikoku Chishiki Rodosha* (Foreign knowledge workers in Japanese enterprises). 1988.

Johnson, C. *MITI & the Japanese Miracle*. Stanford, Calif.: Stanford University Press, 1982.

Jones, H.J. *Live Machines: Hired Foreigners and Meiji Japan*. Tenterden: Norbury Publications, 1980.

Jones, Stephanie. *Working for the Japanese: Myths and Realities*. London: Macmillan, 1991.

"Kaigai Hakensha no tame no Joken Seibi" (Adjusting conditions for employees sent overseas). Tokyo: Nihon Zaigai Kigyo Kyokai, 1990.

"Kaigai ni Hataraku Nihonjin" (Japanese Working Abroad). Nikkei Publishing, 1983.

Kasuya, Koichi. *De-ai to Fure-ai* (Encounters and getting along). Tokyo: Kodansha, 1986.

Kawanishi, K. "Needed: Cool Heads in Washington & Tokyo." *Japan Economic Journal*, 27 October 1990, 9.

Kawanuma, A., ed. *Law & Business in Japan*. The Japan-Australia Business Cooperation Committee, 1982.

Kealing, Jeffrey. "Culture Spanners." *Intersect*, January 1992, 17–18.

Kilbon, P.T. "Long on Japanese Management, Short on Labor Law." *International Herald Tribune*, 4 June 1991, 1.

Kobayashi, Y. "Towards True International Exchange." *Japan Echo*, 3, no. 4 (1976).

"Kokkyo o Koe, Hakushu" (Applause for transcending national borders). *Mainichi Shimbun*, 10 June 1986, 15.

"Kokusai Bijinesuman Yosei ano te kono te" (Aspects of the development of international businessmen). *Asahi Shimbun*, 18 June 1984.

"Kokusaika Jidai no Kaigai Kogaisha Kanri" (Managing overseas subsidiaries in the age of internationalization). *Nihon Keizai Shimbun* (Japan Economic Newspaper), 21 December 1990.

"Kokusaika? Mada, mada!" (Internationalization? Not yet!). *Sankei Shimbun*, 13th October 1990.

Kolata, Gina. "Japanese Labs in US Luring Americans." *New York Times*, 11 November 1990.

Koller, Miki. "Japanese Companies Reluctant to Give Foreign Managers Real Authority." *Asahi Evening News*, 8 June 1990, 4.

Komai, Hiroshi. *Japanese Management Overseas*. Tokyo: Asian Productivity Organization, 1989.

Kuwabara, K. "Homecoming: Japanese Emigrants and their Descendants Returning to the Fold." *Japan Economic Journal*, 28 April 1990.

Kuwabara, K. "Cultural Friction Grates on Neighborhood." *Japan Economic Journal*, 14 October 1989.

"Kyoiku ni Kikokushijo no Koe o" (The views of returnees on education). *Mainichi Shimbun*, 1 July 1986, 12.

Labaton, S. "Bias Rulings and Japan's US Units." *New York Times*, 19 June 1989, 22.

"Lean, Mean and through your Windscreen." *Economist*, 23 February 1991, 68–74.

"Learning Experiences." *Look Japan*, January 1989, 23–25.

Lee, S.M., and G. Schwendiman, eds. *Japanese Management: Cultural and Environmental Considerations*. Praeger, 1982.

Leibowitz, M. "Japan in America: Living in the USA." *Electronic Business*, 1 August 1987, 44–56.

"Lesson for Japan in Discrimination, A" *Forbes*, May 1991.

March, R.M. "Expatriate Managers and Their Japanese Staff." *Winds* 3 (August 1983): 29–33.

March, R.M. "International Training in Leading Japanese Companies." Aoyama Gakuin University, 1986. Xerox.

March, R.M. *The Japanese Negotiator*. Tokyo: Kodansha International, 1988.

March, R.M. "Manpower and Control Issues in International Business." In *Breaking Down Barriers*, by Gower Press, 1980. B. Garratt and J. Stopford.

March, R.M. "Opportunities and Problems for the Foreign Business in Japan." Business Paper No. 7, Dept. of Management, University of Queensland, 1977.

March, R.M. "Osutorariajin kara Mita Osutorariajin no Jozu na Tsukai Kata" (How to manage Australian staff effectively). *Kaigai Iju*, August 1989, 10–13, and September 1989, 9–11.

March, R.M. "The Performance of Foreign Capital and Foreign Enterprises in Japan." Business Paper No. 13, University of Queensland, 1978.

March, R.M. "Western Manager, Japanese Boss." *Intersect*, January 1992, 11–16.

March, Roger. "Survey on Working Conditions of Foreigners in Japanese Companies." Tokyo, February 1990.

Marshall, L. "Japanese Companies in Australia: Their Employment Practices." Sydney, 7 May 1990.

Maruyama, M. "Nihonjin no Kokusaika no Joken" (Conditions for the internationalization of the Japanese). *Shukan Toyo Keizai*, 29 November 1987.

Maruyama, M. "Mindscapes: How to Understand Specific Situations in Multicultural Management." *Asia Pacific Journal of Management* 2, no. 3 (May 1985): 125–149.

Massarella, D. *A World Elsewhere*. New Haven: Yale University Press, 1990.

Matsuoka, M. "Nani ga Hatarakisugi no Nihonjin o Tsukutte Kita ka" (What brought about the overworking Japanese?). *JMA Journal*, January 1990, 20–23.

Matsusaka, M. "Understanding is Key to Bridging Gaps." *Japan Economic Journal*, 2 August 1986, 18.

"Maybe Blood Isn't Thicker than Water." *Japan Free Press*, no. 2, 1991, 3.

Milgram, S. *Obedience to Authority*. Tavistock, 1974.

Miyamoto, S.F. *Social Solidarity among the Japanese in Seattle*. Seattle: University of Washington Press, 1984.

Miyauchi, Y. "Can There be Harmony between Japanese-style Management and the International Marketplace?" *JMA Newsletter*, 1 October 1988.

Moffat, Susan. "Working for the Japanese." *Fortune*, 3 December 1990, 30–36.

Morita, Akio. *Made in Japan*. London: Collins, 1987.

Nakamura, Megumi. "Kaigai Hakensha no Senbatsu to Kigyonai Karia Keisai" (The selection of overseas appointees and their in-company career development). *Nihon Rodo Kyokai Zasshi*, no. 357, June 1989, 3–12.

Nakane, C. *Japanese Society*. London: Weidenfeld & Nicolson, 1970. Revised edition. Penguin Books, 1973.

Nathanson, Donald. "Shame: A Review Article." *Psychiatric Clinics of North America* 12 (1990): 381–388.

Neilan, Edward. "U Md Teaches Top Tokyo Executives." *Washington Times*, 13 June 1990, 5.

News from MITI. "The 19th Survey on Japanese Business Activities Abroad." MITI, March 1990.

"Nikkei Kigyo 17000 Sha no Saishin Joho" (The latest data on 17,000 Japanese-related companies). Toyo Keizai, 1989.

Niskansen, W. "Patience is Needed as Anti-Japan Mood Swells." *Japan Economic Journal*, 3 March 1990, 9.

"Nissan to Pay $605,600 to Settle Race and Age Bias Case." *New York Times*, 4 February 1989, A8.

Noble, K.B. "A Clash of Styles: Japanese Companies in US under Fire for Cultural Bias." *New York Times*, 25 January 1988, A16.

"On the Job Learning." *Look Japan*, August 1989, 32–33.

"The 100-Year History of Mitsui & Co., Ltd." Mitsui & Co., 1977.

Pear, Robert. "Diplomats at Japan's Embassy Worry about Anti-Tokyo Sentiment in US." *New York Times*, 24 November 1989, A12.

Plath, D.W., ed. *Work and Lifecourse in Japan*. Albany: State University of New York Press, 1983.

Pucik, V., M. Hanada, and G. Fifield. *"Management Culture and the Effectiveness of Local Executives in Japanese-owned US Corporations."* Egon Zendor International, 1989.

Rehfeld, John E. "What Working for a Japanese Company Taught Me." *Harvard Business Review*, Nov.–Dec. 1990, 167–176.

Reischauer, H.M. *Samurai and Silk*. Cambridge, Massachusetts: Harvard University Press, 1986. Reprint. Tokyo: Tuttle, 1986.

Risen, J. "US-Japanese Firms Segregate the Americans." *New York Times*, 24 May 1990, 1.

Robinson, G. "People Like Unimportant Australia: Survey." *Japan Economic Journal*, 16 March 1991, 2.

Rohlen, T.P. *For Harmony and Strength*. Berkeley: University of California Press, 1974.

Sansom, G.B. *The Western World and Japan*. Cresset Press, 1950.

Sasaki, Takeshi "Konki ni yoru Sukinshippu" (Skinship depends on perseverance). *Zaigai Kigyo*, November 1989.

Schwind, H.F., and R.B. Petersen. "Personal Value Systems of Japanese." Academy of Management, International Business Division, undated.

Sekiguchi, W. "Bilinguals: From Outcasts to Celebrities." *Japan Economic Journal*, 7 October 1989, 28.

"Shame: an Oft-hidden Affliction; A Psychiatrist Describes Its Impact." *Brain/Mind Bulletin*, November 1990, 3.

Shimada, Haruo. "Gaikokujin Shain kara Mita Nihon Kigyo no Jinji Kanri" (Japanese personnel management as seen by foreign employees). *Nihon Rodo Kyokai Zasshi*, Feb.–Mar. 1989, 34–43.

Simon, James H. "US-Japanese Management Enters a New Generation." *Management International Review*, 1991, 2.

Skinner, K.A. "Aborted Careers in a Public Corporation." In *Work and Lifecourse in Japan*. See Plath, 1983.

Sofue, T. *Nihonjin no Kokusaisei* (The internationalism of the Japanese). Kumon Shuppan, 1989.

Sono, Fukujino. *Stages of Growth: Reflections on Life and Management*. Tokyo, 1981.

Statler, O. *Shimoda Story*. New York: Random House, 1980.

Szymkowiak, Ken. "Japanese Executives: Some Strengths and Weaknesses." Hotel Okura *News*, 13, no. 10, (October 1989): 4.

"Takamaru Kokusai ka no Nami" (The swelling wave of internationalization). *Mainichi Shimbun*, 16 June 1986, 13.

Takashima, A. "Why Japanese Can't Speak English." Translated by A. Takashima. *Asahi Shimbun*, 12 April 1987.

Takemura, K. "How Do the Japanese View Foreigners?" *PHP*, October 1981, 48–51.

Tanaka, H. "Legal Discrimination in Japan." *Japan Times*, 7 August 1986, 12.

Treece, J.B. "What the Japanese Must Learn about Racial Tolerance." *Business Week*, 5 September 1988, 41.

"Trouble Abroad." *Wall Street Journal*, 29 August 1989, 1.

Turner, R. "Ex-Employees Say They Were Beaten by Their Three Bosses." *Wall Street Journal*, 9 August 1989, A5.

"US Official Accuses 2 Companies of Bias." *New York Times*, 1 June 1989, 22.

Van Dyck, Judith. "Problems in Multicultural Organizations." Tokyo: Aoyama Gakuin University, November 1987.

Van Wolferen, Karel. *The Enigma of Japanese Power*. London: Macmillan Paperback, 1990.

Watanabe, Naoto. "Ibunkakan Shokumu Kunren ni Tai suru Pilot Study." (A pilot study on cross-cultural differences in work training), Aoyama Kei-ei Kenkyu 3, no. 2 (August 1988).

Watts, William. "Initiatives for Improving Japan-US Communication." *IHJ Bulletin* II, no. 2 (Spring 1991): 1–3.

White, Merry. *The Japanese Overseas: Can They Go Home Again?* New York: The Free Press, 1988.

Williams, H.S. *Tales of the Foreign Settlements in Japan*. Tokyo: Tuttle, 1958.

Williams, H.S. *Foreigners in Mikadoland*. Rutland, Vermont: Tuttle, 1963.

Wilson, Dick. *The Sun at Noon: An Anatomy of Modern Japan*. London: Hamish Hamilton, 1986.

Yamaguchi, Tamotsu. "The Challenge of Internationalization: Japan's Kokusaika." *Academy of Management Executives* 2, no. 1, February 1988.

Yamamoto, M. "Internationalization: Thin Disguise for Nationalism." *Japan Times*, 22 March 1982, 18.

"Zaibei Nikkei Seizo Keiei no Jittai" (Present Conditions of Manufacturing Management of Japanese Firms in the USA). *JETRO* March 1990.

"Zaigai Kigyo ni Nihonteki Keiei wa Najimu ka" (Will Japanese-style Management Take on in Enterprises Abroad?) *Zaigai Kigyo*, March 1990, 2–13.

INDEX

同じ釜の飯を食う
WORKING FOR A JAPANESE COMPANY

1996 年 7 月 1 日　　第 1 刷発行
2000 年 8 月 25 日　　第 3 刷発行

著　者　　ロバート・マーチ

発行者　　野間佐和子

発行所　　講談社インターナショナル株式会社
　　　　　〒112-8652 東京都文京区音羽 1-17-14
　　　　　電話：03-3944-6493

印刷所　　株式会社　平河工業社

製本所　　株式会社　堅省堂

Printed in Japan
ISBN 4-7700-2085-6

Japan's Modern Writers

BLACK RAIN

Masuji Ibuse
Translated by John Bester

Based on actual diaries and interviews with the survivors of Hiroshima, a literary masterpiece about friends, neighbors, and a city that suddenly ceased to be.

PB, ISBN 0-87011-364-X, 304 pages

CASTAWAYS   Two Short Novels

Masuji Ibuse
Translated by David Aylward and Anthony Liman

The story of a castaway who travelled the world and returned to a secluded island nation on the brink of westernization.

PB, ISBN 4-7700-1744-8, 160 pages

SALAMANDER AND OTHER STORIES

Masuji Ibuse
Translated by John Bester

An engaging collection of short stories ranging from biting satire to wry lyricism. "A brilliance and humour which is frequently memorable."   *—Times Literary Supplement*

PB, ISBN 0-87011-458-1, 136 pages

WAVES   Two Short Novels

Masuji Ibuse
Translated by David Aylward and Anthony Liman

A brilliant retelling of the 12th-century war between the Heike and Genji clans. "Subtle ironies and unsentimental sympathy."
—New Statesman

PB, ISBN 4-7700-1745-6, 176 pages

LOU-LAN AND OTHER STORIES

Yasushi Inoue

Translated by James Araki and Edward Seidensticker
A series of tales about lost worlds and epic battles by one of Japan's most popular writers.

PB, ISBN 0-87011-472-7, 164 pages

Social Sciences and History

THE ANATOMY OF DEPENDENCE

Takeo Doi, M.D.
Translated by John Bester

A definitive analysis of *amae*, the indulging, passive love which supports an individual within a group, a key concept in Japanese psychology.

PB, ISBN 0-87011-494-8, 184 pages

THE ANATOMY OF SELF

The Individual Versus Society

Takeo Doi, M.D.
Translated by Mark A. Harbison

A fascinating exploration into the role of the individual in Japan, and Japanese concepts of self-awareness, communication, and relationships.

PB, ISBN 0-87011-902-8, 176 pages

BEYOND NATIONAL BORDERS

Kenichi Ohmae

"[Ohmae is] Japan's only management guru." — *Financial Times*

PB, ISBN 4-7700-1385-X, 144 pages
Available only in Japan.

THE BOOK OF TEA

Kakuzo Okakura
Foreword and Afterword by Soshitsu Sen XV

The seminal text on the meaning and practice of tea, illustrated with eight historic photographs.

PB, ISBN 4-7700-1542-9, 160 pages

THE COMPACT CULTURE

The Japanese Tradition of "Smaller is Better"

O-Young Lee
Translated by Robert N. Huey

A provocative study of Japan's tendency to make the most out of miniaturization, that reveals the essence of Japanese character.

PB, ISBN 4-7700-1543-3, 196 pages

Social Sciences and History

THE JAPANESE NEGOTIATOR
Subtlety and Strategy Beyond Western Logic

Robert M. March

Shows how Japanese negotiate among themselves and examines case studies, providing practical advice for the Western executive.

PB, ISBN 0-87011-962-1, 200 pages

THE JAPANESE THROUGH AMERICAN EYES

Sheila K. Johnson

A revealing look at the images and stereotypes of Japanese produced by American popular culture and media.

PB, ISBN 4-7700-1450-3, 208 pages   Available only in Japan.

JAPAN'S LONGEST DAY

Pacific War Research Society

A detailed account of the day before Japan surrendered, based on eyewitness testimony of the men involved in the decision to surrender.

PB: ISBN 0-87011-422-0, 340 pages

MANGA! MANGA!
The World of Japanese Comics

Frederick L. Schodt
Introduction by Osamu Tezuka

A profusely illustrated and detailed exploration of the world of Japanese comics.

PB, ISBN 0-87011-752-1, 260 pages

NEIGHBORHOOD TOKYO

Theodore C. Bestor

A highly readable glimpse into the everyday lives, commerce, and relationships of some 2,000 neighborhood residents of Tokyo.

PB, ISBN 4-7700-1496-1, 368 pages   Available only in Japan.

THE INLAND SEA

Donald Richie

An award-winning documentary—part travelogue, part intimate diary and meditation—of a journey into the heart of traditional Japan.

PB, ISBN 4-7700-1751, 292 pages

THE THIRD CENTURY
America's Resurgence in the Asian Era

Joel Kotkin and Yoriko Kishimoto

Argues that the U.S. must adopt a realistic and resilient attitude as it faces serious competition from Asia. "Truly powerful public ideas." — *Boston Globe*

PB, ISBN 4-7700-1452-X, 304 pages
Available only in Japan.

THE UNFETTERED MIND
Writings of the Zen Master to the Sword Master

Takuan soho
Translated by William Scott Wilson

Philosophy as useful to today's corporate warriors as it was to seventeenth-century samurai.

PB, ISBN 0-87011-851-X, 104 pages

THE UNSPOKEN WAY
Haragei, or The Role of Silent Communication in Japanese Business and Society

Michihiro Matsumoto

Haragei, a uniquely Japanese concept of communication, affects language, social interaction, and especially business dealings.

PB, ISBN 0-87011-889-7, 152 pages

WOMANSWORD
What Japanese Words Say About Women

Kittredge Cherry

From "cockroach husband" to "daughter-in-a-box," a mix of provocative and entertaining words that collectively tell the story of Japanese women.

PB, ISBN 4-7700-1655-7, 160 pages

WORDS IN CONTEXT
Takao Suzuki
Translation by Akira Miura

One of Japan's foremost linguists explores the complex relationship between language and culture, psychology and lifestyle.

PB, ISBN 0-87011-642-8, 180 pages